EDMUND SPENSER

A BIBLIOGRAPHICAL SUPPLEMENT

BY

DOROTHY F. ATKINSON, Ph. D.

BALTIMORE

THE JOHNS HOPKINS PRESS

1937

PRINTED IN THE UNITED STATES OF AMERICA
BY J. H. FURST COMPANY, BALTIMORE, MARYLAND

TO

J. E. A. AND F. A.

FOREWORD

The present volume is designed as a supplement to Frederic Ives Carpenter's *A Reference Guide to Edmund Spenser*, published in 1923. The need for such a supplement is obvious, for it is hardly an exaggeration to say that the Spenseriana published since 1923 equals in volume all that had hitherto been printed on the subject. To be sure Miss Alice Parrott's *Spenser Bibliography*, published in 1928, and the annual bibliographies supplied by the Modern Language Association and the Modern Humanities Research Association have been most helpful, but at the best these are scattered and, as a matter of fact, not altogether complete. The present volume, therefore, covers the bibliography from 1923 to the present, and adds considerable material overlooked or omitted from previous compilations. In no sense is it a revision of Carpenter's *Reference Guide*.

In order to minimize the inconvenience of using two books, the present volume follows as nearly as possible the organization of Carpenter's work, with which scholars are already familiar. The same sectional headings have been used so that the two books may dovetail as fully as possible.

Since the preparation of the *Spenser Allusion Book* covering items down to 1800 is now well along, I have incorporated only such items from this projected volume as are critical in character, these finding their natural place in the section " Criticism, Influence, Allusions." Allusions subsequent to 1800, however, have been included, so that in this respect the volume supplements the *Spenser Allusion Book*. This is virtually necessary if scholars are to be informed of all known material bearing on the subject of Spenser's literary reputation. Acknowledgement of all allusion items is made by printing the initials or name of the finder in brackets on the right-hand margin. Items which I have been unable to check with the originals are indicated by an asterisk on the left-hand margin.

I wish to express here my appreciation of the interest and assistance of many who have contributed to make this volume possible. Dr. Frederick M. Padelford has encouraged the work throughout, reading the manuscript and the proofs and making many helpful suggestions. Dr. Ray Heffner has rendered valuable services too numerous to mention, and has read the manuscript and supplied notices from the Public Record Offices in Dublin and London. To both of these scholars I am under deep obligation. Others whose varied assistance I wish to acknowledge include: Dr. Brents Stirling, who has also read the manuscript, Dr. Percy W. Long, Dr. George R. Coffman, Dr. Allen R. Benham, Dr. C. Bowie Millican, Mr. J. C. Wyllie, Mr. R. W. Church, Mrs. Lucille O. Hogan, Mr. William Jackson of the Grolier Club, Dr. Leicester Bradner, and Mrs. Lois J. Wentworth. To my mother, who has read the proofs, I am especially grateful.

For many services I am indebted to the staffs of The Library of Congress, The Folger Shakespeare Library, The Newberry Library, The Johns Hopkins Tudor and Stuart Club Library, The Peabody Institute Library, the Carnegie libraries of Spokane and Seattle, and the libraries of Yale University, the University of Chicago, and the University of Washington.

D. F. A.

TABLE OF CONTENTS

ABBREVIATIONS

Amer. Lit.	American Literature
Anglia	Anglia Zeitschrift
Anglia Beibl.	Anglia Beiblatt
A. P.	Alice Parrott
Archiv	Archiv für das Studium der Neueren Sprachen und Literaturen
CJ	Classical Journal
CP	Classical Philology
CR	Classical Review
CSP, Ire.	Calendar of State Papers for Ireland
CW	Classical Weekly
EHR	English Historical Review
ELH	English Literary History
Eng. Stud.	English Studies, Amsterdam
Engl. Stud.	Englische Studien
F. I. C.	Frederic Ives Carpenter
German.-Roman. Monatss.	Germanisch-Romanische Monatsschrift
Fortn. Rev.	Fortnightly Review
J. Cork Hist. and Arch. Soc.	Journal of the Cork Historical and Archaeological Society
JEGP	Journal of English and Germanic Philology
Lit. Rev.	Literary Review, New York Evening Post
Lit. Zentralb.	Literarisches Zentralblatt für Deutschland
Literaturb. f. Germ. u. Rom. Phil.	Literaturblatt für Germanische und Romanische Philologie
Lond. Merc.	London Mercury
MLN	Modern Language Notes
MLQ	Modern Language Quarterly
MLR	Modern Language Review
MP	Modern Philology
NQ	Notes and Queries
PMLA	Publications of the Modern Language Association
PQ	Philological Quarterly
RES	Review of English Studies
Rev. ang.-amér.	Revue anglo-américaine
Rev. crit.	Revue Critique
Rev. hist.	Revue Historique
Rev. de l'Enseign. des Lang. Viv.	Revue de l'Enseignement des Langues Vivantes
Rev. de Litt. Comp.	Revue de Littérature Comparée
Roy. Soc. Antiq. Ire.	Journal of the Royal Society of Antiquaries of Ireland
SAB	Shakespeare Association Bulletin
SAQ	South Atlantic Quarterly
Shakes. Jahr.	Shakespeare Jahrbuch
SP	Studies in Philology

TLS	London Times Literary Supplement
Univ. of Cal. Chron.	University of California Chronicle
West. Rev.	Westminster Review
YWES	Year's Work in English Studies

Certain items will be found marked " F. I. C. and A. P." By this device I acknowledge entries from Miss Alice Parrott's *Critical Bibliography* which were obtained from manuscript notes by Dr. Carpenter and identified by affixing his initials.

A small number of titles are printed in abridged form, without date and place of publication, or, in the case of periodical entries, without page references. This abridgment serves merely to identify supplementary reviews or notices. In such instances the full entry may be found in the *Reference Guide*.

I.
THE LIFE

I. THE LIFE

CHRONOLOGICAL OUTLINE

1569		Sp secretary to the ambassador to Rimia.

Cf. Harman, E. G. Gabriel Harvey and Thomas Nashe. 1923. 5-6.

May 20   Matriculation as sizar.

Cf. Venn (1927). Pt. I, vol. iv, 132.

1577   Was Sp in Limerick?

Cf. Welply, W. H. Spenser in Ireland. TLS 32 (May 18, 1933). 348; Harman, E. G. Gabriel Harvey and Thomas Nashe, 5-7.

1579   Sp in residence at Leicester House.

Cf. Kingsford, C. L. Essex House, Formerly Leicester House and Exeter Inn. Archaeologia LXXIII (1923). 8, 10.

Oct. 27   Sp's first marriage to Machabyas Chylde.

Cf. Eccles, Mark. TLS 30 (Dec. 31, 1931). 1053; Hamer, Douglas. TLS 31 (Jan. 14, 1932). 28, and RES VII (1931). 271 ff.

1580 Nov.   Sp at Smerwick.

Cf. B. M. Addit. MS 33, 924, fol. 6. Letter of Grey to Burghley, Nov. 28, 1580. Cited by Raymond Jenkins. Spenser at Smerwick. TLS 32 (May 11, 1933). 331.

1581 Mar. 27   Sp at Cullenswood on Easter Monday with Grey.

Cf. Covington, F. F., Jr. Biographical Notes on Spenser. MP XXII (1924). 63-6.

1581 April-May   Grey's letter to Walsingham from Dublin, May 12, encloses three letters. One is dated April 29, Cork, and is listed as " Copy, under the hand of Spenser." A second, undated, is listed as " Copy, certified by Edmund Spenser."

Cf. CSP, Ire. vol. LXXXIII, item 6; Carpenter, F. I. Ref. Guide, 16, where it is stated that a paper was certified *at Cork* on April 29 by Spenser.

Sept. 13   " Captaine Garrat fitz Garret . . . He oweth
and is indebted viz. . . . to . . . Edmunde
Spencer p pst bill xiijᶜⁱᵒ. Sept. 1581 . . . iiijˡⁱ
viijˢ ster facir . . . cxvijˢ iiijᵈ." *Wage Book
for Ireland,* 1584-5, fol. 49ᵛ.

> Cited by Ray Heffner in review of B. E. C. Davis,
> *Edmund Spenser.* MLN L (1935). 194.

Nov. 28   Grey's letter to Burghley apparently in Spenser's hand.

> *Cf.* Hist. MSS Comm. " Cecil Papers," *Hatfield
> House.* II (1888). 443; Jenkins, Raymond. Spenser's
> Hand. TLS 31 (Jan. 7, 1932). 12.

Dec. 6   Sp's lease of Enniscorthy Castle.

> *Cf.* Cal. Fiants, Eliz., No. 3785 (3223) in *XIII
> Report of the Deputy Keeper of the Records in
> Ireland.* 1881. Carpenter, Ref. Guide, 16-7, gives
> the date of this lease as 1582 and of the conveyance
> as Dec. 1581.

1581 Dec. 9   Sp conveyed his lease of Enniscorthy Castle
to Sir Richard Synnott of Ballybrennan.
Synnott made over this property on Mar. 8,
1586, to Sir Henry Wallop. Bodl. MS Addit. C. 39, dated and signed 10 Decembʳ·
1586, lists Enniscorthy among the principal
castles and describes it as " reedefyed lately
by Sʳ He. Wallop."

> *Cf.* Flood, Wm. H. G. Enniscorthy . . . Roy. Soc.
> Antiq. Ire. XXXIV (1904). 380-3 and XXXV
> (1905). 178.

Dec. 10   Grey's letter to Burghley apparently in Sp's
hand.

> *Cf.* Jenkins, Raymond. Spenser's Hand. TLS 31
> (Jan. 7, 1932). 12; Hist. MSS Comm. " Cecil
> Papers," *Hatfield House.* II (1888). 447.

1582   " A Custody of John Eustace his Lande of
the New land to Edmund Spenser one of the
L: Deputies Secretaries."

> [R. Heffner] *Cf.* CSP, Ire. 1574-85, p. 345.

"John Eustace of Newland" perhaps the original owner of estate granted to Sp by Grey.

Cf. Covington, F. F., Jr. Biographical Notes on Spenser. MP XXII (1924). 63-6.

Sp may have been at Court after 1582 until Elizabeth granted him land in Ireland.

Cf. Smyth, George L. The Monuments and Genii of St. Paul's Cathedral and Westminster Abbey. 1839. II, 865-8.

Aug. 22   "He [Nicholas Dawtrye, Seneshall of Clandeboye] is further owinge to . . . Edmonde Spencer p bill dated xxijdo Augustij 1582 signed to Walter Sedgrave . . . xiijli vjs viijd." *Wage Book* . . . 1584-1585, fol. 40r.

Cited by R. Heffner. MLN L (1935). 194.

1584-8   Sp probably not resident near Dublin, but serving as Bryskett's deputy as clerk in the Council of Munster. New evidence.

Cf. Jenkins, Raymond. Spenser and the Clerkship in Munster. PMLA XLVII (1932). 109 ff.

1584 Feb. 1   " Edw : Barkley esquier constable of Askeatin . . . He owethe and is indebted viz. . . . to Edmunde Spencer by bill of the firste of februarij 1584 . . . vijli." *Wage Book* . . . 1584-85, fol. 45v.

Cited by R. Heffner. MLN L (1935). 194.

1586 June 27   There is no evidence to support statement that Sp received a grant of the lands of Kilcolman on this date.

Cf. Carpenter, Ref. Guide, 17; Heffner, R. Spenser's Acquisition of Kilcolman. MLN XLVI (1931). 493 ff.

1587-8   Sp as Bryskett's deputy. Possibility supported by letter of Thomas Norris to Burghley, Mar. 31, 1585, and by entries in *Book of Wages, Ireland,* October 1, 1587 to Mar. 31, 1588.

Cf. Jenkins, Raymond. Spenser's Hand. TLS 31 (Jan. 7, 1932). 12.

1588 Sept. 3-Mar. 24, 1588/9　Sp first occupied Kilcolman.

> *Cf.* CSP, Ire. vol. CXLIV, item 70. Cited by R. Heffner. Spenser's Acquisition of Kilcolman. MLN XLVI (1931). 493-8.

1589 May 22　　　Sp first acquired Kilcolman.

> *Cf.* Heffner, R. Spenser's Acquisition of Kilcolman. MLN XLVI (1931). 493-8.

1589 Oct. 12　　　Counter-suit of Sp *vs.* Roche. Sp charges Roche, among other things, with killing " a fat beef of Teig Olyve's, because Mr. Spenser lay in his house one night as he came from the sessions at Limerick." Roche has forbidden his people to " have any trade or conference " with Sp or his tenants.

> *Cf.* CSP, Ire. vol. CXLVII, item 16.

　　　　　　　　　Sp had at this time six English households (no Irish are mentioned) on his land.

> *Cf.* Dunlop, R. The Plantation of Munster, 1584-1589. EHR III (1888). 267.

　　　　　　　　　Grant by Sp to Mr. Fienny of property and rights in Balligamin and the " baun of Richardston." Roche MSS, B. M.

> *Cf.* Smith, Charles. Ancient and Present State of . . . Cork. II, 345-6.

June 10　　　　　Recognizance by Edmund Spenser and Richard Roche in relation to controversy depending between Sp and Hugh Strawbridge.

> *Cf.* B. M. Addit. MS 19,837 [Cat. 1875]. Cited by W. H. Welply. Edmund Spenser . . . NQ, ser. xiv. VI (1932). 149.

June 18　　　　　Edmund Spenser, gent., bound to Richard Spence in £100 for (1) recovery of £30 due by Richard Brysse to Richard Crowther deceased; and (2) for delivery of body of James Shropp into Newgate Prison, Dublin.

> *Cf.* B. M. Addit. MS 19,837. Cited by Welply. NQ, ser. xiv. VI (1932). 150.

1590 May　　　　Bill presented to Sp, probably in person, in Ireland. *Cf.* MS Rawl. A. 317 (Bodl.) " Receipts and charges " of the Treasurer at Wars in Ireland, Sir Henry Wallop, from Sept. 30, 1588 to Sept. 30, 1591.

Cited by F. P. Wilson. Spenser and Ireland. RES II (1926). 456-7.

1592   Publication of *Axiochus*.

Cf. Reprint, ed. F. M. Padelford.

1594   Sp used by Sir Thomas Norreys to take letters to England.

Cf. CSP, Ire. 1598-9. vol. CCII, pt. 4, no. 36. Cited by H. F. Berry. The English Settlement in Mallow. . . . J. Cork Hist. and Arch. Soc. XII (1906). 1-26.

Feb. 12   " Decree 12 February 1594 that the pltf shall recover two plowlands of Kilvallinge and Classigny in the Co. of Cork agst the Deft and as to the value of the trees cut or waste committed by the Deft. corne growing upon the land converted by the Deft. to his own use. A commission shall issue under George Thornton, Provost Martial of Mounster and William Roch of Cork Gent. to enquire thereof and Costs £3."

On the right side is

    " Cork

      Kilcolman

      Kilvallinge

      Classigany."

Cf. Repertory to the Decrees of Chancery, I (28 Henry VIII to 1624), 231 for this, No. 656.

" Mirishe Lord

      Roch

      Pltf

      Edmond Spenser of Kilcolman

                 Deft."

[Original in PRO, Dublin. Transcript by R. Heffner.]

1594 May 23   Sp's official visit to Mallow.

Sept. 16   *ibid.*

> *Cf.* Plea Rolls (Miscel.) Eliz., No. 34. Cited by H. F. Berry. J. Cork Hist. and Arch. Soc. XII (1906). 1-26.

1596 Nov. 20   A Chancery suit. Plaintiffs: Edmund Sp and wife, and her brothers George and Alexander. Defendants: Thomas Emyly and John Mathewe.

> *Cf.* Carpenter, Ref. Guide, 31; Welply, W. H. Edmund Spenser ... NQ, ser. xiii. II (1924). 445-7.

1598 Sept. 30   Letter [from Privy Council?] urging appointment of Sp as sheriff of Cork.

> *Cf.* Cal. Harleian MS 286, item 152: "Part of a Collection of Letters, Warrants, &c., for the most part relating to the Lords of the Privy-Council, or to the business transacted at that Board. Amongst others, is a Letter to the Justices of Ireland, requiring them to make Edmund Spencer Gentleman, Sheriffe of the Countie of Corke. Dat. ult. Sept., 1598, fol. 271. (Qu. if this was not Spencer the Poet?)."

Aug.-Sept.   Accounts and letters pertaining to the rebellion of 1598.

> *Cf.* MacCarthy, Daniel. The "Jorney" of the Blackwater: from the State Papers of Queen Elizabeth. J. Kilkenny ... Arch. Soc., n. s. I (1856-7). 256-82. No mention of Sp, but important data for the period. [R. Heffner]

1599 Jan. 13   Sp's death.

> *Cf.* Zeitler, W. I. The Date of Spenser's Death. MLN XLIII (1928). 322-4.

MISCELLANEOUS AND GENERAL REFERENCES

LIFE

See "Spenser and Sidney," "Spenser and Harvey," Nos. 1-3, 9-10; "Spenser and Raleigh," Nos. 11, 20; "View of Ireland," Nos. 1, 13, 44; "Editions," i, Nos. 5, 21 and iii, No. 10; "Criticism, General," No. 18; "Addenda," Nos. 1, 32.

1. Add. MSS 25,079-83, Brit. Mus. Vol. II (1877). Letters
   and papers chiefly to and from Sir John Spencer of
   Althorp, relating to the musters in the county of Northampton.

2. ALBRIGHT, EVELYN MAY. Dramatic Publications in
   England, 1580-1640. MLA Monograph, 1927.
   150-2: Quotes James VI's complaint against Sp for his attack
   upon the king in FQ.

3. An Account of Middlesex: the monumental inscriptions
   in Westminster Abbey. Universal Mag. XI (1752).
   309 ff.
   313: Sp's burial-place.

4. ARCHDALL, MERVYN and P. F. MORAN. Monasticon
   Hibernicum. Dublin, 1873-6. Only Vol. I and Vol.
   II, 1-288, were published. *Cf.* Cat. Trin. Coll., Dublin.

5. Baconiana, n. s. I (1894). 119, 120.
   Sp's grave.

6. BAYLEY, M. F. The English Rénaissance. Baconiana
   XXI (1933). 139, 141.
   Sp's name as a "label" for Francis Bacon.

7. BEGLEY, JOHN (Canon). The Diocese of Limerick in
   the Sixteenth and Seventeenth Centuries. Dublin, 1927.
   No mention of Sp. Background for Sp's years in Ireland.

8. BENNETT, GEORGE. History of Bandon.
   4-5: Scheme of the undertakers.

9. BERKENHOUT, JOHN. Biographia Literaria; or a Biographical History of Literature: containing the Lives
   of English, Scotish, and Irish Authors. London, 1777.
   378-80: Sp's life.

10. BERRY, HENRY F. Sheriffs of the County Cork—Henry
    III to 1660. Roy. Soc. Antiq. Ire. XXXV (1905).
    39 ff.
    Quotes *Memoranda Roll, Hil. 21 Eliz.* (1579). Sheriffs of Cork:
    " 1594-5: No name
    1595-6: Richard Barrie, Esq.
    1597-8: Edmund Gibbon, Esq.
    1598-9: Francis Newman, Esq." [R. Heffner]

11. BERRY, HENRY F. The English Settlement in Mallow under the Jephson Family. J. Cork Hist. and Arch. Soc. XII (1906). 1-26.

2: Sp carrying letters to England for Sir Thomas Norreys; Sp's official visits to Mallow, May 23 and Sept. 16, 1594. Cited from *Plea Roll (Miscel.) Eliz.*, No. 34.

12. BLACKHAM, ROBERT J. London For Ever the Sovereign City. London, 1932.

283-4: Life of Sp.

13. BRAYLEY, EDWARD W. (Joseph Nightingale). London and Middlesex . . . Survey. London, 1815.

III, pt. ii, 101: Sp's tomb and the 1778 repairs.

14. BUCK, P. M., Jr. New Facts concerning the Life of Edmund Spenser. MLN XIX (1904).

Cites two new leases of Aug. 24, 1582, and May 12, 1583. *Rev. Shakes. Jahr.* 41 (1905). 288-9: Reprints the leases.

15. Calendars of State Papers relating to Ireland. Henry VIII, Edward VI, Mary, and Elizabeth. London, 1860-1903. Volumes as indicated:

1574-85

345: 1582 "A Custody of John Eustace his Lande of the New land to Edmund Spenser one of the L: Deputies Secretaries."

[R. Heffner]

533: "Kilcoman" is not "Kilcolman." [R. Heffner] *Cf.* Carpenter, Ref. Guide, 31.

1586-8.

261: This letter is printed in full in the Calendar. [R. Heffner]

1588-92

198: Sp's answer to the Articles. Original in PRO, London. Museum, Pedestal 58. [R. Heffner]

1592-6.

60: The list for 1592 of patents to the English undertakers is the same as that of Oct. 29, 1589. (*Cf.* Cal. 1588-92, 258). [R. Heffner]

" Mr. Edmond Spenser hath by particular onlie 4000 acres."

1598-9.

319: The Calendar prints the entire history. [R. Heffner]

16. Calendar of Fiants in the Public Records in Ireland. In Reports of the Deputy Keeper of the Records. Dublin, 1869 +. Index in App. to 21st and 22nd Reports.

Fiants: Elizabeth

No. 3694 (3103): Grant, Mar. 22, 1580-1, to Sp of the office of registrar or clerk in Chancery. (3103 is the no. used in the MS index at PRO, Dublin.) *Cf.* Cottonian MS Titus B. XIII, fol. 263, dated 1577 [Carpenter, Ref. Guide, 37, gives 1578] in *Cat. of MSS in the Cottonian Library,* 1802.

No. 5473 (6536) : Grant of 26 Oct., xxxii (1590), bestowing Kilcolman on Sp. Also in Brit. Mus. Egerton MSS, No. 75, p. 316.
[R. Heffner]
No. 6218 (5599) : License to Henry Wallop to alien to Lodovic Briskett, Oliver Wallopp, Richard Hopper, John Brown . . . " or any others of English blood " the site of the friary of Enescorthy, etc. . . . See No. 5963, which recites Sp's lease. Cf. XVI Report . . . Deputy Keeper.

17. Calendar of the Carew MSS preserved . . . at Lambeth. Ed. J. S. Brewer and Wm. Bullen. London, 1867-73.

449 : MS 636. Certificate of 14 March 1586, of allotment of lands of Killcolman and Rossaghe to Andrew Reade, gent., of Faccombe, Hants. [R. Heffner]

18. Calendar of Patent and Close Rolls of Chancery in Ireland, Henry VIII–Elizabeth. Ed. James Morrin. Dublin, 1861-2. 2 vols.

II, 319 : Nov. 4, xxxvii Eliz. [1595]. Enniscorthy : a grant " in as ample manner as Edmond Spencer (the poet)." . . . [R. Heffner]

19. CAMDEN, WILLIAM. Tomus Alter Annalium Rerum Anglicarum, et Hibernicarum, Regnante Elizabetha. London, 1627 [first edition].

171-2 : Cf. Carpenter, Ref. Guide, 43, for text of this.

20. Catalogue of Additions to the Manuscripts in the British Museum. London, 1875 +.

No. 19,869 : A grant by Sp of rights in lands at Richardston, Co. Cork, to J. McHenry, ca. 1597. With autograph signature.
No. 22,022 : MS View of Ireland. " A View of the present State of Ireland discoursed by way of a dialogue between Eudoxus and Irenaeus " [Almost erased—first page badly damaged]. At top of first page is written "Arthur Chichester "—a copy which belonged, then, to Sir Arthur Chichester, Lord Deputy of Ireland, 1604-13. Folio. [94 folios]. Catalogue [I, 1875] says it contains passages not in other MSS of the View. Several pages torn off at top corner, and many badly blurred by water. [Note by R. Heffner]

21. Catalogue of the Bodleian Library.

MS Addit. C. 39. Description of Ireland by counties, giving the principal Townes, Castles, and Gentlemen, etc. Dated and signed Decemb[r] 10, 1586. Under Co. Wexford, fol. 53 verso, " Principal Castles " is " Inniscorthy, reedefyed lately by S[r] He. Wallop."
[R. Heffner]

22. Catalogue of the Harleian Manuscripts in the British Museum. London, 1808.

II, 355 : No. 1932. 1. MS of the V. of I., dated 10 May 1598.
III, 78 : No. 3787 (21, p. 182) : Sp's brief note concerning Ireland.

III, 447: No. 6910: A Quarto, containing the following:
" Poems : neatly written & ruled.
Nine of Spenser's minor poemes follow fol. 1-73. At the end of
this is written 'Finis 1596,' which is five years after most of them
were printed in 4to. and six after *Muiopotmos* and No. 7 & 9 (*Visions of Bellay* and *V. of Petrarch*) which were printed with it."
[R. Heffner]

23. CAULFIELD, RICHARD. Council Book of the Corporation of Youghal.
Original still at Youghal. [R. Heffner]

24. CHANCELLOR, E. BERESFORD. The Literary Ghosts of London. London, 1933.
48: Sp.

25. CHURCH, R. W. Spenser (English Men of Letters series). London, 1879.
Rev. West. Rev. CXIII (1880). 271-2.

26. COVINGTON, F. F., JR. Biographical Notes on Spenser. MP XXII (1924). 63-6.
Sp perhaps in Dublin on Easter Monday, 1581. Original ownership of Sp's estates by John Eustace. Barnabe Googe in Sp's circle in Ireland. [A. P.]

27. CRAIK, G. L. Spenser and his Poetry.
Rev. Athenaeum. 1846. 172.

28. CRAWFORD, CHARLES. Collectanea. Second Series. Stratford-on-Avon, 1907.
93, 98-9, 146: Sp not a " strong Baconian."

29. CUNINGHAM, GRANVILLE C. Bacon and Edmund Spenser. Baconiana, 3rd. ser. V (1907). 153-77.
153-7: Sp's birth and death dates.
157-66: Short life.

30. ——— Baconiana, 3rd. ser. VI (1908). 134-5.
Sp son of Elizabeth and Leicester!

31. DAVIS, B. E. C. Edmund Spenser: A Critical Study. Cambridge University Press, 1933.
Chs. I, II: The Life.

32. DAVISON, FRANCIS. The Poetical Rhapsody. Ed. Nicholas H. Nicolas. London, 1826. 2 vols.
I, cv-cviii: Sp's life.

33. DAY, ROBERT. Regnum Corcagiense; or, a Description of the Kingdom of Cork. J. Cork Hist. and Arch. Soc., 2nd. ser. VIII (1902). 156 ff.
157: Sp's estate on the Mulla.

34. DOWNS, BRIAN W. Cambridge Past and Present. London, 1926.
121-2: Sp's life.

35. DRAPER, JOHN W. Spenserian Biography . . . The Colonnade XIV (1921).
Rev. Anglia Beibl. 37 (1926). 141, by Walther Fischer.

36. DUNLOP, ROBERT. The Plantation of Munster, 1584-1589. EHR III (1888). 250-69.
"The basic account. That it was suggested by Perrot's Report, 1582. Started at favorable time when Munster was largely depopulated and its lands forfeited by rebellion, but its prospects thwarted by the frequent pardons in subsequent years involving many titles in litigation; the undertakers were left to fight the Irish claims (e. g. Sp *vs.* Lord Roche). A commission on titles, 1588, was ruthless against the Irish (*cf.* p. 266) and so the scheme proved a failure (p. 268). The early survey was incompetent. The various plans ill conceived and poorly supported (p. 269); Sp in 1589 had six households on his land; date of his patent 26 Oct. 1590 (p. 267). Sp's comment on the Plantation (in *V. of I.*)." [F. I. C. and A. P.]

37. ———The Plantation of Leix and Offaly. EHR VI (1891). 61-96.
61-96: "On a survey in 1622 of three principal plantations."
94-6: "List of granters in the Munster plantation."
[F. I. C. and A. P.]

38. FLOOD, WILLIAM H. G. Enniscorthy in the Thirteenth Century—Who Built the Castle? Roy. Soc. Antiq. Ire. XXXIV (1904). 380-3.
383: Sp's lease of the castle.

39. ——— Enniscorthy Castle. Roy. Soc. Antiq. Ire. XXXV (1905). 178.
Sp's lease of Dec. 6, 1581; conveyance, Dec. 9, to Synnott; Synnott's transfer, Mar. 8, 1586, to Sir Henry Wallop.

40. Fratres Roseae Crucis. Secret Shakespearean Seals. Nottingham, 1916.
20, 28, 30, 81 and plates XXII, XXIII, LX, LXI, LXX, Recollections of Rosicrucian Arcana in Sp.

41. FRISBEE, GEORGE. Edward deVere—A Great Elizabethan.
    London, 1931.

    64-75: Edmund Spenser a pen-name for Edw. deVere.

42. ———— Gentle Master de Vere. Sat. Rev. of Lit. IX
    (June 24, 1933). 667.

    Cf. ibid., (Dec. 10, 1932). 323. " Personals "; XI (Feb. 16,
    1935). 499. " Personals "; ibid., (Feb. 23, 1935). 511. " Per-
    sonals." Vide also Tucker Brooke. Sat. Rev. of Lit. IX (June 3,
    1933). 625-6.

43. GAMZUE, B. B. Elizabeth and Literary Patronage. PMLA
    XLIX (1934). 1041-9.

    1047: Sp's relations with Eliz. as patron. Her reputation derives
    " not from her deeds."

44. Gentleman's Magazine. 1848. I. 236.

    Crossley's note on Sp's residence in the north of England. Rejects
    Hurstwood connection.

45. ———— 1864. I. 725-32. The Public Records of Ireland.

    These are now printed in the Cal. of Fiants, Eliz. Cf. 727: Notes
    on Sp documents in Irish records.

46. GLASENAPP, G. Edmund Spenser und die Bartholomaeus-
    Kirche zu Smithfield. Archiv CXII (1904).

    Rev. Shakes. Jahr. 41 (1905). 288.

47. HAMER, DOUGLAS. Edmund Spenser. NQ, ser. xiv.
    VI (1932). 352, 370, 380-4.

    The 1504 grant of arms to Hodnell Spencers; Edmund Spenser-
    Jone Bre'dge marriage; Hodnell Spencers and Edmund Sp not
    related, for Thomas Spenser died 1531/2 without issue; ye aier
    reading of Harvey's letter correct; payments of Nowell money insuf-
    ficient evidence of Sp's poverty; Sp's sister Sarah, and a brother
    (or brothers); "north parts" used by Elizabethans to designate
    Nottingham section; Rosalind; Peregrine not uncommon name in
    Ireland . . . ; Rosalind and the Drydens; names of Stephen Boyle's
    children not given in the register; Prof. Garrod's theory of Eliz.
    Boyle's widowhood untenable; chancery lawsuit insufficient evi-
    dence for prolonging Sp's stay in London into 1597; may Sp have
    been a Westminster man; " Peregrine the second" and certain
    legal records; William Spencer's visit to England; Edm. Spenser's
    projected edition (ca. 1743) of the poet; maternal ancestry of
    Eliz. Boyle; her marriage to Tynte and their children (two or
    three only). Cf. "Parents and Family," No. 54. Rev. YWES
    XIII (1932). 193.

48. HARMAN, EDWARD G. Gabriel Harvey and Thomas Nashe. London, 1923.

5-7: "That Immerito is Bacon; that Sp was in Ireland in 1577 under Sir Henry Sidney; that earlier (1569) he was secretary to the ambassador to Rimia. That he was born nearer '1510 than 1553.'" [F. I. C. and A. P.]

49. ———— The "Impersonality" of Shakespeare. London, 1925.

Sp as Bacon—see index.

50. HARVEY, Sir PAUL. Companion to English Literature. Oxford, 1932.

739: Brief life.

51. HEFFNER, RAY. Spenser and the British Sea-Power. MS essay. University of North Carolina Library, 1925.

52. ———— Spenser's Acquisition of Kilcolman. MLN XLVI (1931). 493-8.

Error of Carpenter and Henley in dating Sp's acquisition of Kilcolman, June 27, 1586. On evidence of Sp's answer to the articles (no. 2) and other documents, the acquisition is set at May 22, 1589; Sp's occupancy between Sept. 3, 1588, and March 24, 1588/9. Quarrel of Sp with Lord Roche concerned the title to the entire Kilcolman estate. Cf. post, No. 59.

53. ———— Did Spenser Die in Poverty? MLN XLVIII (1933). 221-6. Cf. also PMLA XLVI (Proc., 1931). 1436.

Sp left Ireland about Dec. 13, arriving in London about the 24th [documents PRO, Dublin]. Supports tradition of death in poverty by citing contemporary authors. Rev. Shakes. Jahr. 70 (1934). 166; YWES XIV (1933). 224.

54. ———— Review of B. E. C. Davis, Edmund Spenser . . . MLN L (1935). 194-5.

Cites new documents on Sp's life in Ireland. Cf. ante, pp. 2-3, for text of these.

55. HENLEY, PAULINE. Spenser in Ireland. Cork University Press, 1928. Maps.

Presents Sp's Irish career from the Irish point of view. Rev. Studies XVII (1928). 334-6, by M. T. H.; Spectator, No. 5,220. 141 (July 14, 1928). 55; New Statesman 31 (1928). 428-30; Roy. Soc. Antiq. Ire. LVIII (1928). 69-70, by W. F. B.; TLS 27 (1928). 422; YWES IX (1928). 171; Bost. Transcript, Aug. 1, 1928, Pt. II, 4, by G. R. B. R.; EHR XLIV (1929). 493-4, by

G. H. O.; Archiv, n. s. LV (1929). 142; History, n. s. XIV (1929-30). 176, by C. E. M.; MLN XLV (1930). 320-3, by E. A. Greenlaw.

56. *HINCHMAN, WALTER S. Edmund Spenser. In Lives of Great English Writers from Chaucer to Browning. Ed. W. S. Hinchman and F. B. Gummere. New York, 1908. Pp. 44-5. [L. O. Hogan]

57. JENKINS, RAYMOND. New Letters by Spenser. Paper read before the Mod. Lang. Ass., 1932. Cf. PMLA XLVII (Proc., 1932). 1335.

58. ———— Spenser and the Clerkship in Munster. PMLA XLVII (1932). 109-21.

New evidence that Sp was probably not residing near Dublin, 1584-8, but was Bryskett's deputy as clerk in the council in Munster. Rev. YWES XIII (1932). 194. Cf. Plomer, Henry and Cross, T. P. The Life and Correspondence of Lodowick Bryskett. University of Chicago Press, 1927.

59. ———— Spenser's Hand. TLS 31 (Jan. 7, 1932). 12.

i. Two documents support belief Sp was Bryskett's deputy 1584-8. ii. Sp's relations with Andrew Reade and his failure to secure patent for his estate before October 1590 explained by Sp's answer to article two [see PRO for omissions in CSP]. iii. Notes finding of 31 new letters and documents in Sp's hand at PRO. Rev. YWES XIII (1932). 193. Cf. post, Nos. 90, 91; "Spenser's Autographs," Nos. 1, 4; "Other Spensers," No. 6.

60. ———— Spenser at Smerwick. TLS 32 (May 11, 1933). 331.

B. M. Addit. MS 33,924, fol. 6, contains letter of Nov. 28, 1580, which, Mr. Jenkins thinks, proves Sp was at Smerwick. On this evidence, one may conclude Sp is Irenaeus and Veue is a "biographical document" illuminating many incidents in FQ and giving Sp's experiences for 1577. Rev. YWES XIV (1933). 224.

61. ———— Spenser's Travels and Experiences with Lord Grey. Paper read before the Mod. Lang. Ass., 1934. Cf. PMLA XLIX (Proc., 1934). 1326.

62. ———— Newes out of Munster, A Document in Spenser's Hand. SP XXXII (1935). 125-30.

Cotton MS Titus B. XIII, 364 (B. M.) apparently in Sp's secretary hand. Dated March 23, 1582. News of Capt. Fenton's catastrophe, the Jesuit menace, and the danger of a Spanish invasion.

63. JENKINSON, WILBERFORCE. The Royal and Bishops' Palaces in Old London. London, 1921.
84 ff: Describes Leicester House where Sp lived.

64. JONES, H. S. V. A Spenser Handbook. New York, 1930.
Ch. II: The Life.

65. JONSON, BEN. Conversations with Drummond, 1619. In Works, ed. Gifford and Cunningham. London, 1875.
IX, 380: *Cf.* Carpenter, Ref. Guide, 61 (III, 478), for the text.

66. JUDSON, A. C. Spenser in Southern Ireland. Principia Press (Bloomington, Ind.), 1933. Illustrated. Map.
Account of a trip through Sp's Ireland. *Rev.* MLN L (1935). 206, by H. S. V. Jones; MLR XXX (1935). 130, by W. L. R.; Anglia Beibl. XLVI (1935). 43-5, by Rudolf Kapp; YWES XIV (1933). 223.

67. JUSSERAND, J. J. Edmond Spenser. Revue de Paris May, 1903. 58-95.
A life.

68. KEIGHTLEY, T. Edmund Spenser, his Life and Poetry. Brit. Quart. Rev. XXI (1855). 368-412.
Cf. Carpenter, Ref. Guide, 62.

69. KENT, W. CHARLES. Spenser at Kilcolman. New Monthly Mag. CXXI (1861). 170-2.
A dozen Spenserian stanzas on Sp's last days. Negligible.

70. KINGSFORD, C. L. Essex House, Formerly Leicester House and Exeter Inn. Archaeologia LXXIII (1923). 1 ff.
8, 10: Sp lived at Leicester House, 1579.

71. LAWRENCE, C. E. The Personality of Spenser. Quart. Rev. CCXLIX (1927). 154-67.
Tries to discover the personality in the works.

72. LEGOUIS, ÉMILE. Edmund Spenser. New York and London, 1926.
Ch. 1: Spenser's character.

73. The Lismore Papers. . . . Ed. A. B. Grosart. Priv. Print. 1886-8. 10 vols. Index, first series, V; second series, V, 184. Copy in Tudor and Stuart Club Library, Baltimore.
First series.
I, 275: Elizabeth Boyle; II, 354, Kilcolman; II, 363: Ld. Roche named as enemy of Sp; III, 260-61: Sir John Scudamore.

Second series.

I, Frontisp.: Facsimile of letter of Sp's widow to Boyle, Dec. 22, 1615. *Cf.* text given at II, 12-3; I, 19-22: Feb. 8, 1599. A reference to "Edmond Spenser gent. deceased," in Articles of agreement between R. Boyle and Lodowick Bryskett; I, 261: Sp-Roche quarrel.

74. Literary Magazine and American Register V (Feb. 1806). 178-82.

"A Sketch of the Poet Spenser."

75. Littell's Living Age XVIII (1848). 256. A brief note.

Sp's last days.

76. London Mag. XXX (1761). 256. A brief note.

Anecdote of Sp (the old fellowship story, Erasmus Dryden, etc.).

77. LONG, P. W. A Name for Spenser's Rosalind. PMLA XXII (1907). *Proc.,* xiv.

Cf. Long, Spenser's Rosalind. Anglia XXXI (1908). 72 ff.

78. LUCAS, HENRY S. The Renaissance and the Reformation. New York, 1934.

400: Sp.

79. LUNHAM, T. A. Some Historical Notices of Cork in the Seventeenth and Eighteenth Centuries. Roy. Soc. Antiq. Ire. XXXIV (1904). 65 ff.

80. MACCARTHY, DANIEL. The "Jorney" of the Blackwater: from the State Papers of Queen Elizabeth. J. Kilkenny . . . Arch. Soc., n. s. I (1856-7). 256-82.

Conditions in Aug.-Sept. 1598. General.

81. MANNINGHAM, JOHN. Diary. Camden Soc. Pub., London, 1868.

2: Epigram on Sp. *Cf.* Harleian MS 5353, fol. 2.

82. MONTGOMERY, JAMES, and "Others." Dr. Lardner's Cabinet Cyclopaedia. London, 1836.

I, 312-51: Sp in "Lives of the Most Eminent Literary and Scientific Men of Great Britain." *Notice:* TLS 22 (Aug. 23, 1923). 560.

83. The Month X (1869). 354-65. The Poet Spenser in Ireland.

General on Sp's public life and his poetry.

84. Monthly Magazine.
    XVI (1803). 131-2. Cantabrigiana. No. 82. Spenser. Negligible.
    XXV (1808). 331. Sp's epitaph. *Cf. ibid.,* " Shakespeare."
    LVII (1824). 479. Note on life; picture of Kilcolman.

85. MORLEY, HENRY. Ireland Under Elizabeth and James the
    First.
    Rev. J. Cork Hist. and Arch. Soc., 2nd. ser. IV (1898). 145-50,
    " to be continued." Not completed.

86. ———— Spenser. English Writers, IX. London, 1893.
    Rev. The Critic, n. s. XIX (1893). 399-400.

87. MOWAT, R. B. Oxford, Cambridge, and Literature.
    Quart. Rev. CCXLVII (1926). 347-68.
    349-50: Sp's feeling for Cambridge and Oxford.

88. MURPHY, D. The Plantation of Desmond. Amer. Cath.
    Quart. Rev. III (1878). 482-98.
    Gives Desmond history of the period. *Cf.* 491, 496 for Sp.

89. O'MAHONY, CHARLES. The Viceroys of Ireland. Lon-
    don, 1912.
    73: Sp's grant and his life at Kilcolman.

90. PLOMER, HENRY R. Spenser's Handwriting. TLS 22
    (April 26, 1923). 287.
    Notes a document in Irish State Papers which, Mr. Plomer
    thinks, " sets at rest " question of Sp's handwriting.

91. ———— Edmund Spenser's Handwriting. MP XXI
    (1923). 201-7.
    Sp used both Italian and secretary hand; evidence of latter among
    Irish State Papers. *Rev.* YWES IV (1923). 121-2; Shakes. Jahr.
    59/60 (1924). 238. *Cf. ante,* Nos. 58, 59, 60; also " Spenser's Au-
    tographs," No. 1.

92. Polyanthos I (1806). 179.
    Citations from Fuller's account of Sp.

93. REDMOND, G. O'C. Allotments by the Undertakers in
    Munster, Province of Munster, 21st February, 1586.
    J. Roy. Hist. and Arch. Soc. Ire., 4th. ser. IX (1889).
    66-7.
    Regarding Sir Edw. Fytton's portion of land, etc., concealed from
    the Queen. [R. Heffner]

94. Returne from Parnassus, 1601. Dodsley's Old English
    Plays. London, 1874.
    IX, 113: Sp's last days.

3

95. RONAN, MYLES V. The Reformation in Ireland Under Elizabeth, 1558-1580. (From Original Sources.) London, 1930.

> App. IV: "Elizabeth's Court of Faculties" and App. V: "Elizabethan Church in Ireland in 1580." *Cf.* Carpenter, Ref. Guide, 37-8 on "Court of Faculties."

96. RUTHERFORD, MARK (William H. White). Last Pages from a Journal. London, 1915.

> Copy in Peabody Institute Library, Baltimore. Ch. I: Spenser and Kilcolman. [R. Heffner]

97. SANFORD, EZEKIEL. The Works of the British Poets, with Lives of the Authors. "First American Edition of the British Poets." 50 vols. Philadelphia, 1819.

> II, 3-16: Life of Sp. [F. I. C. and A. P.]

98. * SCHMID, CHRISTIAN H. Biographie der Dichter. Leipsig, 1769-70. 2 vols.

> "Zweiter Theil (1770), 148-236, a life of Sp along the lines of the seventeenth and eighteenth century biographies; cites Warton, etc.; analyzes the FQ, with some general criticism. Quotes Hughes (in trans.) at length. Pp. 234-36 on Sp's influence." [F. I. C. and A. P.]

99. SMITH, CHARLES. The Ancient and Present State of the County and City of Cork (1750). Repr. by Cork Hist. and Arch. Soc. with the addition of numerous Original Notes, etc., from the MSS of the late Thomas Crofton Croker, F. S. A., and Richard Caulfield. Cork, 1893. 3 vols.

> I, 6, 31: Sp's grant; 317: Rinny, part of Sp's estate; 311 and II, 327: Kilcolman.

100. SMITH, G. C. MOORE. Printed Books with Gabriel Harvey's Autograph or MS Notes. MLR XXVIII (1933). 78-81; XXIX (1934). 68-70, 321-2; XXX (1935). 209.

> Supplementary lists of Harvey autographs. *Cf.* Camden, C., Jr. Some Unnoted Harvey Marginalia. PQ XIII (1934). 214-8; "Spenser and Harvey," No. 10.

101. SMITH, J. C. Edmund Spenser. Encyclopedia Britannica, 14th ed. London and New York, 1929.

> XXI, 204-8: Sp.

102. SMYTH, GEORGE LEWIS. The Monuments and Genii of St. Paul's Cathedral and of Westminster Abbey. London, 1839. 2 vols.

II, 865-8: Life of Sp. He may have spent some time at Court, 1582-86, before his grant of land was made.

103. SPENCER, NATHANIEL. The Complete English Traveller. London, 1773.

320: Life of Sp.

104. THEOBALD, BERTRAM G. The Monuments to Bacon, Shakespeare and Spenser. Baconiana XX (1929). 14-28.

The "marginal acrostics" and Bacon's three codes of numerical cypher as found on Sp's monument at Westminster.

105. ——— Francis Bacon Concealed and Revealed. London, 1930.

39-80: Sp and Bacon. *Rev.* Baconiana XX (1931). 311, by H. S. Remarks upon difficulty of relating Sp to the Bacon theory. Harvey and Ralegh, however, aided Bacon to conceal his identity under Sp's name.

106. TURBERVILE, GEORGE. Epitaphes and Sonnettes, annexed to the Tragical histories.

Cf. Collier, J. P. Bibliographical Account (1866). III, 86; IV, 178; NQ, ser. iii. XI (1867). 418-9.

107. TWISS, HENRY F. Mallow and Some Mallow Men. J. Cork Hist. and Arch. Soc. XXXI (1926). 61 ff.

61: Sp's official vists to Mallow.

108. Universal Mag., n. s. XX (1813). 298-9. Mr. Edmund Spenser.

The Andrews fellowship once again.

109. VENN, J. and J. A. Alumni Cantabrigienses . . . from the Earliest Times to 1900. Cambridge, 1927.

Pt. I, vol. iv, 132: Sp's matriculation at Pembroke.

110. "Veritas." The Hidden Hand. Baconiana XIX (1928). 205-8.

Francis Bacon's knowledge of Hebrew and Chaldean proved by his use of their sacred symbols in his 1611 " Spenser."

111. WEBSTER, C. M. A note on Alexander Nowell. NQ
CLXVII (1934). 58-9.
    Alex. Nowell's patronage not beneficial in Sp's early years.
    Nowell in Burghley's bad graces, 1563-70. *Rev.* YWES XV (1934).
    210. *Cf. post,* Nos. 112, 114.

112. ——— Robert Nowell. NQ CLXVII (1934). 116.
    Robert Nowell, patron of Sp, may have been the one who intro-
    duced him to the Dudleys. *Cf. post,* No. 114.

113. WELPLY, W. H. The Family and Descendants of Edmund Spenser. J. Cork Hist. and Arch. Soc. XXVIII
(1922). 22-34, 49 ff.
    Cf. Carpenter, Ref. Guide, 75, for notes.

114. ——— Robert Nowell and Edmund Spenser. NQ
CLXVII (1934). 373.
    Robert Nowell not Sp's patron. *Cf. ante,* Nos. 111, 112.

115. WILSON, F. P. Spenser and Ireland. RES II (1926).
456-7.
    Sp probably in Ireland in May 1590. *Cf.* Rawl. MS A. 317.
    Bodl.

116. [WILSON, JOHN (Christopher North)]. Spenser. Blackwood's Mag. XXXIV (1833). 824-56.
    Life, etc.

117. ZEITLER, W. I. The Date of Spenser's Death. MLN
XLIII (1928). 322-4.
    John Chamberlain's "Saturday last" proved to be Jan. 13, 1599,
    rather than Jan. 16. *Rev.* YWES IX (1928). 172.

OTHER SPENSERS CONTEMPORARY WITH THE POET

See "Parents and Family," Nos. 6, 55.

1. ADAMS, R. BINGHAM. Biographic Data for Ferdinando
Freckleton from *Parish Registers of St. Mary Magda-
lene, Bermondsey, Surrey,* 1548-1609. NQ, ser. xiii.
IX (1927). 88.
    An Edward Spenser christened in this parish April 18, 1553. Is
    it the poet?

2. ALLEN, THOMAS. A New History of London, Westminster, and Southwark . . . London, 1837.
    II, 392: An Edmond Spencer is listed in the Cordwainer's Com-
    pany. No date.

3. BURN, JOHN SOUTHERDEN. Livre des Anglois. Appended to *History of Parish Registers in England*. London, 1862. Records of English refugees in Geneva.

> 278-9: Arrival of Thomas Spenser before " 5 November 1556." His marriage (p. 285) in 1557 entered as follows: " Thomas Spenser of Wroghton in Wiltshire, and Ales Agar of Colchester, widowe." Ales Agar's arrival before " 5 June 1557 " with " Johan and Priscilla her daughters, and Thomas her Sonne " (p. 281). Is this Thomas Spenser related to the poet? *Cf.* " Parents and Family," No. 5.

4. Calendar of Fiants Elizabeth. In Reports of the Deputy Keeper of the Records in Ireland. Index in 21st and 22nd Reports.

> No. 3645 (2873): Grant to James Spenscer, esq., of the office of constable of the Castle of Limerick. To hold during good behaviour, . . . with a fee of £10 ster . . . 30 July, xxii (1580). *Cf. post*, No. 9.

5. Catalogue of the Manuscripts of the King's Library: An Appendix to the Catalogue of the Cottonian Library; together with an Account of Books burnt or damaged by a later Fire. Ed. David Casley. London, 1734.

> 275: Lists " 18 A. LIX—Ja. Spenser's Discovery of Frauds in the Revenues of Ireland, A. D. 1610. Pap."

6. HAMER, DOUGLAS. Edmund Spenser; Some Further Notes. NQ, ser. xiv. VI (1932). 380.

> Notes another Edmund Spencer, yeoman of London. (Middlesex Sessions Rolls, Middlesex Co. Records, i, 249.)

7. Historical MSS Commission. Salisbury MSS Preserved at Hatfield House. Part XIII (1915).

> 288: Loan for the Earl of Leicester's expedition. This MS, No. 16. 69, undated, but it includes among "such as were absent" an Alderman Spenser.

8. MACRAY, W. D. Annals of the Bodleian Library. Oxford, 1890.

> 46: A John Spenser appears among signers in 1611 of the agreement of the Stationers' Company to forward their books to the Bodleian. *Cf.* Document A. 27 in *Univ. of Oxford Archives.*

9. WELPLY, W. H. Spenser in Ireland. TLS 32 (May 18, 1933). 348.

> Why was Sp in Limerick in 1577? Was James Spenscer, constable of Limerick Castle, his father? If so, was he visiting home in 1577? *Cf. ante*, No. 4; "Life, Miscellaneous," No. 59. *Rev.* YWES XIV (1933). 224.

Parents and Family

See " Marriage, Wife," Nos. 3, 5, 14, 16.

1. Acts of the Privy Council, 1600-1601. Ed. J. R. Dasent. New Series. London, 1906.

XXXI, 251 : Repeated at 257 : A letter to Sir George Carew from the Lords of the Privy Council dated " 29 Mar. 1601 at Whitehall," asking favor and assistance for Sp's widow and children in recovering things which should be theirs.

2. ADAMS, R. BINGHAM. Biographic Data for Ferdinando Freckleton . . . NQ CLIII (1927). 88.

i. Burial of Ferdinando Freckleton, May 2, 1596; ii. " Edward " Spenser christened at St. Mary Magdalene, Bermondsey, Surrey, April 18, 1553. Is it the poet? Cf. post, No. 54; also p. 32, note by R. B. Adams.

3. Annals of St. Fin Barr's Cathedral, Cork.

A. D. 1623: Grant by Dean and chapter to Robert Travers of Mooretown, of burial-place in South Chancel of " our Church " . . . mentions " Sara Spenser, als Travers." Cited by W. H. Welply. NQ, ser. xiv. VI (1932). 130.

4. Archaeologia XXI (1827). 551-3.

Prints the text of two bills in Chancery. The original of the second, " Petition of Sylvanus Spencer in regard to his father's lands now come into possession of Roger Seckerston," is an undated document preserved in PRO, Dublin (No. 15762. G-1-14. 146).

[R. Heffner]

5. ATKINSON, DOROTHY F. Edmund Spenser's Family and the Church. NQ CLXX (1936). 172-5.

Is Edmund Sp related to Thomas, Richard, and John of Wroughton, Wilts? Associations of Thomas with John Young, Thomas Watts, etc. Is it possible that the poet knew these men through Thomas Spenser? Cf. Bensly, E., ibid., 230-1; Glencross, R. M., ibid., 231.

6. Autobiography of Phineas Pett. Ed. W. G. Perrin. Printed for the Navy Records Society. 1918.

86: Under date of Dec. 6, 1610. Prince Henry's visit to the Straits' voyage ships. Mention of " Lawrence Spencer," a boatswain.

7. BARRY, E. Records of the Barrys. Chapter II. J. Cork Hist. and Arch. Soc., 2nd. ser. VI (1900). 65 ff.

81 : In 22 James I (Mar. 31), inquisition taken at Youghal. " William Wiseman, esquire, escheator for the county of Cork."

8. BARRY, E. Records of the Barrys. Chapter III. J. Cork
Hist. and Arch. Soc., 2nd. ser. VII (1901). 65 ff.

> 74: Under David Nagle of Moneanimney:
> "Ellis [Ellin?], the eldest daughter of the first-mentioned David,
> married unto Sylvanus Spenser, eldest son of Edmond Spenser,
> esquire, the famous poet, by whom she had issue two sons—Edmond
> Spenser and William Spenser; . . ." *Cf.* Trin. Coll. MS F. 3. 27,
> p. 42; *post*, No. 50.

9. BENNETT, GEORGE. The History of Bandon.

> 50, 56, 168: "Catherine, daughter of the poet" Sp, married Wil-
> liam Wiseman (M. P. for Bandon 1634); Sp's second son, Lau-
> rence, died in Bandon in 1654. The poet's third son, Peregrine, was
> firmarius of the adjoining parish of Brinny. [F. I. C. and A. P.]
> 96: "There were several Protestants, also in his [Robert
> Bathurst's] debt in 1642 amongst whom we find the names of
> . . . Spenser . . . all of Bandonbridge."

10. BERRY, H. F. Justices of the Peace for Co. Cork. J. Cork
Hist. and Arch. Soc., 2nd. ser. III (1897). 58 ff., 106.

> 60: On Travers and Nagle appointments of 22 Jan., 1674, and 16
> July, 1686, respectively.

11. Calendar of Fiants Elizabeth.

> No. 5499: "Lease (under Queen's letter, July 1, xxxi) . . . [of]
> the lands of Little Grange, co. Kildare, parcel of the lands of Edm.
> Ewstace, attainted, granted to John Travers, knt., by patent of 13
> Nov., iii, . . . To hold for 31 years . . . 25 Nov. xxxiii (1590)."
> *Cf.* Fiants, Hen. VIII, Nos. 403,404 (Feb. xxxv 1543-4) and 460
> (20 June xxxvii 1545); also No. 6796 (Feb. xxxv Hen. VIII)
> John Travers.

12. CLIFTON, A. S. W. Edmund Spenser, His Connection
with County Northants. NQ, ser. xiii. X (Mar. 17,
1928). 195.

> Cites Round's *Peerage and Family History* on earliest known
> ancestors of Althorp Spencers. Brothers, William of Radbourne
> (founded titled branch) and John of Hodnell. In 1550 John sold
> Hodnell Manor to Thomas Wilkes. If he then went to London,
> Sp's connection with noble Spencers may be explained. *Cf. ibid.,*
> 69, 123.

13. County Cork. Calendar of Inquisitions Postmortem
(Formerly in Rolls Office, now in PRO, Dublin). J.
Cork Hist. and Arch. Soc., 2nd. ser. I (1895). 381 ff.

> The Index gives the following entries:

" William and Mary	Com. Cork.	Name of Deceased	Folio in Roll
1694, 15 Aug.	Old Castle	Hugotin Spencer	13
1694, 15 Aug.	Old Castle	Richard Nagle	16
1692, 19 May	Guildhall	Rīcus Nagle, miles	1
1692, 19 May	Kings Old Castle	Neagle, miles	1 "

14. DAY, ROBERT. Cooke's Memoirs of Youghal, 1749. J. Cork Hist. and Arch. Soc., 2nd. ser. IX (1903). 34 ff.

Lists of mayors and bailiffs. *Cf.* also pp. 109, 111.
54: 1662 " Matthew Spencer"
55: 1673 " Mat. Spencer "
      " John Spencer "
56: 1678 " Jno. Spencer "
    1685 " Jno. Spencer "

15. DEVEREUX, W. *Re* Spencer Pedigree. Portrait. J. Cork Hist. and Arch. Soc., 2nd. ser. XII (1906). 50-1, 152-3.

A pedigree of Joseph Sherlock, husband of Alicia Burne (daughter of Rosamund Spencer and James Burne).

16. ———— Spenser's Pedigree. J. Cork Hist. and Arch. Soc., 2nd. ser. XV (1909). 101-2.

Will of Lawrence Spencer of Bandon. Quotes will of Daniel Adams (dated 25 April 1702) in which Spencers are named.

17. Dublin University Mag. XXXVIII (1851). 233-52. Spenser's Streams—the Mulla and Allo.

240: Sp's wife and children after 1599.

18. EVANS, F. Edmund Spenser, His Connection with Co. Northants. NQ, ser. xiii. X (1928). 29.

If Sp's relation to Burnley Spensers is unproved, perhaps he may be related to Northampton Spensers. *Cf. ante,* No. 12; R. S. B. in NQ, ser. xiii. X (Jan. 28, 1928). 69; Hieronymus, *ibid.* (Feb. 18, 1928). 123.

19. Fasti Ecclesiae Hibernicae. Ed. Henry Cotton. Dublin, 1847-8.

Vol. I, Munster. Under prebendaries of St. Patrick's Cathedral:
36: " 1663. Nathanael Spenser, a Prebendary of Lismore, appears in the Visitation Books of this year. He resigned in, or before, April, 1667."
71: " 1662. Nathanael Spenser, Prebendary of St. Patrick's Cathedral, Waterford; collated and installed 10 Nov."
                                      [Bishops' Returns.]
Vol. II, Leinster.
377: Under Whitechurch. " Nathanael Spenser " is named.

20. FITZGERALD, JOHN J. Documents Found at Castlewhite, Co. Cork. Roy. Soc. Antiq. Ire. LX (1930). 79-83.

> 79: Castlewhite was sold, 1637, to "Sir Robert Travers and Zachary Travers, sons of John Travers who was married to a sister of the poet Spenser . . ."

21. FITZ-ROSE, ——. Gentleman's Mag. 1834. I. 165. The Parentage of the Poet Spenser.

> Sp's relation to noble Spencers "undoubted."

22. FLEMING, HORACE T. (Dean). Some Notes on the Tynte Family. J. Cork Hist. and Arch. Soc., 2nd. ser. IX (1903). 156-7.

> Description of Tynte monument in Kilcredan Church refers to "the second wife of Sir Robert Tynte, who was Elizabeth Boyle, kinswoman of the Earl of Cork, and who was widow of the poet Spenser, and whom Sir Robert Tynte married in 1612." Cf. J. Cork Hist. and Arch. Soc. XXXI (1926). 86; "Spenser's Marriage," No. 15.

23. FLOOD, WILLIAM H. G. The Account-Book of a Dublin Harpsichord Maker, Ferdinand Weber, 1764 to 1783. Roy. Soc. Antiq. Ire. XLIV (1914). 338 ff.

> 340, 344, 346: "Mrs. Spencer" mentioned.

24. GALLWEY, THOMAS. Richard Boyle, First Earl of Cork. The Monitor (Dublin) II (1879). 357 ff., 459 ff.

> 366: Sp's castle sacked. Cf. p. 266.

25. HALPIN, N. J. On Certain Passages in the Life of Edmund Spenser. Proc. Roy. Irish Acad. IV (1850). 445-51.

> Eliz. Boyle's marriage to Seggerston. Cf. Grosart, A. B. Spenser. III, lxxxvi-cii.

26. HAMER, DOUGLAS. Spenser; Travers. NQ, ser. xiv. VI (1932). 352, 370.

> Requests information about recent members of the Sp-Travers families. Cf. Spencer, F. C. Gentleman's Mag., n. s. XVIII (1842). 139. Cf. "Life, Miscellaneous," No. 47.

27. HARDIMAN, JAS. Inquisitionum . . . Cancellariae Hiberniae . . . Repertorium. "By Command." 1826. 2 vols.

> Co. Dublin, Eliz. No. 4 "14 Dec' an' 24." "Postea, viz. 25 Oct' 1561, Joh' Travers mil' in dict' chart' nominat', fecit suā ult. voluntat' (cujus tenor etiam sequit^r in orig.') & obit." Cf. Drog-

heda, Car. 1, [7 Sept. 1630] 3 Joh' Travers; Meath, 4 Eliz. [5 April 1598]; Meath, 71 Jac. 1 [24 May 1624]; Wicklow, 10 Car. 1 [14 April 1632]; Com. Regine, 34 Car. 1 [9 April 1646].

28. HAYMAN, SAMUEL. Ecclesiastical Antiquities of Youghal. No. 1. St. Mary's Collegiate Church. Kilkenny Arch. Soc. Proc. III (1854-5). 96 ff.

On the Boyle family.

29. HENLEY, PAULINE. Spenser in Ireland. Cork University Press, 1928.

Ch. VIII: Sp's Descendants.

30. HICKSON, MARY. The Seggerson or Seckerston Family in Ireland. J. Roy. Hist. and Arch. Ass., 4th. ser. VIII (1887-8). 340-1.

"Cousin Seggerson" [Lismore Papers 2nd. ser. I, 84] is Seckerston. Depositions relating to 1641 [in Trin. Coll. Dublin] use various spellings.

31. Historical MSS Commission Reports.

IV (1874), 594a: Lists MSS in Trin. Coll. Library, *ca.* 1600. Included are: "Treatise on music, by John Travers, *circa* A. D. 1590. Fol."

"Collectanea philosophica. Joh: Travers. Analysis Porphyriana ex P. Ramo. Excerpta ex Aristotele, Lactantio, &c. Fol." [*Qu.* Is this Travers Sp's brother-in-law?]

32. HOWITT, WILLIAM. Homes and Haunts of the British Poets. New York, 1847.

I, 15-44: Descendants.

33. Index Testamentorum olim in Registro Corcagiae, 1600-1802. J. Cork Hist. and Arch. Soc., 2nd. ser. IV (1898). 79 ff.

Several Spensers, some of whom may be related to the poet.
81: 1668—Richard Spencer, of Youghal.
156: 1786 Daniel Pierce Spencer, of Abbey Park, hatter.
1794 Hannah Pierce Spencer, of Abby Park.
158, No. 500: Ebenezer Spencer, of Cork, hatter.

34. Journal of the Cork Hist. and Arch. Soc., 2nd. ser. III (1897). The Windele Manuscripts.

254, 260: Sp's castle.
371-3 :Hugolin, son of Peregrine Sp, in 1702 lost property forfeited in fee by attainder; Sarah Sp's marriage.

35. ———— 2nd. ser. XII (1906). 151, by J. C.

Notice of Gerald H. Supple (d. 1898) and two sisters in New Zealand, 1897. Lineal descendants of Sp.

36. Lismore Papers. Ed. A. B. Grosart . . . priv. print.
    1886-8. 10 vols.
First series.
   I, xiv-xvi; II, 382, 403; III, 238: Seckerstone family.
   I, 189; II, 143, 403; V, 254: Sir Robert Tynte.
   I, 189, 275; II, 402-3; V, 254: Elizabeth Boyle.
   I, 189, 294; II, 94, 96, 143, 360, 374: Peregrine Sp. *Cf.* text below.
   IV, 245: Nagle family.
   IV, 7, 157, 232-3, 242-3: William Wiseman.
   II, 94: In Earl of Cork's Diaries, under "October, 1623":
     "18 [Oct. 1623] I paid pereg   [pres]ance 50^{li} ster.
     being his part [of the C]^{li} my wife did ow the Lady Tynt [which
     C]^{li} the Lady Tent gaue by her las[t will, to be de]vided between
     her two sons p[eregryn Spencer &] Richard Seckerston. So
     peregry[n is paid &] my wife owes Seckers[ton]." (The rest is
     gone.)
   II, 96: Diaries, "15 November 1623":
     "My wife did acknowledge (the whole centre of this entry is
     gone; on either margin words come as put on either side thus)

	"which her
La^p by her last	sonnes
peregryne Spe	erston to be
equally devided	peregryn
this 50^{li}	the Lor^d Roche."

   II, 143: Diaries, "20 October 1624":
     "I paid Sir Robert Tynt, vppon his own acquittance, endorsed
     by Richard seckerstones letter of attorney, 50^{li}, in dischardg of
     my wives debt to my lady Tynt, having formerly paid Peregryne
     Spencer other 50^{li}."
   I, 189: Diaries, "15 May, 1618":
     Note of payment of "v^{li} to peregryne Spencer as interest money
     my wife did owe his mother . . . for geving me up Ballynecourty,
     & he released me Ballymorrisshee."
Second series.
   I, xv-xvii: Eliz. Boyle. Also I, Frontisp.
   I, 261: Sp-Roche quarrel.
   I, xv, xx, 84, 86, 273: Seckerstone.
   II, 284: Peregrinne Sp; *Cf.* III, Frontisp. [text below].
   IV, 75, 123: An Edmond Spencer living *ca.* 1640. His death and
burial. *Cf.* 115 for a lawsuit in which he appears. *Cf.* Welply, W.
H. Edmund Spenser . . . NQ, ser. xiv. VI (1932). 203. Identifies
this man as Sylvanus's son, Edmund.
   III, Frontisp.: Facsimile of receipt, Nov. 1623, sent by Peregrine
Spenser to Earl of Cork. *Cf.* III, 79-80 for text: "Be it knowen
vnto all men by theis present*s* that I Peregrinne Spenser gent, one
of the sonnes of the Lady Elizabeth Tynte deceased, do herby acknowledge to haue here now receaued of the right honorable Richard
Erle of Cork, the some of ffiftie poundes currant money of vse in
England, being the iust moietie of one hundred pound*s* of like Currant money, which was a debt due from the Lady Countess of Cork,

vnto the said Lady Tynte my mother and given by her by will betweene me the said Peregrinne and Richard Seckerston, another sonn
of hers. . . ." 15 November 1623.

37. MacSwiney of Mashanaglass, Marquis of. Notes on
the Formation of the First Two Irish Regiments in the
Service of Spain in the Eighteenth Century. Roy. Soc.
Antiq. Ire. LVII (1927). 7-20.

> 17: Quotes *Regio Archivio di Stato Napoli. S|ezione Guerra e
> Marina. Libretto di Vita e Costumi. Regimento de Dragones de
> Tarragona, An.* 1737, fol. 7. A "Don Hugo Spenser, of the City
> of Cork" appointed a cadet in Mahony's Regiment on June 11,
> 1703. Author announces forthcoming paper in J. Cork Hist. and
> Arch. Soc. showing this to be "An Unknown Descendant of Ed-
> mund Spenser." Apparently the paper has not been published.

38. Miscellanea Genealogia et Heraldica, ser. iv. IV (1910-
1). 360 ff. Travers genealogy.

> Gives Sarah Sp as poet's daughter. *Cf. post,* No. 57, # v.

39. Monthly Mag. XV (1803). 248; XXIV (1807). 51-3.

> A Sp descendant in Ireland, 1724, knew so little English as to
> need an interpreter in court.

40. Moore, Courtenay. Mourne Abbey and Barrett's
Castle, or Castlemore, Co. Cork. J. Cork Hist. and
Arch. Soc., 2nd. ser. VI (1900). 210 ff.

> 213, 214: Sp and Kilcolman.

41. Notes and Queries, ser. vi. X (1884). 86, 333, 434.

> John Travers not connected with Lancashire family.

42. Ó'Ríordáin, Seán P. The Place Names and Antiquities
of Kinalmeaky Barony, Co. Cork. J. Cork Hist. and
Arch. Soc. XXXVIII (1933). 16 ff.

> 16, 18: *Kilbeg* and *Kilbrogan Protestant Church*: Catherine Sp's
> burial-place.

43. P., W. A Note on Spenser in Lancashire (Burnley-
Hurstwood). NQ, ser. i. VII (1853). 303. Reprint
from London Times, Wed., June 16, 1841.

44. Shirley, E. P. Extracts from the Journal of Thomas
Dineley, Esquire, Giving Some Account of his Visit to
Ireland in the Reign of Charles II. J. Kilkenny Arch.
Soc., n. s. IV (1862-3). 320-38.

> 332: Tomb of Jacob Spenser's wife in Youghal. *Cf. ibid.,* n. s.
> V (1864-6). 425 for Boyles, Nagles, and Barrys.

45. SMITH, CHARLES. Ancient and Present State of the County and City of Cork . . . Repr. J. Cork Hist. and Arch. Soc., 1893.

I, 126-7: James Spencer, 1679; I, 468: William Wiseman listed as M. P., 1634, for Bandonbridge.

46. STOKES, G. T. The Antiquities from Kingston to Dublin. Roy. Soc. Antiq. Ire. XXIII (1893). 350.

Sir John Travers obtained his first grant of Monkstown, 1542; estates enlarged, 1545, by grant of property of James Fitzgerald, attainted, and the abbey of Baltinglass. *Cf.* Fiants, Hen. VIII, pp. 61, 78, in *Reports of the Deputy Keeper,* 1875 . . . [R. Heffner]

47. TENISON, C. M. Cork M. P.'s, 1559-1800. J. Cork Hist. and Arch. Soc., 2nd. ser. II (1896). 368-71.

370-1: William Wiseman's descent, marriage to Catherine Sp, residence, positions, etc.

48. TOWNSHEND, DOROTHEA. Notes on the Council Book of Clonakilty. J. Cork Hist. and Arch. Soc., 2nd. ser. I (1895). 385 ff.

395: " Sir R. Travers was member of Parliament for Clonakilty 1634-39, and married Sarah, sister of the poet Spenser."

49. ———— The Great Earl of Cork.

139: Hugolin and Peregrine Spenser.

50. Trinity College Dublin. MS F. 3. 27. p. 42: Nangle (Nagle) genealogy.

Contains marriage of " Elin = Silvanus (*s.* Edmund Spenser, Esq. who wrote yᵉ Fairy Queen) & had issue Edm: Spenser [. . . the rest is illegible]." [*ca.* 1700] [R. Heffner]. *Cf.* Catalogue of the Manuscripts in the Library of Trinity College, Dublin. Ed. T. K. Abbott. Dublin, 1900. MS 1216. Obits, pedigrees, marriages, etc. . . . Ireland, 16th and 17th centuries. This is F. 3. 27; *ante,* No. 8.

51. TWISS, HENRY F. Mallow and Some Mallow Men. J. Cork Hist. and Arch. Soc. XXXI (1926). 61 ff.

68: Edmund Spenser, son of Edmund Sp, who married Anne Freeman, lived in Mallow. He is listed among residents in 1766. Died 23 Oct. 1789. Inscription is said to read:

"Here lies the body of Edmund Spenser,
Great great great grandson of the poet Spenser
Unfortunate from his cradle to his grave."

The stone has not been found.

69: Edmund Spenser who figures among the Mallow Volunteers in 1776 was son of Edmund, son of Nathaniel (of Renny), son of William, son of Sylvanus, son of the poet.

52. W., G. W. Newcomb, Penn, Spenser, and Tesdale. NQ, ser. xiv. VI (1932). 191.

> Rev. Thos. Newcomb, translator of Hervey's *Contemplations on the Night,* descended from Ed. Spenser.

53. WELPLY, W. H. The Family and Descendants of Edmund Spenser. J. Cork Hist. and Arch. Soc. XXVIII (1922). 49-61. *Cf.* Carpenter, Ref. Guide, 83.

> History of Mary Spenser, *ca.* 1736; William Spenser. Brings pedigree down to fairly recent times. Quotes some of records which were destroyed in Four Courts Fire. Important. Genealogical tables for Travers, Tynte, and Spenser families. Quotes Cromwell's letter regarding Wm. Sp's estate.

54. ———— Edmund Spenser; some new discoveries and the correction of some old errors. NQ, ser. xiii. II (1924). 445-7; ser. xiii. III (1924). 35.

> i. PRO, Dublin, preserves Chancery suit of Perregreene Spencer *vs.* Frances Marshiall, 9 July 1622. Peregrine says his mother was wife of Roger Seckerstone in Aug., 1600. Her death given as 23 August 1622. ii. "The Corporate Records of Youghal" contain indenture, dated 3 May 1606, between Sir Richard Boyle of Youghal and Eliz. Boyle als Seckerstone of Kilcoran, *widow.* iii. Lismore Papers record Eliz. Boyle's marriage to Tynte on 3 Mar. 1612. "The Chancery law suit [*Cf.* Carpenter, Ref. Guide, 31] is of great significance. The plaintiffs were Edmond Spencer, his wife Eliz., and George and Alexander Boyle, her brothers. Alexander Boyle migrated to Ireland, accompanied by Eliz., and held land under his kinsman the Great Earl. From evidence obtained in the statement of this suit, it is safe to conclude that the plaintiffs were the poet Sp, his wife, and his brothers-in-law; that Sp's wife was the daughter of Stephen Boyle of Bradden, Northamptonshire (d. 1582), her mother's name was Joan; that Joan Boyle married secondly Ferdinando Freckleton; that Eliz. Boyle became entitled to her legacy of £250, left by her father, when she married Sp 11 June 1594, and that she may have been no more than eighteen . . . a supposition borne out by the fact, that marrying Capt. Tynte in 1612/3, she bore him seven children, and died in 1622. . . ." iv. Lawrence Spenser, yeoman farmer of Kilpatrick, near Bandon, co. Cork, is not the poet's son. [A. P.] *Cf.* Hamer, D., *post,* p. 31; "Life, Miscellaneous," No. 47; "Spenser's Marriage," No. 12.

55. ———— Edmund Spenser: Being an account of some recent researches into his life and lineage, with some no-

tice of his family and descendants. NQ, ser. xiv. VI (1932). 110-14, 128-32, 146-50, 165-9, 182-7, 202-6, 220-4, 239-42, 256-60.

110-14: Sp's claim of relationship to noble Spencers; his descent in relation to that of Althorpe Spencers. Genealogical tables (112-3) of Badby and Everdon Spencers.

128-32: Review of case for Sp's connection with Lancashire; identity of Rosalind. Pedigree of Sir Thos. North.

146-50: Time-chart of Sp's life; the life in Ireland to 1586 from documents; life, 1586-91, noting new documents.

165-9: Eliz. Boyle identified as daughter of Stephen Boyle of Bradden, Northants.

182-7: Sp married twice; Peregrine may be Eliz. Boyle's only child by Sp; character of Eliz. Boyle as revealed in Lismore Papers, etc.; Sir Robert Needham and Ponsonby's preface to *Amoretti* and *Epithalamion*; Sp's life, 1597-99. Chancery suit given in full (Sp, etc. *vs.* Thomas Emyly and John Mathewe, 1596-7); corrections of Sir William Betham's pedigree of Sp, chiefly in regard to his children.

202-6: Silvanus Sp's life and his son Edmund; Peregrine's career, and Catherine's; Peregrine's children, Peregrine and Mary.

220-4: Career of Wm. Sp, the poet's grandson, for whom Cromwell intervened Mar. 27, 1657.

239-42: Sp's great-great-grandson Nathaniel, and his grandson Hugolin; Edmund Sp the third.

256-60: Other Bandon and Youghal Spencers who have no clear connection with the poet's family. Genealogical tables.

Rev. YWES XIII (1932). 193; Shakes. Jahr. 68 (1932). 174. *Cf.* Hamer, D. *ante,* p. 25; also letters as follows:

W., G. H. NQ, ser. xiv. VI (1932). 175-6.
A lease, 4 Nov. 1576, by Lady Anne Catline and John Spencer. Note on Sir Robt. Catline's descent.

Hamer, Douglas. *Ibid.,* 209-11, 231.
Two Ferdinando Freckletons in Sp's day. The one who was military officer in Ireland is Joan Cope (Boyle's) husband. *Cf. ante,* No. 54; and Adams, R. B. below.

A., H. I. Nicholas Spencer of Cheshire, 1510. *Ibid.,* 210-1.
A will, proved Lambeth, Aug. 26, 1510, of Nicholas Spencer. Family and descendants.

B., R. S. Edmund Spenser: Bryan Travers. *Ibid.,* 211.
Is John Travers related to Brian Travers' family?

M., F. R. S. Newcomb, Penn, Spenser, and Tesdale. *Ibid.,* 230.

B., R. S. Seckerston. *Ibid.,* 230.
Seckerstons of Liverpool and Nantwich districts.

S. Seckerston. *Ibid.,* 304, 412.

Smith, G. C. Moore. Seckerston. *Ibid.,* 266.
Cf. note by S., 304, 412.

Adams, R. Bingham. Captain Sir Ferdinando Freckleton. *Ibid.,*
265-6.
A grant of arms. *Cf.* Hamer, D. *Ibid.,* 210, 231; also *ante,*
No. 2.

56. WELPLY, W. H. Spenser in Ireland. TLS 32 (May 18,
1933). 348.

Is James Spenscer, constable of Castle of Limerick, xxii Eliz., the
poet's father? *Cf.* Fiant 3645 (2873).

57. ———— More Notes on Edmund Spenser. NQ, ser. xiv.
IX (1933). 92-4, 111-6.

92-4: i. Grant of arms to Spencers of Hodnall; ii. Th. Spencer
died without issue; iii. *ye aier* correct reading of Harvey's letter;
iv. Sp and "Money of Robert Nowell"; v. Sarah Sp, wife of John
Travers. Proof in funeral certificate of Wm. Wiseman and in his
will; vi. Sp's brothers; vii. CCCHA and Thos. Stuteville's wife;
viii. Rosalind and Sir Erasmus Dryden's wife; ix. could "north
parts" be interpreted to refer to service with Sir Henry Sidney at
Ludlow Castle and in Ireland; x. Matt. Spencer of Cromwell's time;
xi. funeral entry of David Nagle in relation to Sp-de Vere controversy.
111-6: i. Annotated pedigree of Tynte of Wraxall, Co. Somerset;
Tynte genealogical tables; ii. Geo. Boyle, knighted 1620, not Eliz.
Boyle's brother. *Cf. ante,* No. 54; "Life, Miscellaneous," No. 47.
Rev. YWES XIV (1933). 224.

58. WHITE, JAMES G. Historical and Topographical Notes
on Buttevant, Castletownroche, Doneraile, Mallow. . . .
Cork, 1905. 3 vols.

I, 51, 54-6, 57, 260, 353: Sp's descendants. Genealogical tables,
Nagle family.
I, 83: Garrett Nagle's loss of Sp's works.
I, 162: Sp's grant of Ballyellis. *Cf.* Fiants, Eliz. 5473 (6536).
I, 353: Sp's grant of arrearage, 7 Feb. 1597. Peregrine's holding
Buttevant abbey, 1656.
I, 225: Edmund Burke's connection with Sp's family.
II (Cork, 1911), 69: Anne Freeman's marriage to last lineal des-
cendant of poet. *Cf.* I, 260.

59. WOOD, HERBERT. Spenser's Great-Grandson. TLS 28
(Feb. 14, 1929). 118.

Repr. part of letter (3 Aug. 1736) of John Wainwright, Baron of
the Irish Court of Exchequer, in regard to sale for debt of estate of
poet's great-grandson.

SPENSER'S MARRIAGE: HIS WIFE, ETC.

See "Life, Miscellaneous," Nos. 47, 73; "Parents and
Family," Nos. 1, 4, 22, 28, 36, 55, 57.

1. BALL, F. E. Some Notes on the Irish Judiciary . . .
   1660-1685. J. Cork Hist. and Arch. Soc., 2nd. ser.
   VIII (1902). 185.
   Is Tynte's daughter who married Wm. Worth the child of Eliz.
   Boyle?

2. BERRY, HENRY F. Sheriffs of County Cork. Roy. Soc.
   Antiq. Ire. XXXV (1905). 52.
   Note on Sir Robert Tynte and Eliz. Boyle.

3. CARPENTER, FREDERIC I. The Marriages of Edmund
   Spenser. MP XXII (1924). 97-8.
   Two records of an Edmund Spenser's marriage: i. "Edm. Spenser
   & Jone Bre[ttri]dge . . . 21, July, 1586" at West Drayton. Cf. post,
   No. 16. Improbable that Sp was in London on this date. ii. "1590,
   1 December. Edmundus Spencer et Maria Towerson nupti fuerunt."
   Cf. Register of St. Bees, Cumberland. This is not the poet, on
   evidence of other entries in the register. Rev. YWES V (1924).
   153. Cf. post, Nos. 5, 10, 11, 14.

4. DAY, ROBERT. Notes on Youghal. Roy. Soc. Antiq. Ire.
   XXXIII (1903). 325.
   Sp, and later, his widow, Eliz. Seckerston, lived at Kilcoran
   Castle. Amor. LXXV cited as perhaps referring to rock at Youghal
   where names were inscribed.

5. ECCLES, MARK. Spenser's First Marriage. TLS 30
   (Dec. 31, 1931). 1053.
   Cites entry, Parish Registers, 1539-1660, of St. Margaret's, West-
   minster, Oct. 27, 1579. "Edmounde Spenser to Machabyas Chylde."
   Cf. ante, No. 3; post, No. 11. Rev. YWES XII (1931). 192.

6. FRISBEE, GEORGE. Sat. Rev. of Lit. X (Jan. 20, 1934).
   431. "Personals."
   Cf. also Frisbee, ibid., (Jan. 27, 1934). 443, two items in "Personals"; ibid., (Feb. 10, 1934). 483; ibid., XI (Feb. 16, 1935). 499;
   Rosenbach, post, No. 19.

7. GARROD, H. W. Spenser and Elizabeth Boyle. TLS 22
   (May 10 and 24, 1923). 321, 355.
   On evidence in copy of FQ 1596, Eliz. Boyle, when Sp married
   her, was Mrs. Elizabeth Pease, widow (since 1592/3 or earlier) of
   Tristram Pease. Cf. Amor. allusion. [F. I. C. and A. P.] Rev.
   YWES IV (1923). 122-23. Cf. post, No. 20; "Parents and
   Family," Nos. 54, 55.

8. GRISMER, FRANK A. Spenser's Epithalamion. TLS 33
   (April 26, 1934). 303.
   Sp's intention in writing this, the date, etc. Cf. "Epithalamion,"
   No. 12.

9. HALPIN, N. J. On Certain Passages in the Life of Edmund Spenser. Proc. Roy. Irish Acad. IV (1850). 445-51.

Sp's wife; her marriage to Seggerston.

10. HAMER, DOUGLAS. Spenser's First Marriage. RES VII (1931). 271-90.

Sp twice married; first, 1580, to mother of his first three children; secondly, to Eliz. Boyle, mother of Peregrine. *Rev.* YWES XII (1931). 192. *Cf. ante,* Nos. 3, 5; " Life, Miscellaneous, No. 47; " Parents and Family," No. 55.

11. ——— Spenser's First Marriage. TLS 31 (Jan. 14, 1932). 28.

Corroborates facts of St. Margaret's entry. *Cf. ante,* No. 5; "Life, Miscellaneous," No. 59.

12. ——— Sir Robert Tynte's Sons. NQ, ser. xiv. VII (1932). 62-3.

William Tynte of Cahirmony was only son of Sir Robert and Elizabeth Boyle. *Cf.* " Parents and Family," No. 54.

13. Historical MSS Commission. Salisbury MSS. Hatfield House. Pt. XI. Dublin, 1906.

95: Hugh Cuffe, writing to Sir Robert Cecil, Feb. 1, 1600-1, lists a " Mrs. Spencer " among undertakers in Co. Cork.

14. JACKSON, WILLIAM. Marriage of Edmund Spenser. NQ, ser. iv. X (1872). 244.

Sp-Towerson entry. *Cf. ibid.,* 301-2, by T. MacGrath. *Cf. ante,* No. 3.

15. LEE, PHILIP G. The Ruined Monuments of Sir Robert Tynte. . . . J. Cork Hist. and Arch. Soc. XXXI (1926). 86 ff.

Tynte monument (1636), Kilcredan Church, shows Eliz. Boyle as second wife. *Cf.* " Parents and Family," No. 22.

16. Middlesex Parish Registers. Ed. W. P. W. Phillimore and Thomas Gurney. London, 1910.

145: " Edm. Spenser & Jone Bre[ttri]dge 21 July 1586 " under " Marriages at West Drayton." [F. I. C. and A. P.]

17. ORPEN, GODDARD H. Roy. Soc. Antiq. Ire. XXXIII (1903). 418-9.

Eliz. Sp resident at Kilcoran; her marriage to Sp, 1594; to Seckerstone, 1603; to Tynte, 1606; her children. [R. Heffner]

18. PARTRIDGE, A. F. Spenser's Mistress, Rosalind. NQ, ser. xiii. IX (1927). 389-90.

Aubrey's mention of Rosalind as kinswoman of Francis Wilkes. *Cf. ibid.*, 350.

19. ROSENBACH, A. S. W. Books and Bidders. Boston, 1927.

148-51 : Sp's copy of FQ with Greek inscription on title-page: " From the author to himself." This volume presented to Eliz. Boyle. *Amor. I* inscribed under head "A Sa Mistresse" [Facs. opp. 151]. Copy, now in Mr. Rosenbach's library, belonged to I. Gollancz. *Cf.* I. Gollancz, Carpenter, Ref. Guide, 55.

20. WELPLY, W. H. Spenser and Elizabeth Boyle. TLS 22 (May 24, 1923). 355-6.

"Answers Garrod [*ante*, No. 7] with documents as to her third (?) husband, Roger Seckerstone and his wife. As to Sp's purchase of Renny." [F. I. C. and A. P.] *Rev.* YWES V (1924). 152-3.

21. ———— Edmund Spenser: some new discoveries and the correction of some old errors. NQ, ser. xiii. II and III (1924). 445-7, 35.

Cf. "Parents and Family," No. 54.

22. WESTROPP, THOMAS J. Temple-na-Caille, County Limerick. Roy. Soc. Antiq. Ire. XXXIII (1903). 297.

Kilcolman and Kilcoran.

SPENSER'S CIRCLE: FRIENDS, PATRONS, ASSOCIATES, AND ACQUAINTANCES

1. Baconiana, n. s. VIII (1900). 92-3, by C. M. P.

Sp's name does not appear among the lists of secretaries to Anthony and Francis Bacon, though Spenser was the family name of two of these officials.

2. BRUNO, GIORDANO.

Cf. Bhattacherje, M. Studies in Spenser, Ch. 4; Levinson, Ronald B. Spenser and Bruno. PMLA XLIII (1928). 675-81; McIntyre, J. Lewis. Giordano Bruno. London, 1903; Davis, B. E. C. Edmund Spenser: A Critical Study. 235-40; Parmenter, Mary. Bruno's Influence on Spenser's *Mutabilitie*. No. 36. Proceedings of Dr. Greenlaw's Seminary " C," 1928-9. The Johns Hopkins University Library.

3. BRYSKETT, LODOWICK.

Cf. Ritson, Jos. Bibliographia Poetica, 1802, 146 n; Collier, J. P. Poetical Decameron, 1820, I, 95-6, 98; Hunter, Joseph. Chorus Vatum Anglicorum, B. M. Addit. MS 24,489, fols. 308, 309; Gilbert,

J. T. Calendar of Ancient Records of Dublin. Dublin, 1891. " By
Authority." II, xiii: Sp, Bryskett, and Harvey; Jenkins, Raymond.
Spenser and the Clerkship in Munster. PMLA XLVII (1932).
109-21; Plomer, H. R. and Cross, T. P. The Life and Correspondence
of Lodowick Bryskett. Univ. of Chicago Press, 1927; Jones, Deborah.
Lodowick Bryskett and his Family, in *Thomas Lodge and Other
Elizabethans.* Ed. C. J. Sisson. Cambridge, Mass., 1933. 245 ff.;
Spens, J. Spenser's *Faerie Queene.* Appendix.

4. CAMDEN, WILLIAM. ·

> *Cf.* Hunter, Joseph. Chorus Vatum . . . B. M. Addit. MS 24, 487,
> fols. 126-8; Camden's epitaph on Sp " in his own hand " in the vols.
> of his collection in the Bodleian.

5. CAREY, LADY.

> *Cf.* Strathmann, E. A. Spenser and Lady Carey. No. 21. Pro-
> ceedings of Dr. Greenlaw's Seminary " C," 1928-9. The Johns Hop-
> kins Univ. Library; *ibid.*, Spenser and Lady Carey. PMLA XLVIII
> (*Proc.*, 1933). 1430; *ibid.*, Lady Carey and Spenser. ELH II (1935).
> 33-57. Sp's avowed addresses to Lady Carey are adequately ex-
> plained by kinship, conventional practice of literary patronage, and
> the hospitality for which others praise the Careys; Lemming, Edith
> M. Spenser and his Relations with Elizabeth, Lady Carey. M. A.
> Thesis, Columbia University, 1916.

6. CHALKHILL, JOHN.

> *Cf.* Hunter, Joseph. Chorus Vatum . . . B. M. Addit. MS 24, 487,
> fols. 27ᵛ-28; Ritson, Jos. Bibliographia Poetica, 1802, 155; Retro-
> spective Rev. IV (1821). 230-31 and 231 n.

7. COVINGTON, F. F., JR. Biographical Notes on Spenser.
MP XXII (1924). 63-6.

> Suggests that Barnabe Googe may have been in Sp's circle in
> Ireland. [F. I. C. and A. P.]

8. DRANT, THOMAS.

> Hunter, Joseph. Chorus Vatum . . . B. M. Addit. MS 24,487, fol.
> 268ᵛ. Drant's patron was Grindal.

9. FRAUNCE, ABRAHAM.

> Hunter, Joseph. Chorus Vatum . . . B. M. Addit. MS 24,488,
> fol. 193. Fraunce a Shrewesbury man sent by Philip Sidney to St.
> John's Coll. Cambridge. Sp's Corydon in CCCHA.

10. GASCOIGNE, GEORGE.

> Hunter, Joseph. Chorus Vatum . . . B. M. Addit. MS 24,487,
> fol. 267ᵛ. Refers to E. K.'s opinion of Gascoigne in notes on SC
> " Nov."

11. GORGES, SIR ARTHUR.

> The Olympian Catastrophe. Ed. Randall Davies. Kensington,
> 1925. 9 ff. on Sp and Gorges; Hunter, Joseph. Chorus Vatum
> . . . B. M. Addit. MS 24,488, fols. 57ᵛ-9ᵛ, 60ᵛ, 62; Sandison, Helen E.

Arthur Gorges, Spenser's Alcyon and Ralegh's Friend. PMLA XLIII (1928). 645-74. *Rev.* YWES IX (1928). 171; *ibid.,* Ralegh's Orders Once More. Mariners' Mirror XX (1934). 323-30; Fletcher, J. M. J. The Gorges Monument in Salisbury Cathedral. Wiltshire Archaeological and Natural History Mag. XLVI (1932). 16 ff. See "FQ, Sources," No. 26.

12. GREY, ARTHUR LORD.

Cf. Price, John. An Historical Account of the City of Hereford. Hereford, 1796. 210-11: Grey as Sp's patron; Dixon, Wm. Hepworth. Her Majesty's Tower. London, 1901. I, 267: Grey as Sp's patron and Artegall in FQ; Dunlop, Robert. Ireland Under the Commonwealth. Manchester, 1913. I, lix: Sp and Grey. [F. I. C. and A. P.]

13. HARVEY, GABRIEL.

Cf. Hunter, Joseph. Chorus Vatum . . . B. M. Addit. MS 24,489, fol. 208ᵛ-10. Harvey's friendship for Sp is the only praiseworthy thing we know of him. See " Spenser and Harvey," esp. No. 12.

14. HUNTER, JOSEPH. Chorus Vatum Anglicorum. B. M. Addit. MSS. Photostat copies in Library of Congress and Newberry Library.

The following references relate to Sp.
MS 24,487: fol. 27ᵛ-28 (John Chalkhill); 33 (Bp. Still); 115 (Lord Strange); 126, 127, 128 (William Camden); 170ᵛ (Matthew Roydon); 267ᵛ (Gascoigne); 268ᵛ (Thos. Drant).
MS 24,488: fol. 9 (Geo. Turbervile); 57ᵛ-9ᵛ, 60ᵛ, 62 (Arthur Gorges); 91ᵛ (Sylvanus Scory); 193 (Abraham Fraunce); 234 (Edward Knight-E. K.?).
MS 24,489: fol. 109 (Van der Noot); 128, 131, 133-4 (Samuel Daniel); 208ᵛ-10 (Gabriel Harvey); 252ᵛ (Edward Knight); 308, 309 (L. Bryskett).
MS 24,490: fol. 22ᵛ, 25, 29ʳ (Sir Philip Sidney); 256ᵛ (John Parkhurst); 249ᵛ (Edward Knight).

15. JUDSON, A. C. Spenser's Circle in 1578. Paper read before the Mod. Lang. Ass., 1933. *Cf.* PMLA XLVIII (*Proc.,* 1933). 1430.

16. KIRKE, JOHN. The Seven Champions of Christendome. Ed. G. E. Dawson. Western Reserve Bull. 32 (1929). xxxix, 16-82.

Cf. vii: John Kirke may be son of Sp's friend, Edward Kirke.

17. KNIGHT, EDWARD.

Cf. Hunter, Joseph. Chorus Vatum . . . B. M. Addit. MS 24,489, fol. 252ᵛ; 24,490, fol. 249ᵛ; 24,488, fol. 234. The Edward Knight who wrote verses before Anthony Munday's *Mirror of Mutabilitie* may "lay claim to be Sp's friend." Hunter concludes that this Edward Knight is not the Norrey King-at-arms who died in 1593 at Twickenham.

18. LEICESTER, EARL OF.
    Cf. Baconiana, 3rd. ser. V (1907). 173-4.

19. LONG, P. W. Spenser's Early Associates. PMLA XXXI (1916). *Proc., xxiv.*

20. LYON, WILLIAM.
    Cf. Lismore Papers, First Series. IV, 262.

21. ORMONDE and OSSORY, EARL OF (Butler).
    Cf. Gilbert, John T. Facsimiles of National Manuscripts of Ireland. London, 1882. "By Command." Part IV, i, pp. liii, 223: quotes Sp's sonnet to the Earl as a tribute to one of his patrons; Renwick, W. L. Spenser's Galathea and Neaera. TLS 28 (Mar. 14, 1929). 206-7: Identifies Neaera as Countess of Ormonde.

22. PARKHURST JOHN.
    Cf. Hunter, Joseph. Chorus Vatum . . . B. M. Addit. MS 24,490, fol. 256ᵛ: If *Ludicra*, 1576, really alludes to Sp, it is an early notice "if Sp was born as late as generally supposed."

23. PARMENTER, MARY. Colin Clout and Hobbinoll: a reconsideration of the relationship of Edmund Spenser and Gabriel Harvey. Diss., The Johns Hopkins University, 1933.
    Suggests John Dee and Edward Kelley were friends of Sp.

24. PERCY, HARRY.
    Cf. Dixon, Wm. H. Her Majesty's Tower. London, 1901. I, 407: Sp sent a sonnet and a copy of FQ to Percy in the Tower.

25. ROYDON, MATTHEW.
    Cf. Hunter, Joseph. Chorus Vatum . . . B. M. Addit. MS 24,487, fol. 170ᵛ: Roydon's *Elegy or Friend's Passion for his Astrophell* . . . is "found bound up in first edition of Sp's *Colin Clout,* 1595." *Cf.* Library of Congress copy of CCCHA.

26. RUSSELL Family.
    Cf. Wiffen, Je(remiah). Historical Memoirs of the House of Russell. London, 1833. II, 19, 52 n., 54-5, 94 n.: Sp and the Countesses of Cumberland and Warwick. [F. I. C. and A. P.]

27. SALTER, ROBERT.
    Cf. Millican, C. B. Paper read before the Mod. Lang. Ass., 1933. *Cf.* PMLA XLVIII (*Proc.,* 1933). 1430. Cites from Robert Salter's *Wonderfull Prophecies,* 1627, an allusion which seems to add him to Sp's circle.

28. SCORY, SYLVANUS.

> *Cf.* Hunter, Joseph. Chorus Vatum . . . B. M. Addit. MS 24,488, fol. 91^v-2. (The present editor is investigating the relationship between Sp and the Scory family.)

29. SIDNEY, SIR PHILIP. *Cf.* "Spenser and Sidney."

30. STILL, JOHN (Bishop of Bath and Wells).

> *Cf.* Hunter, Joseph. Chorus Vatum . . . B. M. Addit. MS 24,487, fol. 33.

31. TURBERVILE, GEORGE.

> *Cf.* Hunter, Joseph. Chorus Vatum . . . B. M. Addit. MS 24,488, fol. 9: Sp one to whom Turbervile addresses his poems; Hankins, J. E. MLN XLIV (1929). 164-7; NQ, ser. iii. XI (1867). 418.

32. VANDERNOOT, JOHN.

> *Cf.* Hunter, Joseph. Chorus Vatum . . . B. M. Addit. MS 24,489, fol. 109; Bibliotheca Anglo-Poetica. . . . Early English Poetry in the Possession of Longman, Hurst, Rees, Orme, and Brown. London, 1815. 370-1; Pienaar, W. J. B. English Influences in Dutch Literature. . . . Cambridge Press, 1929. ix, 10-11; see "Theatre of Worldlings," Nos. 3, 5-7.

33. WALLOP, SIR HENRY. *Cf.* "Life, General References," Nos. 16, 21.

34. WHITNEY, GEFFREY. Choice of Emblemes. 1586. Facs. repr. Ed. Henry Green. London, 1866.

> Probability of acquaintance between Sp and Whitney suggested by apparent borrowings in *Emblemes.* *Cf.* ix-x, xvi-xvii, xxiv-v, lxiv ff., 253-65, 298, 323-5. *Cf.* Carpenter, Ref. Guide, 202.

35. YOUNG, JOHN (Bishop of Rochester).

> *Cf.* Judson, A. C. A Biographical Sketch of John Young, Bishop of Rochester, with Emphasis on his Relations with Edmund Spenser. Indiana University Studies XXI (1934). No. 103. 1-41. Excellent.

SPENSER AND SIDNEY

See "Areopagus," Nos. 1, 4, 8; "Astrophel," No. 2; "Teares of the Muses," No. 13; "Spenser's Circle," No. 34.

1. ADDLESHAW, PERCY. Sir Philip Sidney. London, 1909.

> 259-71: "Speculations on the nature and degree of their friendship. A superficial and popular book." [F. I. C. and A. P.]

2. ALBRIGHT, EVELYN M. The Dating of Spenser's *Mutabilitie Cantos*. SP XXVI (1929). 491-5.

   Sidney's influence on Sp perhaps reflected in choice of Irish episodes for FQ. Influence dates back to 1579.

3. BEHLER, MALLY. Die Beziehungen zwischen Sidney und Spenser. Archiv CXLVI (1923). 53-9. *Cf. post,* No. 12. [F. I. C. and A. P.]

4. BERKELEY, FRANCES C. The Relation of Spenser's *Faerie Queene* to the *Arcadia* of . . . Sidney. M. A. Thesis, Columbia University, 1904. *Cf. post,* Nos. 9, 26.

5. DENKINGER, EMMA M. Immortal Sidney. New York, 1931. See index for Sp.

6. DRYDEN, ALICE. (ed.) Memorials of Old Wiltshire. London, 1906.

   157: Sp at Wilton on Sidney's introduction.

7. DRYDEN, JOHN. Prose Works. Ed. Malone, 1800. II, 179: Dedication to Earl of Leicester of *Don Sebastian,* 1690.

   On Sidney's patronage of Sp. [R. Heffner]

8. FRIEDRICH, W. G. The *Astrophel* Elegies, a Collection of Poems on the Death of Sir Philip Sidney. Diss., The Johns Hopkins University, 1934.

   Intro: "The Relations of Spenser and Sidney."

9. GREENLAW, EDWIN A. The Captivity Episode in Sidney's *Arcadia*. Manly Anniversary Studies. . . . Chicago, 1923.

   58-62: FQ and Pamela-Cecropia episode of *Arcadia. Rev.* YWES IV (1923). 118. *Cf. ante,* No. 4; *post,* No. 26.

10. HARMAN, E. G. Gabriel Harvey and Thomas Nashe. London, 1923.

    5-7: Sp in Ireland under Sir Henry Sidney, 1577. [F. I. C. and A. P.]

11. HARRISON, T. P., JR. *The Faerie Queene* and the *Diana*. PQ IX (1930). 51-6.

    Sidney probably introduced Sp to Montemayor's *Diana,* which is perhaps source of FQ VI, ix ff. and IV, vii ff.

12. HARRISON, T. P., JR. The Relations of Spenser and Sidney. PMLA XLV (1930). 712-31.

> *Cf.* PMLA XLIV (*Proc.*, 1929). xliii. Comparative study of the writings of the two men in an effort to discover the outlines of their friendship. Finds a "remarkable parallel" in the chronology and nature of their work. *Rev.* Shakes. Jahr. 68 (1932). 173; *ibid.*, 67 (1931). 116-7. *Cf. ante*, No. 3; *post*, No. 21.

13. HEFFNER, RAY. Essex, the Ideal Courtier. ELH I (1934). 7-36.

> Calidore identified as Essex rather than Sidney. *Cf. post*, Nos. 16, 23.

14. HUNTER, JOSEPH. Chorus Vatum. . . . B. M. Addit. MS 24,490, fol. 22v, 25, 29v.

> Sidney and Sp.

15. KITE, EDWARD. Wilton House, and its Literary Associations. Wiltshire NQ No. 58 (June, 1907).

> 436, 439: Sp at Wilton.

16. LONG, P. W. Spenser and Sidney. PMLA XXVIII (1912). *Proc.* xiii.

> *Cf.* Anglia XXXVIII (1914). 173-92 for full account. *Rev.* Shakes. Jahr. 51 (1915). 221-2.

17. MAGNUS, LAURIE. English Literature in its Foreign Relations, 1300 to 1800. London, 1927.

> 33-5: Sp and Sidney.

18. MINTO, WILLIAM. Characteristics of English Poets from Chaucer to Shirley. London, 1874.

> 481-3: "Our Pleasant Willy." Willy = Sidney; Gentle Spirit = Sp.

19. OSBORN, ALBERT W. Sir Philip Sidney en France. Paris, 1932.

> 43: Sp and Sidney. *Cf.* 45, 157, 159.

20. The Phoenix Nest, 1593. Repr. Ed. H. E. Rollins. Cambridge, Mass., 1931.

> See index; Sp's CCCHA and the Sidney elegies; also xxviii ff. and xli.

21. PURCELL, J. M. The Relations of Spenser and Sidney. PMLA XLVI (1931). 940.

> Harrison's materials are practically the same as Behler's but the conclusions are "somewhat opposed." *Rev.* Shakes. Jahr. 68 (1932). 173. *Cf. ante*, Nos. 3, 11, 12; "Astrophel," No. 6.

22. Retrospective Rev. X (1824). 43.

Sidney, except for Sp, the best poet of his time.

23. Rowe, Kenneth. Sir Calidore: Essex or Sidney? SP XXVII (1930). 125-41.

Considers arguments for Essex as Calidore and rejects evidence. Sidney is the prototype of Calidore. *Cf. ante,* Nos. 13, 16.

24. Sargent, Ralph M. At the Court of Queen Elizabeth. Oxford, 1935.

58-65: Sp, Dyer, Sidney, and the Areopagus. *Cf.* Index also. *Rev.* TLS 34 (May 9, 1935). 293-4. Leading article; New Statesman and Nation, May 25, 1935, 758-60, by P. Q.; Spectator, Aug. 16, 1935, 269-70, by A. L. Rowse.

25. Shephard, Oscar H. Sir Philip Sidney. Manchester Quart. L (1931). 1-25.

26. Syford, Constance M. The Direct Source of the Pamela-Cecropia Episode in the *Arcadia.* PMLA XLIX (1934). 472-89.

Relation of *Arcadia* and FQ. The natural philosophy of *Arcadia* implies familiarity with Empedocles, Lucretius, Cicero, Plato, Aristotle. It indicates Sidney's "deep Christian character" and "religious fervor." *Cf. ante,* Nos. 4, 9, 11, 12; "Mutabilitie," Nos. 3, 18; "FQ Sources," Nos. 4, 6.

27. Wilson, Mona. Sir Philip Sidney. London, 1931.

123-6: Sp and Sidney and the new poetry. *Rev.* New Statesman and Nation, n. s. II (1931). 202-3.

28. Wright, George R. Archaeologic and Historic Fragments. London, 1887.

89: Quotes Thomas Wright's *Ludlow Sketches,* on Sidney and possibility of literary figures like Sp visiting at Ludlow Castle.

29. Yart, Abbé Antoine. Idée de la Poësie Angloise. See "Criticism after 1651," No. 163.

AREOPAGUS

See "Spenser and Sidney," Nos. 15, 24.

1. Faverty, Frederic E. A Note on the Areopagus. PQ V (1926). 278-80.

Sp and Harvey use "areopagus" facetiously. Probably not a formal group. Sixteenth century used word to designate "any group of persons which exercised judiciary authority." *Cf. post,* No. 7.

2. FLASDIECK, HERMANN M. Der Gedanke einer englischen Sprachakademie. Jena, 1928.
   6-7: Areopagus.

3. HOLLOWELL, B. M. The Elizabethan Hexametrists. PQ III (1924). 51-7.
   52-3: Sp's interest in the movement, 1570-90, to introduce classical prosody. *Cf. post,* No. 8.

4. KLIEM, HANS. Sentimentale Freundschaft in der Shakespeare-Epoche. Diss., Jena, 1915.
   8 ff.: Areopagus. *Cf.* " Table of Contents " also.

5. MACINTIRE, ELIZABETH J. French Influence on the Beginnings of English Classicism. PMLA XXVI (1911).
   Rev. Shakes. Jahr. 48 (1912). 219.

6. MAGNUS, LAURIE. English Literature in its Foreign Relations, 1300 to 1800. London, 1927.
   Ch. II, esp. 32-5: Areopagus.

7. MAYNADIER, HOWARD. The Areopagus of Sidney and Spenser. Cambridge, 1909.
   Rev. Contemp. Rev. XCVI (July, 1909). 15-6. Lit. Supplement.

8. WILLCOCK, G. D. Passing Pitefull Hexameters. MLR XXIX (1934). 1-19.
   5-6, 7-10, 17-8: Sp-Harvey correspondence on Drant's rules; SC and other experiments in metrical forms. *Cf. ante,* No. 3.

9. WILSON, MONA. Sir Philip Sidney. London, 1931.
   117, 123-6, 156: The new poetry, DuBellay, Sidney, etc.

SPENSER AND HARVEY

See " Life, Miscellaneous," Nos. 100, 105; " Mutabilitie," No. 1; " Letters," Nos. 1-4, 6, 8; " Circle," No. 13; " Areopagus," No. 8.

1. CRAWFORD, CHARLES. Greenes Funeralls. 1594. SP, extra ser. I (1929). 1-39.
   2: Sp interested in Harvey's quarrels. *Cf.* pp. 22, 24, 26, 32, 36, 37-8.

2. CUNINGHAM, GRANVILLE C. Bacon and Edmund Spenser. Baconiana, 3rd. ser. V (1907). 153-77.
   160-1: The correspondence of Sp and Harvey.

3. DISRAELI, ISAAC. The Calamities and Quarrels of Authors. . . . London, 1859.
   117: Harvey the Hobynol whose poem is prefixed to FQ.

4. GREENLAW, EDWIN A. Spenser and Harvey. Paper read before the Mod. Lang. Ass. 1926. *Cf.* PMLA XLII (1927, *Proc.*, 1926). x.

5. HARMAN, E. G. Gabriel Harvey and Thomas Nashe. London, 1923.
   "Further development of the theory that Sp is one of the 'impersonators' of Bacon. That Immerito is Bacon." [F. I. C. and A. P.] *Rev.* YWES IV (1923). 124-5.

6. JOHNSON, FRANCIS R. The First Edition of Gabriel Harvey's *Foure Letters*. The Library, ser. 4. XV (1934). 212-23.

7. Monthly Mag. XXX (1810). 46.
   Sp's sonnet to Harvey quoted.

8. PARMENTER, MARY. Colin Clout and Hobbinoll; a reconsideration of the relationship of Edmund Spenser and Gabriel Harvey. Diss., The Johns Hopkins University, 1933.

9. RITSON, Jos. Bibliographia Poetica. London, 1802.
   237-8, 255: Sp and Harvey.

10. SMITH, G. C. MOORE (ed.). Gabriel Harvey's Marginalia.
    Rev. MLR XII (1917). 218-21, by H. J. C. Grierson; Shakes. Jahr. 50 (1914). 175-8, by A. Brandl; Anglia Beibl. XXV (1914). 259-61, by Friedrich Brie.

11. THEOBALD, BERTRAM G. Francis Bacon Concealed and Revealed. London, 1930.
    38-80: The Spenser Problem. Immerito letters printed deliberately to create doubt as to authorship of SC.

SPENSER AND RALEIGH

See " Life, Miscellaneous," No. 105; " FG, General," No. 73; Muiopotmos," No. 11.

1. COLLIER, J. PAYNE. Additional Information respecting . . . Sir Walter Raleigh. . . . Archaeologia XXXIV (1852). 149 ff.

150: Quotes a note dated on the outside "16th Nov. 1585" and asks if it may not be Sp's note. "My dutie remembred, myselfe would have come craving pardon of your wourship, for that my wife this presente is very extreme sycke. Accordinge to my dutie and promis, made before the honorable Mr. Secreatorie, I have sente the booke which I had from Mr. William Hearle, and the names hereunder, to whom I have delyvered copies:
"To my Mr Sr Walter Ralegh, knight, one booke.
"To Mr Frauncis Knollis, one booke.
"To Mr Cope, my L. Tresorer's Gent. Usher, one booke.
"To a gent. that serveth Sr Phillipp Sydney, sometymes of the Temple, one booke.
"And to Mr Neale, of the Temple, one booke."
Cf. Original in State Paper Office; probably relates to some recently printed work.

2. DOUADY, JULES. "Spenser et la Reine des Fées." La Mer et les Poètes Anglais. Paris, 1912.

66-84: Sp and Raleigh.

3. Edinburgh Rev. LXXI (1840). 16. Sir Walter Raleigh.

Sp's interview with Raleigh.

4. EDWARDS, EDWARD. The Life of Sir Walter Raleigh.

I, 138-40: FQ, Timias, Belphoebe, and Amoret episode describes Raleigh and Mrs. Throckmorton (Amoret) and Elizabeth's (Belphoebe) wrath. Cf. post, No. 14.

5. GUINEY, LOUISE IMOGEN. Sir Walter Raleigh of Youghal in the County of Cork. Atlantic Monthly LXVI (1890). 779-86.

Sp and Raleigh as neighbors and friends. Nothing new.

6. HANNAH, JOHN (ed.). Poems by Sir Henry Wotton, Sir Walter Raleigh and Others. London, 1845.

xl, xliv-v, 115-6: Sp.

7. ——— The Courtly Poets, from Raleigh to Montrose. London, 1870.

xiv, xvii, xxii, 5-9, 215-6: Sp.

8. HAYMAN, SAMUEL. Ecclesiastical Antiquities of Youghal. No. III. J. Kilkenny Arch. Soc., n. s. I (1856-7). 14 ff.

25-6: Raleigh's house; CCCHA and Raleigh; FQ.

9. HEFFNER, RAY. Raleigh and Book III of the *Faerie Queene*. See "FQ, General," No. 75.

10. HENNESSY, SIR JOHN P. Sir Walter Ralegh in Ireland. Nineteenth Cent. X (1881). 678.
    Sp's friendship for Raleigh.

11. Journal of Cork Hist. and Arch. Soc. I (1892). 129. Sir Walter Raleigh's House at Youghal.
    Sp's grant of Desmond lands; his 1589 trip with Raleigh.

12. ———— 2nd. ser. XXVI (1920). 54-9, by G. M. Sir Walter Raleigh. His Connection with Munster.
    56: Sp and Raleigh.

13. KOLLER, KATHRINE. Spenser and Ralegh. Proceedings of Dr. Greenlaw's Seminary " C," 1931. The Johns Hopkins University Library.

14. ———— Spenser and Raleigh. ELH I (1934). 37-60.
    CCCHA a compliment to Sp's friendship with Raleigh. Delay in publication may have been due to desire to assist him regain favor at Court after the Throckmorton affair. Timias episode (FQ) allegory of Raleigh's career. *Rev.* YWES XV (1934). 218. *Cf. ante,* No. 4.

15. Littell's Living Age V (1845). 50-1.
    Sp and Raleigh reading FQ; taken from Campbell's *Specimens.*

16. POLLARD, A. F. The Elizabethans and the Empire. Raleigh Lecture on History, 1921. Proc. of Brit. Acad. X. London, 1921.
    144: Sp's " Shepherd of the Ocean " is Raleigh.

17. Retrospective Rev. VII (1823). 400.
    Raleigh's " Vision upon the Conceipt of the FQ."

18. RITSON, JOS. Bibliographia Poetica. London, 1802.
    255: Raleigh and " Ignoto " (FQ); 307: Sp and Raleigh. *Cf.* 307 n.

19. Roy. Soc. Antiq. Ire. XLII (1912). 272.
    Sp and Raleigh, in an account of Lismore.

20. WESTROPP, THOMAS J. Notes on Askeaton, County of Limerick. Roy. Soc. Antiq. Ire. XXXIII (1903). 159.
    Sp and Raleigh as undertakers.

21. WILSON, F. P. Spenser and Ireland. RES II (1926). 456-7.
    Sp's supposed departure with Raleigh, 1589, in relation to possibility of Sp's being in Ireland in May, 1590. *Rev.* YWES VII (1926). 162; Proceedings of Dr. Greenlaw's Seminary " C," 1926. No. 10, by Charles G. Smith.

Spenserian Place-Names

1. Brash, Richard R. Antiquities of Buttevant. J. Kilkenny Arch. Soc. II (1852-3). 83 ff.
   84-5: Sp's "Mulla, the daughter of Old Mole" as reference to Buttevant. *Cf.* pp. 94, 265-76.

2. Butler, W. F. The Clan Carthy. J. Cork Hist. and Arch. Soc. XXIX (1923-4). 51 ff.
   Sp's Irish rivers.

3. Dublin University Mag. XXXVIII (1851). 233-52.
   Sp's streams—the Mulla and Allo.

4. Evans, R. W. Notes on River Bregog. J. Cork Hist. and Arch. Soc., 2nd. ser. XVIII (1912). 201-3.
   Quotes CCCHA 104-8, 116-7, 137-55.

5. Flood, William H. G. Identification of the Spenserian "Aubrian" River. J. Cork Hist. and Arch. Soc., 2nd. ser. XXII (1916). 143-4.
   Suggests the Urrin. *Cf.* "View of Ireland," No. 49.

6. Hickson, Mary. The Blackwater, Cappoquin, and the Barons of Burnchurch. Roy. Soc. Antiq. Ire. XX (1890). 244-6.
   Sp's references to Blackwater.

7. Jones, H. S. V. A Spenser Handbook. Pp. 385-6.

8. Johnston, Swift P. On a Manuscript Description of the City and County of Cork, *cir.* 1685, Written by Sir Richard Cox. Roy. Soc. Antiq. Ire. XXXII (1902). 353-76.
   355, 356: Sp's Awbeg, Buttevant, etc.

9. Journal Cork Hist. and Arch. Soc. I (1892). 149-50; II, 353; III, 126-8, 247, 250, 254, 285-6. Local Names of Rivers of County Cork.
   Sp's Awbeg, Awniduff, etc.

10. Kilkenny Arch. Soc., n. s. IV (1862-3). 320n: The Blackwater; V (1864-6). 289n: The Liffy.

11. Lismore Papers. Ed. A. B. Grosart.
    First series II, 358: "Lugg"; II, 391: "Awniduff."
    Second series II, 279: "Chaple Isold" on the Liffy.

12. MOORE, COURTENAY. The Bregoge. J. Cork Hist. and Arch. Soc., 2nd. ser. XIX (1913). 40-2.
Some of Sp's river names.

13. O'Brien's Irish-English Dictionary. Paris, 1768.
Clódeach—" the name of a river in the county of Cork, near Mallow, celebrated in Spenser's *fairy Queen.*" *Cf.* Joyce. Spenser's Irish Rivers. Proc. Roy. Irish Acad. X (1866-9). 13.

14. O'DONOVAN, DR. Annals by the "Four Masters." Vol. IV.
701: Hill of Croghan in the north of King's County celebrated by Sp. Cited in Proc. Roy. Irish Acad. X (1866-9). 13.

15. Ó'RÍORDÁIN, SEÁN P. The Place Names and Antiquities of Kinalmeaky Barony, Co. Cork. J. Cork Hist. and Arch. Soc. XXXVII (1932). 1-7.
5-6: Kilcolman.

16. SMITH, CHARLES. Ancient and Present State of . . . Cork. Repr. Cork Hist. and Arch. Soc. 1893 +.
I, 292: Buttevant was Kilnemullagh in Sp; I, 296-7: Some of Sp's rivers; III, 208: The Dripsey.

17. SMITH, ROLAND M. Spenser's Irish River Stories. PMLA L (1935). 1047 ff.

18. TWISS, HENRY F. Mallow and Some Mallow Men. J. Cork Hist. and Arch. Soc. XXXI (1926). 81 ff.

19. WESTROPP, THOMAS J. The Name "Buttevant." Roy. Soc. Antiq. Ire. XXXI (1901). 87.
Buttevant perhaps from the Barry's war-cry: Boutez en avant.

20. WHITE, JAMES G. Historical and Topographical Notes. Cork, 1905.
I, 221 and 301: Awniduff and Bregog.

II.
THE WORKS

II. THE WORKS

1. Athenaeum. 1920-1. 81-2. English Classics at the British Museum.

   Notes of first editions of FQ, SC, Amor., and Daph.

2. Bibliotheca Anglo-Poetica . . . Early English Poetry in the Possession of Longman, Hurst, Rees, Orme, and Brown. London, 1815.

   302-6: Sp entries.

3. Catalogue of Early English Books, Chiefly of the Elizabethan Period. Collected by William Augustus White and Catalogued by Henrietta C. Bartlett. New York, priv. print., 1926.

   145-6: Early Sp editions.

4. COLLIER, J. P. (ed.). A Catalogue of [Richard] Heber's Collection of Early English Poetry. . . . London [n. d.].

   212, 303, 310-2: Sp editions.

5. ———— The Registers of the Stationers' Company. NQ, ser. ii. XII (1861). 362, 514; ser. iii. III (1863). 2.

   Cites in full the entries for Sp's works.

6. Grolier Club. Catalogue of Original and Early Editions of some of the Poetical and Prose Works of English Writers from Langland to Wither. New York, 1893.

   198-210: Several facsimiles of original edition title-pages.

7. JOHNSON, FRANCIS R. A Critical Bibliography of the Works of Edmund Spenser Printed before 1700. The Johns Hopkins Press, 1933.

   Rev. MLR XXIX (1934). 448, by W. L. Renwick; New York Times, Book Rev., May 6, 1934, p. 23, by Philip Brooks; Anglia Beibl. XLV (1934). 45-6, by Walther Fischer; Lond. Merc. XXIX (1934). 449, by I. A. Williams; Eng. Stud. XVI (1934). 112-4, by A. G. Van Kranendonk; Sat. Rev. of Lit. X (Feb. 17, 1934). 496, by Bertha C. Slade; Library Quart. IV (1934). 518-20, by Arthur Berthold; Archiv CLXVI (1934). 103-5, by A. Brandl; Johns Hopkins Alumni Mag. XXIII (1934). 93-6, by Frederick Hard; The Book-Collectors' Quart. No. XIV (1934). 79-83, by Harold Stein; RES XI (1935). 479-82, by Douglas Hamer;

JEGP XXXIV (1935). 449-51, by C. B. Millican; MLN L (1935). 206-7, by H. S. V. Jones; YWES XIV (1933). 225. See also TLS 33 (Mar. 8, 1934). 168, by F. R. Johnson. *Cf.* "Addenda," No. 2.

8. LOWNDES, WILLIAM T. The Bibliographers' Manual of English Literature. London, 1865.

Pt. IX, 2476-9, 2480: Sp editions. No mention of *Axiochus*.

9. OSBORNE, LUCY EUGENIA. Report for 1933-34, Chapin Library (Williams College).

Exhibit III: Sp. *Cf.* New York Times, Book Rev., Dec. 9, 1934. 27.

10. PILLSBURY, STANLEY R. The Four Hundredth Anniversary of Queen Elizabeth. New York Pub. Lib. Bull. XXXVII (1933). 859.

FQ in exhibit.

11. Tudor and Stuart Club. The Book of the . . . The Johns Hopkins University. Baltimore, 1927.

30-3: Lists of Spenser items among additions to " Rare Books . . ."

EDITIONS OF SPENSER

I. COLLECTIONS

COMPLETE WORKS, POETICAL WORKS, EDITIONS OF SEPARATE WORKS BEFORE 1700

1. AXIOCHUS. A most excellent Dialogue, written in Greeke by *Plato* the Phylosopher : concerning the shortnesse and vncertainty of this life, with the contrary ends of the good and wicked. Translated out of Greeke by *Edw. Spenser. Heereto is annexed a sweet speech or Oration, spoken at the Tryumphe at Whitehall before her Maiestie, by the Page to the right noble Earle of Oxenforde.* At London, Printed for Cuthbert Burbie, and are to be sold at the middle shop in the Poultry, vnder S. Mildreds Church. *Anno* 1592.

A very rare copy in library of Dr. Frederick M. Padelford. *Cf.* New York Times, Dec. 30, 1932, p. 13, col. 6. "Finds Spenser Book Missing Since 1758." [L. O. Hogan]. But see "Addenda," No. 33.

2. The Faerie Queene, 1590. *Cf.* Lond. Merc. XII (1925). 302: Notice by I. A. Williams. In Quaritch's Catalogue, No. 392, is listed what seems to be the largest known copy of the first, 1590, edition.

3. ANDREWS, CHARLES M. An Early Edition of Spenser's Poems. Yale University Library Gazette IX (July, 1934). 20-2. [L. O. Hogan.]

   A copy of 1611 edition which lacks *Mother Hubberds Tale.*

4. The Works. Ed. John Hughes.

   Rev. The Daily Courant. Aug. 22, 1715. Cited by Wurtsbaugh, J. *Two Centuries of Spenserian Scholarship*, 35; London Evening-Post, Dec. 6-8, 1750; cited by Wurtsbaugh, J., *op. cit.,* 60: Announcements of Hughes's ed. and the reprint; NQ, ser. ii. IX (1860). 420.

5. Pue's Occurrences. Dublin, 23 January 1744.

   Proposal for printing 6 volume edition of Sp's Works with "a more exact account of his life by his great grandson Edmond Spencer who has undertaken this work at the desire of several persons of distinction, who are admirers of that celebrated poet and willing to show a mark of favour to his descendants." The edition was not made. *Cf.* Welply, W. H. NQ, ser. xiv. VI (1932). 240-1.

6. Whitehall Evening-Post. July 27-30, 1751. Proposals for John Upton's edition.

   Cited by Wurtsbaugh, J. *Two Centuries of Spenserian Scholarship,* 60.

7. MEEN, . . . Letter to Bishop Percy. Jan., 1803. In John Nichols's *Illustrations of the Literature of the Eighteenth Century*, VII, 58. Cited by Wurtsbaugh, J. *Two Centuries of Spenserian Scholarship*, 141.

   On Todd's projected edition.

8. Poetical Works. Pickering.

   Rev. Blackwood's Mag. XXIII (1828). 9.

9. Poetical Works . . . J. Mitford.

   Rev. Spectator XII (1839). 1187-8.

10. Poetical Works . . . G. S. Hillard.

    Rev. The Knickerbocker (New York) XV (1840). 162.

11. The Works of Edmund Spenser. Frontisp. portrait. Pp. lx, 562. London, 1845 (Moxon).

12. Poetical Works . . . F. J. Child.

> Rev. North American Rev. LXXXII (1856). 284; West. Rev. XXXI (1867). 133-50. Reviews also Todd's and Corbould's (1866) editions.

13. Poetical Works . . . G. Gilfillan.

> Rev. Littell's Liv. Age LXI (1859). 374; Gentleman's Mag., n. s. X (1861). 267-71.

14. Poetical Works . . . J. Payne Collier.

> Rev. NQ, ser. ii. XII (1861). 511-2; West. Rev., n. s. XXXI (1867). 133-50.

15. Brit. Quart. Rev. XLII (1865). 29-47.

> General essay on ed. 1611.

16. Athenaeum. 1869. I. 23.

> Notice of forthcoming cheap ed.

17. Complete Works . . . Morris and Hales.

> Rev. NQ, ser. iv. IV (1869). 351; West. Rev., n. s. XXXVII (1870). 323; Brit. Quart. Rev. LI (1870). 253; Quart. Rev. CCXLIX (1927). 154-67, by C. E. Lawrence. Rev. of 1927 impress. of 1893 ed.

18. Poetical Works . . . J. C. Smith.

> Rev. Athenaeum. 1912. II. 687, by Frowde; Nation (N. Y.) XC (1910). 93.

19. The Poetical Works . . . Ed. J. C. Smith and E. de Sélincourt. London, 1926.

20. The Complete Works. Ed. W. L. Renwick. Scholartis Press, London. 1928 +. Two editions; one of 95 copies, numbered . . . , and one of 1660 copies. Vol. I. The Complaints. London, 1928.

> Rev. YWES IX (1928). 169-70; TLS 28 (Mar. 14, 1929). 203, 210. Interesting; TLS 29 (Feb. 27, 1930). 149-50. "The Poets' Poet," by J. Middleton Murry; Proc. Eng. Journ. Club, The Johns Hopkins Univ., 1929-30. April 8, Discussion of Murry's article, by R. Heffner; Rev. ang.-amér. 6ᵉ· an. (1928-9). 538-9, by É. Legouis; Lond. Merc. XX (1929). 633, by E. G. Twitchett; Criterion IX (1929-30). 171-2; Anglia Beibl. XLI (1930). 20, by S. B. Liljegren; MP XXVIII (1930). 235-9, by Harold Stein; MLN XLV (1930). 323-8, by E. Greenlaw.

Vol. II. Daphnaida and Other Poems. London, 1929.

> *Rev.* YWES X (1929). 217; YWES XI (1930). 193-5; MLR
> XXV (1930). 347-8, by B. D. Wright; MLN XLV (1930). 323-8,
> by E. Greenlaw. Discusses the Burghley matter; TLS 29 (Feb.
> 27, 1930). 149-50. Leading article; RES VI (1930). 340-42, by
> Helen Darbishire; Spectator No. 5,347 (Dec. 20, 1930). 985-6,
> "The Sophist's and Shepherd's Calendar," by Richard Church;
> Rev. ang.-amér. 8è· an. (1930-1). 57, by É. Legouis.

Vol. III. The Shepherd's Calendar. London, 1930.

> *Rev.* YWES XI (1930). 193-5; TLS 30 (Feb. 5, 1931). 95.
> E. K.'s identity and the arrangement; *cf.* Arber, Agnes. TLS 30
> (April 2, 1931). 271 and Herbert, A. S., *ibid.,* (Mar. 19, 1931).
> 234; Sat. Rev. CLI (1931). 544; Quart. Rev. CCLVI (1931).
> 411-2; MLR XXVI (1931). 456-9, by G. C. Moore Smith; Archiv,
> n. s. CLX (1931). 124-6, by A. Brandl; MLN XLVII (1932).
> 473-5, by A. C. Judson; RES VIII (1932). 326-9, by Helen Darbi-
> shire; Rev. ang.-amér. 9è· an. (1931-2). 546, by A. Digeon.

Vol. IV. A View of the Present State of Ireland . . .
from MS Rawlinson B. 478 in the Bodleian and MS
188. 221 in Caius College, Cam. Map. London, 1934.

> *Rev.* TLS 33 (July 19, 1934). 506, 515. "Spenser on Ireland";
> Fortn. Rev., n. s. CXXXVI (1934). 489-92, by Stephen Gwynn;
> Quart. Rev. CCLXIII (1934). 360-1. Rev. ang.-amér. 12è· an. (1935).
> 240-1, by E. L.; Rev. hist. 60è· an. CLXXVI (1935). 349, by A.
> Rivoallan; YWES XV (1934). 211.

21. Complete Works, with the correspondence of [the
author] and Harvey. With Glossary, introduction,
biographical and critical. Decorated with facsimile
pages. Portrait. Cornhill, Boston, 1929.

22. Works. Ed. W. L. Renwick. Wood cuts by Hilda Clark.
Shakespeare Head. Oxford, 1930-32. 8 volumes.

> Text follows first editions. *Rev.* YWES XI (1930). 195; TLS
> 29 (Nov. 20, 1930). 971; *cf. ibid.,* 30 (Mar. 26, 1931). 255; 30 (May
> 21, 1931). 411; 30 (Sept. 3, 1931). 667; 30 (Dec. 10, 1931). 1011;
> 31 (Nov. 24, 1932). 880; 32 (Sept. 28, 1933). 637-8; Spectator
> No. 5,347 (Dec. 20, 1930). 985-6, "The Sophist's and Shepherd's
> Calendar," by Richard Church; *ibid.,* CXLVI (April 18, 1931). 624;
> *ibid.,* CXLVIII (Jan. 23, 1932). 122; Lond. Merc. XXIV (1931).
> 96, 576.

23. Works. With hand-coloured decorations engraved on
wood by Hilda Quick, and initial letters engraved from
designs by Joscelyne Gaskin. Shakespeare Head. Oxford, 1930. 8 vols. Folio.

24. The Works . . . A Variorum Edition. Ed. by Edwin Greenlaw, C. G. Osgood, and F. M. Padelford. The Johns Hopkins Press, 1932 +. Vol. I. The Faerie Queene, Book I. Ed. F. M. Padelford. Baltimore, 1932.

Rev. YWES XIII (1932). 190-1; More Books (Bost. Public Libr. Bull.) VIII (1933). 232-3; Sat. Rev. of Lit. IX (June 3, 1933). 625-6, by Tucker Brooke. "Gentle Master Spenser"; New York Times, Book Rev., July 30, 1933. 2, by P. M. Jack; MLN XLVIII (1933). 253-8, by H. J. C. Grierson; Lond. Merc. XXVIII (1933). 180, by John Sparrow; MLR XXVIII (1933). 508-11, by W. L. Renwick; JEGP XXXII (1933). 616-8, by H. S. V. Jones; Rev. ang.-amér. 11è· an. (1933). 52, by É. Legouis; New York Herald-Tribune Books IX (June 4, 1933). VII, 13, by Samuel C. Chew; PQ XII (1933). 415-6, by E. N. S. Thompson; German.-Roman. Monatss. XXI (1933). 250; Archiv CLXIV (1933). 133, by A. B.; TLS 32 (Sept. 28, 1933). 637-8. "The New Poet"; RES X (1934). 217-23, by Douglas Hamer; cf. RES XI (1935). 81, by C. G. Osgood and F. M. Padelford for answer to this; Eng. Stud. XVI (1934). 112-4, by A. G. Van Kranendonk; Anglia Beibl. XLV (1934). 44-5, by Walther Fischer; Rev. de Litt. Comp. XIIIè· an. (1933). 364; MLN L (1935). 186-91, by H. J. C. Grierson; SP XXXII (1935). 245-58, by William F. Thrall; MP XXXIII (1936). 322-34, by E. M. Albright. Cf. "Addenda," No. 3.

Vol. II. The Faerie Queene, Book II. Ed. Edwin Greenlaw. Assisted by Ray Heffner, James G. McManaway, and Ernest A. Strathmann. Baltimore, 1933.

Rev. TLS 33 (Jan. 11, 1934). 31; Eng. Stud. XVI (1934). 112-4, by A. G. Van Kranendonk; Anglia Beibl. XLV (1934). 44-5, by Walther Fischer; Rev. de Litt. Comp. 14è· an. (1934). 386; JEGP XXXIII (1934). 578, by H. S. V. Jones; MLR XXIX (1934). 346-8, by B. E. C. Davis; PQ XIII (1934). 317-8, by E. N. S. Thompson; Archiv CLXVI (1934). 103-5, by A. Brandl; SP XXXII (1935). 245-58, by William F. Thrall; MLN L (1935). 186-91, by H. J. C. Grierson; MP XXXIII (1936). 322-34, by E. M. Albright. Cf. "Addenda," No. 3.

Vol. III. The Faerie Queene, Book III. Ed. F. M. Padelford. Baltimore, 1934.

Rev. TLS 33 (June 14, 1934). 427; The Johns Hopkins Alumni Mag. XXIII (1934). 93-6, by F. Hard; New York Herald-Tribune Books (Aug. 26, 1934). 13, by Samuel C. Chew; Rev. ang.-amér. 12è· an. (1934). 57-8, by É. Legouis; MLN L (1935). 186-91, by H. J. C. Grierson; SP XXXII (1935). 245-58, by William F. Thrall; MLR XXX (1935). 517-9, by W. L. Renwick; Archiv CLXVII (1935). 275-9, by A. Brandl; Anglia Beibl. XLVI (1935). 48-9, by W. Fischer; MP XXXIII (1936). 322-34, by E. M. Albright. Cf. "Addenda," No. 3.

Volume IV. The Faerie Queene, Book IV. Ed. Ray Heffner. Baltimore, 1935.

Rev. New York Herald-Tribune Books XII (Feb. 16, 1936). 14. VII, by Samuel C. Chew.

II. The Faerie Queene, editions since 1700

See " Complete Works "; " Addenda," Nos. 35-7.

1. *Proposals for printing by subscription Spencer's Fairy queen, in three volumes in 4°, from his own edition in 1590 and 1596, adorned with 32 copper plates, designed by Mr. Kent. [With a specimen leaf of the fairy queen]. n. p. [1750?] Copy in Harvard Coll. Library.

2. The Faerie Queene . . . Ed. Dr. T. Birch.

Rev. Journal Britannique, par M. Maty (à la Haye). V (Juillet 1751). 323-4; ibid., VI (Nov. 1751). 345-64. Gives a life, etc.; London Mag. XX (1751). 480. No. 16; Gentleman's Mag. XXI (1751). 479; Quaritch's Gen. Cat. 1887, Vol. IV, 2182.

3. The Fairy Queen. Tonson's, 1758.

Rev. The Daily Advertiser. April 13, 1758. Cited by Wurtsbaugh, J. Two Centuries of Spenserian Scholarship, 73.

4. The Faerie Queene . . . Ralph Church.

Rev. The Daily Advertiser. Jan. 22, 1759. Cited by Wurtsbaugh, J. Two Centuries of Spenserian Scholarship, 73.

5. The Faerie Queene . . . John Upton.

Rev. Journal Britannique, par M. Maty (à la Haye). V (Juillet 1751). 324. Notice of Upton's " A Letter concerning a new Edition of Spenser's Faerie Queene, to Gilbert West, Esq., London, 1751 "; Gentleman's Mag. XXIX (1759). 38; The Daily Advertiser. Jan. 13, 1759. Cited by Wurtsbaugh, J. Two Centuries of Spenserian Scholarship, 73.

6. The Faerie Queene. With a Glossary. London (Routledge), 1843.

7. The Faerie Queene: disposed into twelve Books, . . . to which is added his Epithalamion. Illustrated by Edward Corbould. London (Routledge), 1869.

8. The Faerie Queene . . . and Epithalamion. In " Sir John Lubbock's Hundred Books," No. 53. London (Routledge), 1893.

9. The Faerie Queene . . . T. J. Wise. Illustrated by Walter Crane.

Rev. The Critic, n. s. XXVI (1896). 26; *ibid.*, n. s. XXVII (1897). 387; Spectator LXXVII (1896). 904; *ibid.*, LXXIX (1897). 380.

10. The Faerie Queene . . . John W. Hales.

Rev. The Critic, n. s. XXVIII (1897). 302.

11. The Faerie Queene . . . Kate M. Warren.

Rev. Literature (Amer. ed.). II (1898). 316.

12. *The Faerie Queene. Disposed into twelve bookes, Fashioning XII Moral vertues. London, 1596. Repr. 2 vols. Cambridge University Press, 1909.

Includes letter to Raleigh and fragment of Bk. VII from 1609 ed.

13. The Faerie Queene, disposed into twelve books fashioning xii. moral vertues. Chelsea (Ashendene Press), 1923.

Folio ed. based on text of J. C. Smith.

14. The Faerie Queene. Ed. R. Morris. London (Dent), 1933. 2 vols.

Rev. YWES XIV (1933). 226.

15. HEFFNER, RAY. The Printing of John Hughes' Edition of Spenser, 1715. MLN L (1935). 151-3.

16. WURTSBAUGH, JEWEL. Upton's Edition of the *Faerie Queene* (1758). Pp. 56. Proc. of Dr. Greenlaw's Seminary " C ". [n. d.] The Johns Hopkins University Library.

17. ———— The 1758 Editions of *The Faerie Queene.* MLN XLVIII (1933). 228-9.

Explains why Church and Upton do not refer to each other's work. Rev. YWES XIV (1933). 225-6.

18. ———— Textual Interest in Spenser, 1609-1805. Paper read before the Mod. Lang. Ass., 1934. *Cf.* PMLA XLIX (*Proc.*, 1934). 1326.

19. ———— Thomas Edwards and the Editorship of the *Faerie Queene.* MLN L (1935). 146-51.

20. WURTSBAUGH, JEWEL. Two Centuries of Spenserian Scholarship (1609-1805). Baltimore, 1936. Pp. xii + 174. Also Diss., The Johns Hopkins University, 1932.
   1) The First Hundred Years. 2) John Hughes. 3) Improvement of the Text. 4) The High-Tide of Interest. 5) Studies in Spenser's Sources. 6) The First Variorum (1805).

III. FAERIE QUEENE, EDITIONS OF SEPARATE BOOKS AND SELECTIONS

See " Addenda," Nos. 4-5.

1. Faery Queene. Book I. Ed. G. W. Kitchin.
   Rev. Brit. Quart. Rev. XLVII (1868). 548.

2. Faerie Queene. Book I. Ed. H. M. Percival.
   Rev. Athenaeum. 1893. II. 64.

3. Faery Queene, Book I. Ed. W. H. Hudson.
   Rev. Academy LXVI (1904). 195.

4. The Faerie Queene, Book II. Ed. Lilian Winstanley.
   Rev. Anglia Beibl. XXV (1914). 365, by Frank Gschwind; MLN XXXI (1916). 189-91, by J. W. B. Reviews Book I, 1915.

5. The Faerie Queene. Books I and II. Ed. Lilian Winstanley. Cambridge, 1928.

6. The Faerie Queene. The Second Booke, Contayning The Legend of Sir Guyon; or Of Temperaunce by Edmund Spenser; with notes and comments by George R. Potter and James Cline. New York, 1929.
   Rev. YWES XI (1930). 195.

7. The Faerie Queene, Book I. Ed. Guy N. Pocock (King's Treasuries). London, 1930.
   Rev. YWES XI (1930). 195.

8. *The Lady Una and the Red Cross Knight. A Fairy Tale, in Three Acts. Ed. J. Barfield. 1806.
   " Anonymous, founded on Sp's Faerie Queene (in a London bookseller's Cat., 1923." [F. I. C. and A. P.] Copy in Newberry Library, presented by Dr. Carpenter.

9. Knight of the Red Cross of Holiness. Book I. In a modernized text. Preface signed by William Horton. London, 1850. [F. I. C. and A. P.]

10. *The Faerie Queene cantos i and ii and the Prothalamion. Life by G. W. Kitchin. New York, 1891. (Maynard's English Classics.)

11. Baconiana, n. s. IX (1901). London.
Selections from Sp.

12. Day Book of Passages from the Faery Queene. Ed. Alice Cowell. Edinburgh and London, 1905. [F. I. C. and A. P.]

13. Britomart, selections from Spenser's Faerie Queene, Books III, IV, V. Ed. Mary E. Litchfield. Boston, 1906.

14. Selections from Spenser's The Faerie Queene. Ed. John Erskine. New York, 1921.

15. Chaucer and Spenser, contrasted as narrative poets. Introduction and notes. Ed. Guy Boas. Edinburgh, 1926.

16. *Legends and Pageants from The Faerie Queene. Selections by J. C. Smith. London, 1932.

IV. Faerie Queene, Paraphrases

See " Pseudo-Spenser "; " Addenda," No. 4.

1. Una and Arthur, An Allegorical Romance. The Story from Spenser. London, 1779. 2 vols.
Copy in Tudor and Stuart Club Library, and in Harvard Coll. Library. Cf. Cat. of Elkin Mathews, No. 39. 1931. Item 9; Lowndes, IX (1865). 2480, ascribes this to Alexander Bicknell; Carpenter, Ref. Guide, 119, " Prince Arthur." Rev. Monthly Rev. LX (1779). 324.

2. Corns, Albert R. and A. Sparke. A Bibliography of Unfinished Books in the English Language. London (Quaritch), 1915.
215: " Spenser (Edmund). Spenser's Fairy Queen attempted in blank verse, with notes critical and explanatory. No. I. London, 1783." Includes four cantos of Bk. I.

3. Peabody, Mrs. Holiness; or the Legend of St. George: A Tale from Spencer's Faerie Queene, by A Mother.
Cf. " Preface": MS of Legends of Temperance, Chastity, Justice, &c. await publication at popular demand. Cf. Carpenter, Ref. Guide, 119.

4. Towry, M. H. Spenser for Children.
   Rev. Spectator L (1877). 1625; Nation (N. Y.) LVII (1893). 101.

5. Maclehose, Sophia H. Tales from Spenser chosen from the Faerie Queene.
   Rev. The Critic, n. s. XIII (1890). 206; Athenaeum. 1905. II. 332.

6. Thomson, Clara L. Tales from the Fairie Queene. Illustrated by Helen Stratton. Sheldon, South Devon. 1902. (2nd. ed.)

7. *Durrant, W. S. The Red Cross Knight, a Play. (Scenes from Spenser's Faerie Queene.) London, 1913. Also W. H. Baker Co., New York, 1936.
   "An attempt to dramatize the story of the First Book of the FQ. His own lines have been used whenever possible." [F. I. C. and A. P.]

8. Underdown, Emily. The Faerie Queene.
   Rev. Athenaeum. 1911. II. 730.

9. Pierce, G. A. The Red Cross Knight and the Legend of Britomart (The Lady Knight) being Tales from Spenser's Faerie Queene, done into simpler English . . . New York, 1924.

10. *Sturt, M. and E. C. Oakden. Faerie Queene. Paraphrases: The Knights of the Faerie Queene, Tales retold from Spenser. (Treasuries of Literature). London, 1924. [A. P.]

11. Underdown, Emily. Faerie Queene. Paraphrases: the Approach to Spenser (Formerly the "Gateway to Spenser"). Prose Tales with Extracts from the Faerie Queene. "Teaching of English Series," No. 7. London, 1925. [A. P.]

12. *Royde-Smith, N. G. Una and the Red Cross Knight, with other Tales from Spenser's Faery Queene. Illustrated by T. H. Robinson. London, 1927.
    Rev. TLS 26 (Nov. 24, 1927). 882.

13. Stories from the Faery Queen. Illustrated. (Epworth Children's Classics.) London, 1929.

14. *Dawson, Lawrence H. Stories from the Faery Queene . . . Illustrated by G. D. Hammond. London, 1932.

V. Minor Poems and Prose

See " Editions," i, iii, vi; " Addenda," No. 34.

1. Catalogue of the Additions to the Manuscripts in the British Museum. London, 1882.
   MS 31,626: " Sonnets of Edmund Spenser, set for a single voice by Maurice Greene. Dedicated to [Harriet Pelham-Holles], Duchess of Newcastle; 1 Sept. 1738. . . ."

2. Maggs Brothers Catalogue. No. 505, Pt. II. London, 1928.
   No. 2250: The Shepherd's Calendar, Containing Twelve Aeglogues, proportionable to the Twelve Months. 12 plates; a portrait by G. Vertue. Royal 8ᵛᵒ. London, 1732. Printed by Will. Bowyer.
   No. 2251: The Shepherd's Calendar. With fine engraved portrait of Spenser by George Vertue and engraved plate by P. Fourdrinier to each of 12 months. 8ᵛᵒ. London, 1732.

3. The Shepherdes Calendar. Edition of 1579 . . . Ed. H. O. Sommer.
   Rev. Athenaeum. 1889. II. 857; The Critic, n. s. XII (1889). 281.

4. The Shepheardes Calender. Illustrated by Walter Crane.
   Rev. The Critic, n. s. XXVIII (1897). 343.

5. Amoretti, Including Prothalamion and Epithalamion. Preface signed R. B. J. London, 1904. [F. I. C. and A. P.]

6. *Amoretti, Including the Prothalamion and Epithalamion. London, 1905.

7. The Shepheards Calendar. (Cambridge Plain Texts.) Foreword by A. Attwater. Cambridge, 1923.
   Rev. Engl Stud. LIX (1925). 107, by J. H.[oops].

8. *The Wedding Songs of Edmund Spenser; being the Prothalamion & Epithalamion: printed from the best editions with wood-cuts by Ethelbert White. Waltham St. Lawrence, Berkshire, 1923.

9. Myers and Co. London. An Illustrated catalogue of illuminated and other Manuscripts. London, 1924. No. 241.

> Description of a MS of Sp's "Complaints containing sundrie small poemes of the world's vanitie. 1591." Facsimile reproduction of original t.-p. and parts of text.

10. *Sonnets and Poems (Selected), with biographical introduction by Hannaford Bennet. (The Carlton Classics.) London, 1924. [A. P.]

11. *The Sonnets and Poems of Edmund Spenser. (The Pilgrim's Books.) London, 1925.

> *Notice*: TLS 24 (1925). 523.

12. Spenser's Minor poems, containing the *Shepheardes Calender, Complaints, Daphnaida, Colin Clovts Come Home Again, Amoretti, Hymnes, Epithalamion, Prothalamion*, Sonnets, and svndrie other verses. Chelsea (Ashendene Press), 1925. Folio ed.

13. *The Shepheards calendar: conteyning twelve aeglogues, proportionable to the twelue moneths. Entituled, To the Noble and vertuous gentleman, most worthy of all tytles, both of learning and chiualrie, Maister Philip Sidney. Lond., 1597. Reproduced, San Marino, Cal., 1926.

> Photostat facs. of copy in Henry E. Huntington Library. *Cf. post*, No. 18.

14. Epithalamion, with introduction and notes by Cortlandt van Winkle. New York, 1926. Also Diss., Princeton University, 1926.

> *Rev.* MLR XXII (1927). 243, by W. L. R.[enwick]; YWES VII (1926). 160; TLS 25 (June 3, 1926). 379.

15. *Daphnaida: an elegie vpon the death of the noble and vertuous Douglas Howard, daughter and heire of Henry Lord Howard, Viscount Byndon and wife of Arthure Gorges, esquier. Dedicated to the Right Honorable the Lady Helena, marquesse of Northampton, by Ed. Sp; . . . Lond. 1591. Reproduced, San Marino, Cal., 1927.

> Photostat facs. of copy in Henry E. Huntington Library.

16. *Fovvre Hymnes, made by Edm. Spenser. Lond., 1596. Reproduced, San Marino, Cal., 1927.

    Photostat facs. of copy in Henry E. Huntington Library.

17. *Prothalamion: or A spousall verse made by Edm. Spenser. In honovr of the dovble mariage of . . . the Ladie Elizabeth and the Ladie Katherine Somerset . . . espoused to . . . M. Henry Gilford, and M. William Peter esquyers, Lond., 1596. Reproduced, San Marino, Cal., 1927.

    Photostat facs. of copy in Henry E. Huntington Library.

18. *The Shepheardes calender, conteyning tvvelue aeglogues proportionable to the twelue monethes. Entitled to the noble and vertvous gentleman most worthy of all titles both of learning and cheualrie M. Philip Sidney. Lond., 1579. Reproduced, San Marino, Cal., 1927.

    Photostat facs. of copy in Henry E. Huntington Library. *Cf.* another ed., *ante*, No. 13.

19. Amoretti and Epithalamion. Noel Douglas Replicas. London, 1927. (Facs. of B. M. copy, 1611.)

    Rev. YWES VIII (1927). 186; TLS 26 (Nov. 24, 1927). 861.

20. Amoretti and Epithalamion; the edition of 1595 (English Replicas). London, 1927. Incorporated as Vol. 32, Publications of the Facsimile Text Soc., New York. Limited ed. (Ballou), 1927.

21. *Poems. (The Augustan books of English Poetry, ser. ii. No. 25.) London (Benn), 1927.

22. Complaints. Ed. W. L. Renwick. Elizabethan Gallery, No. 1. Oxford, 1928.

23. Epithalamion. Illustrated with wood-cuts by Maud Wethered. (The Helicon Series, V.) London (John Lane), 1928.

24. Daphnaida. Ed. W. L. Renwick. Elizabethan Gallery, No. 4. Oxford, 1929.

25. Shepherds Calendar. Ed. W. L. Renwick. Elizabethan Gallery, No. 5. Oxford, 1930.

26. Critical Edition of Spenser's *Muiopotmos*. MS Diss., by E. A. Strathmann, 1930. The Johns Hopkins University Library.

27. *Shepheards Calender. Illustrated in color by John Nash. London (Cresset Press), 1930.
    Rev. TLS 30 (Feb. 5, 1931). 95. Calls text poor.

28. The Fowre Hymnes. Ed. Lilian Winstanley. Cambridge University Press, 1930.

29. The Shepherds Calendar, and other Poems. Ed. with an introduction by Philip Henderson. London and New York (Everyman's Library), 1932.
    Rev. TLS 31 (Feb. 25, 1932). 139; Lond. Merc. XXV (1932). 512; Rev. ang.-amér. 9è· an. (1931-2). 546, by A. Digeon.

30. Thalamos, The Brydall Boure; Being the Epithalamion and Prothalamion, with 5 wood engravings by Lettice Sandford. Limited edition. Heathercombe, Manaton, Devon (Boar's Head Press), 1932.
    Rev. Lond. Merc. XXVII (1933). 259, by B. H. Newdigate.

31. The Astrophel Elegies, a Collection of poems on the death of Sir Philip Sidney. Diss., by Walter G. Friedrich, 1934. The Johns Hopkins University Library.

32. The View of Ireland. Ed. Cliff Martin. Diss. (Cornell University) announced 1924 in Bull. Mod. Lang. Ass., Spenser-Milton Group. [A. P.]

33. BERRY, ALBERT M., JR. Edition of Spenser's Colin Clout's Come Home Again. M. A. Thesis, Columbia University, 1932.

34. Axiochus. Ed. F. M. Padelford. The Johns Hopkins Press, 1934.
    Rev. Archiv CLXVI (1934). 138-9, by A. B.[randl]; Boston Herald, July 21, 1934, p. 11, by John C. Minot; New York Herald-Tribune Books X (Aug. 26, 1934). p. 13, by Samuel C. Chew; TLS 33 (Sept. 6, 1934). 600; The Johns Hopkins Alumni Mag. XXIII (1934). 93-6, by Frederick Hard; Anglia Beibl. XLVI (1935). 49-51, by W. Fischer; MLN L (1935). 191-2, by Douglas Bush; Rev. belge de phil. et d'hist. XIV (1935). 131-3, by E. Buyssens; MLR XXX (1935). 519-20, by B. E. C. Davis; SAB X (1935). 115, by Samuel A. Tannenbaum; RES XII (1936). 84-6, by D. Hamer. *Cf.* " Addenda," No. 6.

6

VI. Selections, Miscellaneous

See " Editions," iv, v, vi; " Addenda," No. 7.

1. *Mother Hubberd's Tale of the Ape and the Fox, abbreviated from Spenser. London, 1715. Copy in Bodleian. [Leicester Bradner.]

2. The Muses Library. Ed. Wm. Oldys. 1737. Life and selections.

3. Ritson, Joseph. The English Anthology. London, 1793-4.
   I, 7, 11: Minor poems; III, 81 ff.: FQ.

4. Gentleman's Mag. LXXIII. i. (1803). 159-60. Amor. XIII, LXXV " modernized."

5. Elegant Extracts. Ed. Vicesimus Knox. London and Edinburgh, 1805.
   Bk. IV: " Various Descriptions from Spenser."

6. Laura, or an Anthology of Sonnets (in Petrarchan model). Ed. Capel Lofft. London, 1814.
   Nos. 123, 679, 680, 692, 696, 697, 864: Sp.

7. Sanford, Ezekiel. The Works of the British Poets, with lives of the authors. 50 vols. Philadelphia, 1819. " First American edition of the British Poets." [F. I. C. and A. P.]
   II, 3-282: FQ, Amor., Epithalamion, Hymns.

8. Selections from the English Poets from Spenser to Beattie. London, 1834.
   Rev. Spectator VII (1834). 1023.

9. Select Poetry. Parker Society. Cambridge, 1845.
   Selections from FQ, Amor., Hymns.

10. A Garland For The New Royal Exchange, Composed of the Pieces of divers Poets made in Memory of the first Opening thereof, 1571, with the choice Verses and Devices of sundry fine Wits of later Times; written in honour of the Second Opening, 1669, now first collected and printed complete. 1845.
    Cf. Howes, Cat. 42, No. 789. Sp selections.

11. The Wedding-Day Book with the Congratulations of the
Poet. Ed. Katherine Lee Bates. Boston, 1882.
Sp *passim* and title-page.

12. WISE, DANIEL. Edmund Spenser. Home College Series.
(A brief pamphlet.) New York, 1883.

13. *HARRISON, LUCY. Spenser for Home and School. Poems
of Edmund Spenser, selected and arranged, with notes
by . . . London (Bentley), 1883. [F. I. C. and A. P.]
Rev. Athenaeum. 1883. II. 271.

14. Heroines of the Poets. Drawing by Fernand Lyngren.
Boston, [1885].
163: Spenser's Una.

15. Through the Year with the Poets. Ed. Oscar F. Adams.
Boston, [1886].
Sp entry for each volume.

16. The Sonnets of Europe. A Volume of Translations. By
Samuel Waddington. New York, 1887.
128: Sp's *Visions of Bellay*, I, II, quoted as translations. *Cf.* pp.
129, 132.

17. *Fairy Queen: Selections and Passages. With Notes by
T. E. Jacob. London, 1891.

18. Januarie: A song from Spenser. Music by H. A. Clarke.
Poet Lore IV (1892).
Frontisp: From SC " Jan." 31 ff.

19. GROSART, A. B. The Poet of Poets. The Love Verses
from the Minor Poems of Edmund Spenser. 1894.
Rev. The Critic, n. s. XXII (1894). 446.

20. RHYS, ERNEST. Lyric Poems.
Rev. The Critic, n. s. XXII (1894). 426; Nation (N. Y.) LIX
(1894). 463.

21. SELLON, G. B. Selections from the Poetry of Edmund
Spenser. London, 1893, 1905. [F. I. C. and A. P.]

22. PANCOAST, HENRY S. Standard English Poems. Spenser
to Tennyson. New York, 1899.
Amor., FQ, MHT.

23. ARBER, EDW. The Spenser Anthology, 1548-1591.
Rev. Spectator LXXXIV (1900). 97.

24. WARD, THOMAS H. The English Poets. Selections with
Critical introduction by various writers. New York,
1901 (first ed. 1880).
    I, 275-340: Sp (FQ, SC, TM, sonnets, Epith.)

25. KIRKE, EDWARD (?) Epistle Dedicatory to the Shepheards Calendar. In Elizabethan Critical Essays. Ed.
G. G. Smith. Oxford, 1904. [L. O. Hogan] I, 127-34.

26. YEATS, W. B. Poems. . . .
    Rev. Spectator XCVII (1906). 627.

27. Prefaces and Prologues to Famous Books. With introduction, notes, and illustrations. New York, 1910.
    Sp's letter to Raleigh.

28. HEPPLE, NORMAN. Lyrical Forms in English. Cambridge
University Press, 1911.
    Two of Sp's sonnets.

29. GOSSET, ADELAIDE L. J. Shepherd Songs of Elizabethan
England. London, 1912.
    93: SC; 108: Daphnaida.

30. Cambridge Readings in Literature. Ed. by George Samp-
son. Cambridge, 1919.
    V, 209 ff.: *Mutabilitie* selections.

31. RENWICK, W. L. Edmund Spenser; Selections, with Essays by Hazlitt, Coleridge, and Leigh Hunt. Introduction and notes by W. L. Renwick. Oxford, 1923.

32. England's Helicon. Repr. from the Edition of 1600 with
Additional Poems from the Edition of 1614. London,
1925.
    18, 27, 49: Sp selections.

33. Edmund Spenser's Letter to Sir Walter Raleigh, a letter
prefatory to the Faerie Queene, edited with introduction
and notes by Evelyn Boatwright. M. A. Thesis, The
Johns Hopkins University, 1928.

34. Golden Book Mag. 13 (May, 1931). 29. "May Day: a
poem."
    SC "May" 1-36.

35. WITTS, WILLIAM. An Anthology of Poetry from Spenser to Arnold. London, 1932.
> 1-279: Sp. *Cf.* 917-24: "Glossary to the Poems of Spenser."

36. CHAMBERS, SIR E. K. The Oxford Book of Sixteenth Century Verse. Oxford, 1932.
> 247-343: Sp. An excellent selection. *Rev.* Commonweal XVII (1932). 196; PQ XIII (1934). 91-2, by Hoyt H. Hudson; MLN XLVIII (1933). 263-5, by Douglas Bush.

37. GEBERT, CLARA. An Anthology of Elizabethan Dedications and Prefaces. Philadelphia, 1933.
> Unimportant.

38. GAWSWORTH, JOHN. [pseudon.] Terence I. F. Armstrong. The Poets of Merchant Taylors' School. London, 1934.
> 13-121: Sp (SC, Proth., Amor. Muiopot.).

39. Up from the Earth. A Collection of Garden Poems 1300 B. C.-A. D. 1935. Boston, 1935.
> 51-5: Sp's Garden of Adonis and Garden of Venus.

40. HAMER, ENID. The English Sonnet. An Anthology. Ed. with introduction and notes by Enid Hamer. London, 1936.
> *Rev.* Quart. Rev. CCLXVI (1936). 308, by C. E. Lawrence.

41. The New Book of English Verse. Ed. Charles Williams. Associate eds. Lord David Cecil, Ernest de Sélincourt, E. M. W. Tillyard. New York, 1936. FQ and SC selections.
> *Rev.* New York Times, Book Rev., Feb. 2, 1936, p. 4, by P. H.

VII. TRANSLATIONS

1. Catalogue of MSS in the Library of Gonville and Caius College, Cambridge.
> II, 627. No. 595: John Dove's translation of the entire SC. Probably written at Christ Church, Oxford, between 1584 and 1586. *Cf.* Leicester Bradner, MP XXXIII (1935). 21-6; Carpenter, Ref. Guide, 195, dates this *ca.* 1590.

2. Catalogue of the Harleian MSS in the British Museum. London, 1808.
> No. 532: Hymnus Pastoralis in laudem Serenissimae Reginae Elizabethae, ex Anglico sermone, in Latinum traductus. Anon.

Late 16th. or early 17th. century version of song on Eliz. in April eclogue. *Cf.* Leicester Bradner, MP XXXIII (1935). 21-6.

3. *HACKET, BP. JOHN. Letter to Dillingham. Nov. 23, 1653. Cited by Wurtsbaugh, J. *Two Centuries of Spenserian Scholarship*, 10.
> On Bathurst's translation of SC.

4. Catalogue of the Pamphlets, Books, Newspapers, and Manuscripts Relating to the Civil War, the Commonwealth, and Restoration, Collected by George Thomason, 1640-1661. London, 1908.
> II, 42: [Nov. 1]. The Shepherds Calendar. By Edmund Spencer. [Translated into Latin verse by Theodore Bathurst.] With the English Text. Pp. 147. E. 1437 (1).

5. Pembroke College, Cambridge. MS of Bathurst's translation of SC, dedicated to Harsnet, Master of Pembroke 1605-1616. Probably written *ca.* 1608.
> *Cf.* Leicester Bradner, MP XXXIII (1935). 21-6; Carpenter, Ref. Guide, 201. Two other copies of this translation extant at B. M. interleaved in 1597 edition of SC.

6. Shepheardes Calendar. MS of Theodore Bathurst's translation. The Britwell copy, sold at Sotheby's, April 4, 1924, Lot 721. In the Library of Mr. Carl H. Pforzheimer, New York City.
> Quarto, paper, 42 leaves. Numerous blank pages (35, 36, 39 etc.). "October" has one stanza only. The MS is in several hands. Description by Mr. William A. Jackson, Grolier Club.

7. Teutscher Merkur. 1788.
> I, 237-49: Partial translation of FQ. Cited by Price, Mary B. and L. M. Price. The Publication of English Literature in Germany in the Eighteenth Century, 224. Univ. of Cal. Pub. Mod. Phil. XVII, 1934.

8. Spensers Feenkönigin, I, i. Probe einer Übersetzung, von Eschenburg. Deutsche Monatsschrift, 1795. 313-31.
> Cited by Price, Mary B. and L. M. Price. The Publication of English Literature in Germany in the Eighteenth Century, 224. Univ. of Cal. Pub. Mod. Phil. XVII, 1934.

9. Bruiloftsdag. Translation of Sp's Epithalamion by Willem Bilderdijk. Printed in *Nieuwe Dichtschakeering*, 1819, II, 59 and in *De Dichtwerken van Bilderdijk*. Haarlem, 1858. X, 159-71. *Cf.* Catalogue of Addit.

MSS in the British Museum, London, 1933. Addit.
MS 39, 301, fol. 55: autograph MSS of Bilderdijk's Sp.

10. Il Cavaliero della Croce Rossa . . . de T. Jacopo Mathias.
Napoli, 1830.

11. Amoretti d'Edmund Spenser . . . Traduit . . . par F.
Henry.
Rev. Athenaeum. 1914. I. 37.

12. Edmund Spenser; introduction, traduction et notes, par
Paul de Reul. Paris, 1933.
Rev. TLS 32 (Sept. 28, 1933). 637-8. "The New Poet"; Rev.
Hist. ·58è· an. CLXXII (1933). 359; Rev. crit. 67è· an. (1933).
510, by A. Koszul.

VIII. Pseudo-Spenser

For obvious imitations, see sections on "Criticism, Influence, Allusions." See also "Apocrypha."

1. A Supplement of The Faery Queene in three Bookes.
Cambridge Univ. MS Ee. iii. 53. 576 fol.
Cat. describes it as a Supplement portraying allegorically the civil
and military affairs of the times. ca. 1635. Photostat copy, Tudor
and Stuart Club, Baltimore. Cf. Carpenter, Ref. Guide, 123, where
this is tentatively ascribed to Robert Jegon, and 150. These are
identical MSS. Cf. Hunter, Chorus Vatum . . . MS 24,490, fol.
245; NQ, ser. viii. I (1892). 273. Mr. Heffner supplies the following note: "Finished in 1633, MS Ee. 3. 53. was in the possession of Bp. Moore in 1697 whose Library was presented to Cambridge University in 1715 by George I." Cf. Brinkley, R. F.
Arthurian Legend in the Seventeenth Century, 108-11; post, No. 3.

2. [Croxall, Samuel]. An Original Canto of Spencer:
Design'd as Part of his Fairy Queen, but never Printed:
. . . by Nestor Ironside . . . London, 1714.

3. Millican, C. Bowie. Ralph Knevett's "Supplement of
the Faery Queene." TLS 34 (Oct. 10, 1935). 631.
Author of MS Ee. iii. 53. is Ralph Knevett of Norfolk. Cf. ante,
No. 1, and RES article forthcoming.

4. [West, Gilbert]. A Canto of the Fairy Queen. Writ-
ten by Spenser. Never Before Published. London, 1739.
Advertisement, p. 1: "A Friend of mine who lives in
Ireland, having communicated to me the following
Poem, which he said was given him by a Descendant of

that great Poet, whose Name it bears; I thought it too
extraordinary not to be presented to the Publick. I shall
not enter into the Question whether this canto be really
his, to whom it is ascribed. . . ."

Copies in Yale University Library and Tudor and Stuart Club.
Cf. Pickering and Chatto, Catalogue No. 238. London, 1926-8.
Addenda.

LOST WORKS

See " Axiochus," and " Editions," v, No. 34.

1. BUCK, P. M., JR. Addit. MS 34,064 and Spenser's *Ruins
of Time.* . . . MLN XXII (1907).

   Rev. Shakes. Jahr. 44 (1908). 284.

2. ———— Spenser's Lost Poems. PMLA XXII (1907).
Proc. xxix.

3. BURKE, CHARLES B. Spenser's Nine Lost Comedies
Again. Paper read before the Mod. Lang. Ass., 1931.
Cf. PMLA XLVI (*Proc.*, 1931). 1436.

4. PADELFORD, F. M. One of Spenser's Lost Works Comes
to Light. Paper read before the Mod. Lang. Ass., 1932.
Cf. PMLA XLVII (*Proc.*, 1932). 1335.

5. STRATHMANN, ERNEST A. Spenser's *Legends* and *Court
of Cupid.* MLN XLVI (1931). 498-501.

   Sp's lost works regarded as available as late as 1597-1603, on
evidence of Douce MS 280.

6. VALLANS, W. Tale of Two Swannes, 1590.

   Cf. Hunter, Jos. Chorus Vatum . . . B. M. Addit. MS 24,488,
fol. 105ᵛ.

APOCRYPHA

See " Pseudo-Spenser."

i. *Britain's Ida*

1. BOAS, FREDERICK S. Poetical Works of Giles and
Phineas Fletcher. Cambridge Press, 1909.

   II, xiii ff.: States case for Fletcher's authorship.

2. ———— TLS 22 (Mar. 29, 1923). 216.

   Phineas Fletcher's authorship proved by Sion Coll. MS. *Cf. post,*
Nos. 3, 4. *Rev.* YWES IV (1923). 125-6.

3. SEATON, ETHEL. Phineas Fletcher—a new MS. TLS 22 (Mar. 22, 1923). 199.

A Fletcher MS in Sion Coll. Library includes *Brittain's Ida* under title *Venus and Anchises*. Proof of Fletcher's authorship removes this entry from category of *pseudo*-Sp. *Cf. ante,* No. 2.

4. ———— Venus and Anchises. Preface by F. S. Boas. Oxford University Press, 1926.

v-viii, xlix-li: Sp's authorship completely disproved. *Rev.* The Library, ser. 4. VII (1926-7). 329-32. Trans. Bibl. Soc., n. s. VII. No. 3 (1926), by W. W. Greg; *Rev.* ang.-amér. 4è· an. (1926). 240-1, by É. Legouis.

ii. *The Doleful Lay of Clorinda*

5. JONES, H. S. V. A Spenser Handbook. Ch. XXIV.

Cf. "Hymnes," No. 11.

iii. *Edward II*

6. Catalogue of the Library of the late Winston H. Hagen. Anderson Galleries. New York, 1918.

No. 650: The Deplorable Life and Death of Edward the Second, King of England, Together with the Downefall of the Vnfortunate Fauorites, Gravestone and Spencer. Engraved portrait of Edward the Second. . . . London, 1628. This, sometimes ascribed to Spenser, here is attributed to Sir Francis Hubert. *Cf.* Hunter, Jos. Chorus Vatum . . . B. M. Addit. MS 24,491, fol. 136. Hunter ascribes the poem to Ralph Starkey, born *ca.* 1560-70, and describes it as Spenserian stanza. Ritson, Bibliographia Poetica, 256 and 352, says a seven-line stanza.

iv. *De Rebus Gestis Britanniae*

7. CARPENTER, FREDERIC I. Spenser Apocrypha. Manly Anniversary Studies in Language and Literature. Chicago, 1923.

64-9: Sp's authorship possible but doubtful. *Rev.* YWES IV (1923). 123; Shakes. Jahr. 59/60 (1924). 239.

v. *Various Scattered Verses*

8. Paradise of Dainty Devices, 1576-1606. Ed. Hyder E. Rollins. Harvard Press, 1927.

lxii: On poems signed " E. S."

vi. *A Dialogue on Ireland*

9. A breife note of Ireland [by E. Spenser; and, a book on
the state of Ireland, addressed to Robert, earl of Essex,
by " H. C." The first page of the MS bears the signature " Tho. Wilson," i. e. Edmund Spenser; the preface
is initialled " H. C." Dec., 1598, March, 1599]. 158 pp.
A photostat copy of a MS preserved in the PRO. Di-
vided into 4 books, the whole in the form of a dialogue
between Peregryne and Sylvyn.
    Copy in Newberry Library, presented by Dr. Carpenter. *Cf.* Car-
    penter, Ref. Guide, 132, No. VIII; " View of Ireland," No. 45.

SOURCES IN GENERAL, READING, SPENSER'S LIBRARY

See sections on separate works; also " Spenser and Dante ";
" Spenser and Chaucer," Nos. 2, 3, 5-6, 9-10; " Spenser and
Shakespeare," Nos. 2, 4, 6; " Spenser and Sidney," Nos. 2, 4,
8-11, 21, 26; " Spenser and Platonism," Nos. 1, 2, 8; " Edi-
tions," ii, No. 20, ch. 5; " Addenda," Nos. 8-10; " Axiochus,"
No. 5.

1. *Abbott, W. R. Studies in the Influence of DuBartas
in England, 1584-1641. Diss., University of North
Carolina, 1931.

2. Anderson, Ruth L. Elizabethan Psychology and
Shakespeare's Plays. Univ. of Iowa, Humanistic
Studies III (1927). No. 4.

3. Apperson, George L. English Proverbs and Proverbial
Phrases: A Historical Dictionary. London and New
York, 1929.

4. Ashton, Harry. DuBartas en Angleterre. Paris, 1908.
Diss., University of Paris.
    References to Spenser, *passim*.

5. Baroway, Israel. Studies in the Bible as poetry in the
English Renaissance. Diss., The Johns Hopkins University, 1930.

6. BAROWAY, ISRAEL. Spenser and the *Song of Songs*. Paper read before the Mod. Lang. Ass., 1933. *Cf.* PMLA XLVIII (*Proc.*, 1933). 1430.

7. —— The Imagery of Spenser and the *Song of Songs*. JEGP XXXIII (1934). 23-45.

    Possibility that Sp translated *S. of S.* Its influence seen in many of his works. *Cf.* Baroway, I. The Hebrew Hexameter: A Study in Renaissance Sources and Interpretation. ELH II (1935). 66-91. *Rev.* YWES XV (1934). 213.

8. BEUTNER, SISTER MARY LOUISE. Spenser and the Emblem Writers. M. A. Thesis, 1933. St. Louis University Library. [R. Heffner]

    Cf. ibid., Paper read before the Mod. Lang. Ass., 1933. PMLA XLVIII (*Proc.*, 1933). 1430.

9. BHATTACHERJE, MOHINIMOHAN. Studies in Spenser. Calcutta, 1929.

    Ch. II: Pico della Mirandola; Ch. IV: Bruno.

10. BOATWRIGHT, EVELYN. A Note on Spenser's Use of Biblical Material. MLN XLIV (1929). 159.

    Correction of Miss Landrum's article, *post,* No. 25. *Rev.* YWES X (1929). 216.

11. BULLOCK, WALTER L. A Comment on Criticism in the Cinquecento. PMLA XLII (1927). 1057-60.

    Theories of literary language in Bembo, *ca.* 1525, and in Speroni, *ca.* 1542. Sp's knowledge of these works.

12. BUSH, DOUGLAS. Mythology and the Renaissance Tradition in English Poetry. Univ. of Minnesota Press, 1932.

    86-123: Some aspects of Sp's treatment of mythology and of certain poets (Homer, Virgil, Ovid). Sp far less dependent on classical than on medieval and modern literature. His treatment of myth is largely influenced by these latter. *Cf. post,* No. 26. *Rev.* TLS 31 (July 21, 1932). 521-2. The Matter of Britain. (A good article); Commonweal XVII (1932). 194, by George N. Shuster; Criterion XII (1932-3). 701-3, by W. L. Renwick; MLN XLVIII (1933). 261-3, by C. G. Osgood; Lond. Merc. XXVIII (1933). 180, by John Sparrow; JEGP XXXIII (1934). 130-2, by Warner G. Rice; *Rev.* ang.-amér. 11è. an. (1934). 445-7, by Floris Delattre; CJ XXX (1934). 46-8, by Robert V. Cram; CW XXVIII (1934). 53, by J. P. Pritchard; MLR XXX (1935). 228-9, by G. D. Willcock; RES XI (1935). 214-8, by E. Bensly, esp. 216-7. *Cf.* "Addenda," No. 9.

13. CONINGTON, JOHN. "The English Translators of Virgil." Miscellaneous Writings of John Conington. Ed. J. A. Symonds. London, 1872. Repr. from Quart. Rev. CX (1861). 73 ff.

I, 137-97: Some reference to Sp.

14. CRANE, RONALD S. The Vogue of Guy of Warwick. . . . PMLA XXX (1915). *Proc.*, xlviii. "Thomas Warton and Eighteenth Century Interest in Medieval Romances."

15. DEBLACAM, HUGH. The Secret of Spenser. Lit. Rev. V (Dec. 6, 1924). 1-2.

Sp the first great Englishman whose work bore the mark of Ireland. His poetry is the "pure creation of the Celtic spirit." [A. P.]

16. Edinburgh Rev. LVII (1833). 419.

Sp knew well Ariosto and Tasso, but was not so familiar with Dante.

17. FAIRCHILD, HOXIE NEALE. The Noble Savage. A Study in Romantic Naturalism. New York, 1928.

Unimportant, but see index for Sp.

18. FINSLER, GEORG. Homer in der Neuzeit von Dante bis Goethe. Italien. Frankreich. England. Deutschland. Leipsig and Berlin, 1912.

277-80: Sp's knowledge of Homer is both direct and from intermediaries. Also *passim*.

19. GREENLAW, EDWIN A. The New Science and English Literature in the Seventeenth Century. Tudor and Stuart Club Lecture, 1925. Also The Johns Hopkins Alumni Mag. XIII (1925). 331-59.

Echo of new scientific learning in MHT and FQ.

20. HARD, FREDERICK. Studies in Aesthetic Influences on Edmund Spenser. Diss., The Johns Hopkins University, 1928.

21. HARRISON, T. P., JR. The Latin Pastorals of Milton and Castiglione. PMLA L (1935). 480-93.

480: Sp and the Muses. *Cf.* "FQ, General," Nos. 8, 142; "Teares of the Muses," No. 9.

22. HAWES, STEPHEN. The Pastime of Pleasure. Ed. W. E. Mead. Oxford University Press, 1928. [L. O. Hogan]
cxi-cxii: Sp probably knew Hawes's work, but his so-called borrowings from it can be traced as well to the work of other writers.

23. *HOYLOR, AUGUST. Gentleman-Ideal und Gentleman-Erziehung. Erziehungs-geschicktliche Untersuchungen, hrsg. von A. Fischer, O. Kroh, P. Luchtenberg. Bd. 1. Leipsig, 1933.
Copy in Henry E. Huntington Library.
Rev. Eng. Stud. XVI (1934). 194-6, by P. Meissner.

24. JOHNSON, FRANCIS R. The Progress of the Copernican Astronomy among English Scientists to 1645 and Its Reflection in Literature from Spenser to Milton. Diss., The Johns Hopkins University, 1935.
Cf. "FQ, General," Nos. 30, 31.

25. LANDRUM, GRACE W. Spenser's Use of the Bible and his Alleged Puritanism. PMLA XLI (1926). 517-44.
Sp seems more familiar with the Great Bible than with any other version. *Cf. ante,* No. 10.

26. LOTSPEICH, HENRY G. Classical Mythology in the Poetry of Edmund Spenser. Princeton Studies in English, No. 9. Also Diss., Princeton University, 1932. Princeton University Press, 1932.
A study of the presence and significance of classical myth in Sp. Sources, esp. Boccaccio, Comes, Petrarch, Ronsard, etc. *Rev.* YWES XIII (1932). 194; MLR XXIX (1934). 229-30, by B. E. C. D.[avis]; MLN XLVIII (1933). 263-5, by Douglas Bush; CR XLVII (1933). 147-8, by H. J. Rose; PQ XIII (1934). 223-4, by A. H. Gilbert; RES XI (1935). 92, by E. B.; JEGP XXXIV (1935). 116-7, by Clark S. Northup. *Cf. ante,* No. 12; Sawtelle, Alice E. The Sources of Spenser's Classical Mythology. 1896.

27. MATTHIESSEN, FRANCIS O. Translation an Elizabethan Art. Cambridge, Mass., 1931.
15: Sp and the *Courtier;* 124: Sp and DuBartas.

28. MEZGER, FRITZ. Kannte Spenser irische Gedichte? Archiv CL (1926). 232-3.

29. ——— Spenser's Quellenangaben. Archiv CL (1926). 233-4.

30. MURRY, J. MIDDLETON. "The Poet's Poet." Countries of the Mind, second series. Oxford University Press, 1931.

No. V: Repr. of lead. article, TLS 29 (Feb. 27, 1930), reviewing W. L. Renwick. The Works of Edmund Spenser.

31. OSGOOD, C. G. "Virgil and the English Mind." The Tradition of Virgil. With Junius S. Morgan and Kenneth McKenzie. Princeton University Press, 1930.

26-31: Sp found three-fold significance in Virgil as moralist, imperialist, and poet.

32. OWST, GERALD A. Literature and Pulpit in Medieval England. Cambridge University Press, 1933.

See index for Sp.

33. PEARSON, LU EMILY. Elizabethan Love Conventions. University of California Press, 1933.

See index for Sp. Rev. RES XI (1935). 230-1, by Nadine Page.

34. Retrospective Rev. IX (1824). 291.

Sp's borrowings from Ariosto.

35. ROBIN, PERCY A. Animal Lore in English Literature. London, 1932.

Sp's use of animals and his debt to traditional materials. See index.

36. RUSSELL, I. WILLIS. Influence of Huguenot Thought on English Literature of the Sixteenth Century. No. 48. Proceedings of Dr. Greenlaw's Seminary "C," 1926-7. The Johns Hopkins University Library.

37. SCHULZE, IVAN L. The Relationship between Spenser and Elizabethan Pageantry and Chivalry. No. 34. Proceedings of Dr. Greenlaw's Seminary "C," 1928-9. The Johns Hopkins University Library.

38. ———— Elizabethan Chivalry, Pageantry, and Masque in Spenser. Diss., The Johns Hopkins University, 1930.

39. SESSUMS, A. C. Spenser's Use of Proverbs. No. 55. Proceedings of Dr. Greenlaw's Seminary "C," 1926-7. The Johns Hopkins University Library.

40. SHEPARD, ODELL. The Lore of the Unicorn. Boston, 1930.

Cites FQ II, v, 10 as characteristic unicorn simile.

41. SMITH, G. C. MOORE. Printed Books with Gabriel Harvey's Autograph or MS Notes. MLR XXVIII (1933). 78-81; XXIX (1934). 68-70, 321-2; XXX (1935). 209.

> Additional books which Sp may have known through Harvey's reading of them. Supplements *Gabriel Harvey's Marginalia.*

42. ST. CLAIR, FOSTER Y. The Myth of the Golden Age from Spenser to Milton. Diss., Harvard University, Summaries of Theses, 1931. 242-4.

> Ovid and DuBartas lead as sources for golden age myth which became frequent vehicle of expression for discontent of a social or political nature, esp. in last decade of the 16th century.

43. TRENEER, ANNE. The Sea in English Literature from Beowulf to Donne. University of Liverpool Press, 1926.

> Sp's description of the sea and use of sea legend. See index.

44. TUVE, ROSEMOND. Spenser's Reading: The *De Claris Mulieribus.* SP XXXIII (1936). 147-65.

45. UPHAM, ALFRED H. The French Influence in English Literature from the Accession of Elizabeth to the Restoration. Diss., Columbia University, 1908. Also Columbia University Press, 1908.

46. WEBB, W. S. Spenser and Vergil. No. 67. Proceedings of Dr. Greenlaw's Seminary " C," 1926-7. The Johns Hopkins University Library.

47. ———— Spenser's Acquaintance with Hebrew. No. 32. Proceedings of Dr. Greenlaw's Seminary . . . *Loc. cit.*

48. ———— Spenser and Vergil. Diss., The Johns Hopkins University, 1928.

49. ———— Mulcaster and Spenser. No. 36. Proceedings of Dr. Greenlaw's Seminary . . . *Loc. cit.*

SPENSER AND CHAUCER

See "FQ, Sources," Nos. 15, 39; "Mutabilitie," Nos. 30, 34; "Language, Archaism," Nos. 9, 43; "Style, Diction," No. 10; "Versification," Nos. 10, 18, 26, 28, 33, 37, 41.

1. Bayne, Thomas. "Well of English Undefyled." NQ, ser. x. IX (1908). 267-8.
   On misquotation of this.

2. Broadus, Eleanor H. The Influence of Chaucer on Spenser's Poetry. In MS material relating to E. Spenser by students of the University of Chicago.
   Copy in Newberry Library, presented by Dr. Carpenter.

3. Burt, M. K. Verse ancient and modern. Rev. de l'Enseign. des Lang. Viv. 50è· an. (1933). 420-2.

4. Franklin, Viola B. Romance Allegory from Chaucer to Spenser. Paper read before the Mod. Lang. Ass., 1895. Cf. PMLA Proc. XI (1896). lxxii.

5. Hales, J. W. Folia Litteraria. London, 1893.
   97,108: Sp and Chaucer.

6. Harrison, T. P., Jr. Spenser and Boccaccio's Olympia. University of Texas Studies in English XIV (1934). 5-30.
   15-9: Daphnaida cast in mold of Chaucer's Book of the Duchess; use of Boccaccio's materials.

7. Hazlitt, William. On Chaucer and Spenser. Notice of Mr. Hazlitt's Lectures on English Poetry. Blackwood's Mag. II (1818). 558-60.

8. Landor, Walter S. Letter to Richard H. Horne [partly printed in Letters of Elizabeth Barrett Browning addressed to Richard Hengist Horne. Ed. S. R. Townshend Mayer, 1877. I, 99].
   Cited in Spurgeon, C. F. E., post, No. 15, II, 238-9. Sp and Chaucer contrasted in ability to portray human nature.

9. Magoun, F. P., Jr. The Chaucer of Spenser and Milton. MP XXV (1927). 129-36.
   A Chaucerian source for Blandamour. Speght (1602 or 1687) only edition using Blandamour for Pleyndamour (C. T., B. 2090). Rev. YWES VIII (1927). 185.

10. Nelson, Louise A. Muiopotmos. Calcutta Review, 3rd. ser. XXXVII (1930). 339-41. [L. O. Hogan]
    Resemblances of Muiopotmos to Chaucer's Sir Thopas and Nun's Priest's Tale.

11. RENWICK, W. L. Edmund Spenser: An Essay on Renaissance Poetry.

See index for Sp and Chaucer. *Rev.* TLS 24 (April 30, 1925). 296. " Edmund Spenser." Contends Chaucer is greater than Sp.

12. Rev. de l'Enseign. des Lang. Viv. 52è· an. (1935). 56-60.

Assignment to illustrate difference between medieval and Renaissance poetry by a comparison of SC and *Parl. of Fowles.*

13. SAINTSBURY, GEORGE. Chaucer and Spenser. Athenaeum. 1920. I. 698-9.

14. SMITH, ALEXANDER. Dreamthorp: A Book of Essays Written in the Country. Boston, 1864. Also ed. Christopher Morley. Garden City, 1934.

216-7: Sp and Chaucer compared.

15. SPURGEON, CAROLINE F. E. Five Hundred Years of Chaucer Criticism and Allusion. Cambridge University Press, 1925. 3 vols.

See III, index, for numerous allusions linking Chaucer and Sp.

SPENSER AND DANTE

See " Addenda," Nos. 11-2.

1. BAYNE, THOMAS. Spenser and Dante. NQ, ser. viii. I (1892). 439.

Sp apparently knew Dante well; evidence in his adaptations.

2. BRESLAR, M. L. R. Spenser and Dante. NQ, ser. xi. IV (1911). 447. Also 515, by A. R. Bayley.

Sp does not allude to Dante in Letter to Raleigh. *Cf. post,* No. 6.

3. Edinburgh Rev. LVII (1833). 419 and CCVII (1908). 398 ff.

Sp did not know Dante well.

4. FLETCHER, J. B. Dante and Spenser. Lecture delivered at Vassar College, April 6, 1934.

5. *GALIMBERTI, ALICE. Dante nel pensièro inglese. Florence, 1922.

Copy in Columbia University Library. [F. I. C. and A. P.]

6. LANGDON, IDA. Spenser and Dante. NQ, ser. xi. V (1912). 33.

Allusions to Dante in English literature. *Cf. ante,* No. 2.

7

7. SILLS, KENNETH C. M. Virgil in the Age of Elizabeth. CJ VI (1910). 123-31.

127-8: Sp's debt to Dante and Virgil.

SPENSER AND SHAKESPEARE

See "Colin Clout's Come Home Again," No. 17, and "Teares of the Muses," No. 6; "Addenda," No. 38.

1. ACHESON, ARTHUR. Shakespeare's Sonnet Story 1592-1598. London, 1922.

6-7, 12-3, 194, 249, 272: Sp and Shakespeare on John Florio, etc.

2. ALLEN, PERCY. Anne Cecil, Elizabeth & Oxford. London, 1934.

Chs. VII-IX: Sp's treatment of materials also used by "Shakespeare" or DeVere.

3. Baconiana XIX (1927). 113-22. Who Wrote Shakespeare? Repr. from Chambers' Edinburgh Journal, Aug. 7, 1852.

119: Sp's omission of Shakespeare's name.

4. BUSH, DOUGLAS. Mythology and the Renaissance Tradition.

142-5: Sp and Shakespeare contrasted in use of Venus and Adonis theme.

5. FORREST, H. T. S. The Five Authors of Shake-speare's Sonnets. London, 1933.

203, 206, 215: Sp's sonnets illustrated by Nos. 19-20. Sp a candidate for "Rival Poet."

6. Love's Labour's Lost. Ed. H. C. Hart. London (Arden ed.), 1930.

xxiv: FQ V and LLL parallels.

7. NEEDHAM, FRANCIS. The Rival Poet. TLS 32 (Oct. 12, 1933). 691.

Quotes Sir E. K. Chambers, Shakespeare, I, 568 on the "rival poet" who may be Sp.

8. PAGE, THOMAS. Spenser and Shakespeare. Their Lives and Literary Work. London, 1894.

3-16: Sp. Negligible. *Rev.* The Critic XXIII (1895). 276.

9. RICKERT, EDITH. Political Propaganda and Satire in *A Midsummer Night's Dream*. II. MP XXI (1923). 133-54.

> 137-8, 148 n, 154: Sp's influence. Shakespeare uses one of Sp's "tricks" here. *Cf. post*, No. 14.

10. RUSHTON, W. L. "Shakespeariana." NQ, ser. iv. XI (1873). 192.

> Parallels between *Richard III*. IV, iv and FQ VI, xii, 44; V, iv, 12, and HHL.

11. THALER, ALWIN. Shakspere and Spenser. SAB X (1935). 192-211. *Cf*. PMLA L (*Proc.*, 1935). 1359.

> Shakespeare's indebtedness to Sp, esp. in situations, settings, and phrasing.

12. THEOBALD, BERTRAM G. Shakes-peare's Sonnets Unmasked. London, 1929.

> Sp and Bacon, *passim*.

13. Times Literary Supplement 24 (April 30, 1925). 296. Review of Renwick, W. L. Edmund Spenser.

> Sp and Shakespeare.

14. VANKRANENDONK, A. G. Spenserian Echoes in *A Midsummer Night's Dream*. Eng. Stud. XIV (1932). 209-17.

> Influence of FQ I and II on MND. *Cf. ante*, No. 9.

SPENSER AND PLATONISM

See "Mutabilitie," Nos. 7, 32; "Hymnes," Nos. 1-4, 10, 15, 18, 28; "Spenser's Philosophy," Nos. 1-4, 6, 8, 10, 15; "FQ, Sources," Nos. 110-13.

1. BHATTACHERJE, MOHINIMOHAN. Studies in Spenser. Calcutta, 1929.

> Chs. II, IV: Bruno and Pico della Mirandola and Platontism.

2. ———— Platonic Ideas in Spenser. Pp. xii + 200. London, 1935.

3. BULLOUGH, GEOFFREY (ed.). The Philosophical Poems of Henry More. University of Manchester Press, 1931.

> xlii-xliii: Ficino's ideas in Sp's last two *Hymnes*; lxiii-lxviii: FQ allegory in relation to doctrines of purification and illumination. *Cf*. lxxv-lxxvii.

4. CASSIRER, ERNST. Die Platonische Renaissance in England und die Schule von Cambridge. Leipsig, 1932.
   79-87: "Seele und Eros bei Spenser." On FQ and *Hymnes*. *Rev*. Eng. Stud: XV (1933). 228-30, by Mario Praz.

5. DAVIS, B. E. C. Edmund Spenser: A Critical Study.
   210-7: Sp's Platonism.

6. DELATTRE, FLORIS. Rev. de l'Enseign. des Lang. Viv. 51è. an. (1934). 145-57.
   Platonism in Sp.

7. DOGGETT, FRANK A. Donne's Platonism. Sewanee Rev. XLII (1934). 274-92.
   Compares Donne and Sp in regard to Platonism.

8. *FRITTS, KATHERINE T. Spenser and Platonism. M. A. Thesis, Columbia University, 1929.

9. GLOVER, T. R. The Ancient World. A Beginning. New York, and Cambridge University Press, 1935.
   355: FQ full of teaching of Porphyry and Plotinus, etc.

10. LAMB, CHARLES. Version Popular Fallacies. Also, Corrigé de la version. Rev. de l'Enseign. des Lang. Viv. 50è. an. (1933). 232-3.

11. Variorum I, App. viii. "The Platonic Element."

PUBLISHERS AND PRINTERS

See "Editions," ii, Nos. 15-20, for editors.

1. BAILEY, JOHN E. Hugh Singleton, the Printer of *The Shepherds Calendar*. NQ, ser. vi. X (1884). 178.

2. BYROM, H. J. Edmund Spenser's First Printer, Hugh Singleton. Paper read before the Bibliographical Soc., London, Feb. 20, 1933. The Library XIV pt. 2 (1933). 121-56.
   Sp's choice of Singleton not accidental. Is Sp connected with Puritan protests *vs*. the Anjou marriage? *Cf*. Lond. Merc. XXIX (1933). 158-9. *Rev*. YWES XIV (1933). 225.

3. PEARSON, A. F. SCOTT. Thomas Cartwright and Elizabethan Puritanism. Cambridge University Press, 1925.
   188-9: Printing of SC.

PICTORIAL ILLUSTRATIONS

See " Editions," iii, iv, v.

1. [FENTON, R.] A Tour in Quest of Genealogy, through several Parts of Wales, Somersetshire, and Wiltshire, in A Series of Letters to a Friend in Dublin . . . by a Barrister. London, 1811.

> 184: Letter dated "November 8, 1807" from Stourhead, Wilts. Speaks of pictures at Stourhead Mansion; "the subject of the other is the Death of the Dragon by Red-cross Knight from Spenser, both productions of the pencil of Mr. H. Thompson, of the Royal Academy."

2. HOWARD, FRANK. "Una seeking the Assistance of Gloriana." A Cartoon exhibited at Westminster Hall, 1843.

3. Epithalamion, with illustrations by G. W. Edwards.

> Rev. The Critic, n. s. XXVI (1896). 441.

4. The Faerie Queene. Pictured and Decorated by L. F. Muckley.

> Rev. Spectator LXXVII (1896). 904.

5. OPIE, JOHN. The Freeing of Amoret (Bk. III, xii). ca. 1790.

> See Earland, Ada. John Opie and his Circle. London, 1911. p. 338.

6. ——— Serena Rescued by Sir Calepine (Bk. VI, vii-viii). 1798.

> See Earland, Ada. John Opie and his Circle, p. 344; Cottle, Joseph. Reminiscences of S. T. Coleridge and R. Southey.

7. RIDEOUT, EDNA. The Chester Companies and the Old Quay. Trans. Hist. Soc. Lancashire and Cheshire. LXXIX (1928). 156.

> Sp illustrations listed in Catalogue of "Works of Henry Melling in paintings . . . At Old Quay House, Neston, River Dee, Chester, 1874."

FAERIE QUEENE, GENERAL REFERENCES

See " Spenser and Raleigh," Nos. 17, 18; " Editions," i, ii, iii; " Mutabilitie," Nos. 1, 24, 32; " Language," Nos. 11-2, 19, 23, 27; " Style, Diction," Nos. 1, 2, 9, 13-6, 19, 21, 22, 26-7; " Versification," Nos. 1, 3, 5, 8-12, 14-5, 19, 20, 25,

27-9, 31, 33, 35, 39, 43, 45, 46; "Shepherd's Calendar," No. 56; "Addenda," Nos. 13-4.

1. Ackermann's Repository. VI (1811). 190.

    FQ's portrayal of Suspicion.

2. ALBRIGHT, EVELYN M. The *Faerie Queene* in Masque at the Gray's Inn Revels. PMLA XLI (1926). 497-516.

    Pub. of 2nd. part FQ announced by Francis Davison's "Proteus Masque," 1594-5. Possible friendship of Sp and Davison and effect of this on Sp's attittude to Burghley, Mary Stuart, etc. *Rev.* Shakes. Jahr. 64 (1928). 218-9; Proceedings of Dr. Greenlaw's Seminary "C," 1926-7. No. 13, by James M. Edmunds.

3. ―――― Review of Variorum, I-III. MP XXXIII (1936). 322-34.

4. ALLEN, PERCY. Anne Cecil, Elizabeth & Oxford. London, 1934.

    Ch. IX: "Scudamore and Amoret." Interprets FQ III-IV. Timias = Oxford; Amoret = Anne Cecil; Scudamore = Oxford; Belphoebe = Elizabeth; Duessa = Mary Stuart; Blandamour = Arundell; Paridell = Howard; Artegall = Leicester.

5. AMISS, MARGARET. The Pageant in literature with particular relation to the *Faerie Queene*. M. A. Thesis, Columbia University, 1917.

6. BALL, LEWIS F. The Morality Theme in Book II of *The Faerie Queene*. MLN XLVI (1931). 371-9.

    Structure of II follows "regular formula" of moralities. Analogues, to show that Sp probably received ideas of despair, forgiveness, etc., from late scholastic works and moralities. *Rev.* YWES XII (1931). 192. *Cf. post,* No. 87; "FQ, Sources," Nos. 90, 93; Variorum II, App. vi.

7. ―――― The Background of the Minor English Renaissance Epics. ELH I (1934). 63-89.

8. BENNETT, JOSEPHINE W. Spenser's Muse. JEGP XXXI (1932). 200-19.

    Argues for Clio rather than Calliope; Virgil is authority for Clio's pre-eminence. *Cf. post,* No. 142; "Sources, General," No. 21; "FQ, Sources," No. 120; Variorum I, 506.

9. BENSEL, E. (Ven-Ten Bensel). The Character of King Arthur in English Literature. Paris and Amsterdam, 1925.

    Ch. VII: Arthur in Tudor and Elizabethan Literature. Sp's Arthur and that of the chronicles.

10. BHATTACHERJE, MOHINIMOHAN. Studies in Spenser. Foreword by W. S. Urquhart. Calcutta, India, 1929.

Chs. I, V: Justice and Courtesie. *Rev.* NQ, ser. xiv. I (1929). 180; YWES X (1929). 216; MLR XXV (1930). 244-5, by W. L. R.[enwick].

11. Blackwood's Mag. XXVI (1829). 949; XXX (1831). 489-90; XLIV (1838). 468; XLVI (1839). 145. "Our Pocket Companions."

On Sp's impersonation of Hope in FQ. Other various notes. Negligible.

12. BLAIR, LAWRENCE C. The Plot of the *Faerie Queene*. PMLA XLVII (1932). 81-8.

Shows how Sp departed from his "avowed" plan; Ariosto's plan fails to account for that of FQ. *Rev.* YWES XIII (1932). 193; Shakes. Jahr. 69 (1933). 196. *Cf. post,* Nos. 28, 33, 146.

13. —————— The Plot of the *Faerie Queene,* Reply to Mr. Perkinson. PMLA XLVIII (1933). 297-9.

Cf. post, No. 146.

14. Bodleian Quarterly Record. VII (1933). 292-3.

FQ noted among rare books in 1933 "Elizabethan Exhibit" at Bodleian.

15. BOUGHNER, DANIEL C. The Psychology of Memory in Spenser's *Faerie Queene*. PMLA XLVII (1932). 89-96.

FQ II, ix analyzed to see how Sp's descriptions tally with psychological concepts of the time. Sp's memory seems selective and the basis of selection is ethical. *Rev.* YWES XIII (1932). 193; Shakes. Jahr. 69 (1933). 196. *Cf.* Variorum II, App. ix.

16. BOYS, H. WARD. Name-Puzzle in Early Spenser. NQ, ser. x. IX (1908). 48.

Cf. ibid., 114, by H. E. D. Blakiston; *ibid.,* ser. x. XI (1909). 334, by Edw. Bensly. Ownership of copy of 1617 edition.

17. British Quart. Rev. XXII (1855). 400-12; XLVIII (1868). 92-124. "Camilla and her Successors."

93-117: Sp's heroines; 122-4: Compared with Ariosto's.

18. BURKE, CHARLES B. Humor in Spenser. NQ 166 (1934). 113-5.

Rev. YWES XV (1934). 214.

19. BUYSSENS, E. Calvinism in the *Faerie Queene* of Spenser. Rev. belge de Phil. et d'Hist. V (1926). 37-69, 381-400.

Bk. I an allegorical but detailed statement of Calvinistic doctrine of Salvation. Sp's Calvinism compared with Milton's.

20. ―――― The Symbolism in *Faerie Queene*, Book I. PQ IX (1930). 403-6.

Key to symbolism is Calvin's *Institution Chrétienne*. Identifications, in the light of this work, of several characters. *Rev.* YWES XI (1930). 197. *Cf. post*, Nos. 110, 140; "FQ, Sources," Nos. 45, 46.

21. ―――― Spenser's Allegories. TLS 33 (Jan. 11, 1934). 28.

Insists upon *Institution Chrétienne* as key to Sp's allegory. Interpretations of Bk. I in this connection. *Rev.* YWES XV (1934). 215-6; Shakes. Jahr. 71 (1935). 145. *Cf. ante*, Nos. 19, 20.

22. ―――― Aristotelianism and Anti-Puritanism in Spenser's Allegory of the Three Sisters. Eng. Stud. XVIII (1936). 68-73.

23. C., W. H. The Faery Queen, II, ix, 22. NQ, ser. v. VII (1877). 509.

24. CALCOTT, EMILY S. Costumes of the *Faerie Queene*. M. A. Thesis, University of Virginia, 1929.

25. Catalogue of the MSS in University Library, Cambridge.

Ee. iii. 53: *Cf.* Carpenter, Ref. Guide, 123, 150; also " Pseudo-Spenser," No. 1; NQ, ser. x. XI (1909). 190.

26. CHAMBERS, SIR E. K. Sir Thomas Wyatt and Some Collected Studies. London, 1933.

Ch: "The Disenchantment of the Elizabethans " on Sp's place in 16th century literature. *Rev.* TLS 33 (Jan. 18, 1934). 41.

27. CHRISTIE, RICHARD C. The Old Church and School Libraries of Lancashire. Chetham Soc. Pub., Vol. 7. 1885.

81, 93: The Cartmel copies of FQ identified. *Cf.* New York Times, Nov. 26, 1930, p. 5, col. 2: Theft and recovery of these copies.

28. COLLINS, JOHN CHURTON. Ephemera Critica. New York, 1902.

123-4: Structure of FQ contrasted with that of Tasso and Ariosto in the epics. See pp. 112-3. *Cf. ante*, No. 12; *post*, No. 33.

29. Covington, F. F., Jr. A Note on *Faerie Queene,* IV, iii, *27.* MLN XL (1925). 253.

This stanza is one of earliest references to Sp's Irish environment. *Cf. post,* Nos. 61, 112, 124. *Rev.* YWES VI (1925). 168.

30. DeLacy, Hugh. Astrology in the Poems of Edmund Spenser. M. A. Thesis, University of Washington, 1932.

31. ——— Astrology in the Poetry of Edmund Spenser. JEGP XXXIII (1934). 520-43.

Shows Sp was interested in the subject and discusses chief passages in Sp's poetry which employ astrology. *Cf.* " Sources, General," No. 24. *Rev.* YWES XV (1934). 214.

32. Dodge, R. E. N. The Well of Life and the Tree of Life. MP VI (1909).

Rev. Shakes. Jahr. 45 (1909). 289.

33. Draper, John W. The Narrative Technique of the *Faerie Queene.* PMLA XXXIX (1924). 310-24.

Symmetry particularly marked in Bks. I, II, and VI, but present throughout. Sp's plan shows he could have drawn from previous generation of Italian theorists. Their opinions on the whole closer to his practice than is *Orl. Fur.* [A. P.] *Rev.* Shakes. Jahr. 63 (1927). 230-1. *Cf. ante,* No. 12; *post,* No. 133; Variorum I, App. i; II, App. x; III, App. i; IV, App. i.

34. ——— The Allegory of the *Faerie Queene,* Book I. Three mimeographed sheets. *Cf.* PMLA XLV (*Proc.,* 1930). xxiv, footnote.

Summary in 3 parallel columns of three-fold allegory, Bk. I.

35. ——— Classical Coinage in the *Fairie Queene.* PMLA XLVII (1932). 97-108.

On evidence of the diction, concludes that FQ may be regarded as a document of " social reaction." *Rev.* YWES XIII (1932). 193; Shakes. Jahr. 69 (1933). 196.

36. ——— Spenser's Talus Again. PQ XV (1936). 215-7.

37. Durning-Lawrence, E. J. Baconiana, n. s. X (1902). 98.

FQ I, i, 5 cited in connection with Bacon theory.

38. Edinburgh Rev. XXXI (1818-9). 476. Campbell's notes on poetic power and quality of FQ.

Ibid., LIV (1831). 451. Tediousness of FQ allegory; XC (1849). 174. FQ does not retell old story of Arthur; *ibid.,* 413-4. Sp's imagination is Gothic. *Cf.* Campbell, Thomas. Specimens of the British Poets. I, 124-7.

39. EDMUNDS, JAMES M. A Study of the Amoret Story in the third and fourth Books of the *Faery Queene*. M. A. Thesis, The Johns Hopkins University, 1927.

40. ────── The Amoret Story. No. 56. Proceedings of Dr. Greenlaw's Seminary "C," 1926-7. The Johns Hopkins University Library.

41. EINSTEIN, LEWIS. Tudor Ideals. New York, 1921.
    Passim but unimportant.

42. ELIOT, T. S. The Use of Poetry and the Use of Criticism. Cambridge, Mass., 1933.
    Ch: "Apology for the Countess of Pembroke." Also *passim.*

43. ELLIOTT, P. L. *Faerie Queene,* II, x. No. 41. Proceedings of Dr. Greenlaw's Seminary "C," 1927-8. The Johns Hopkins University Library.

44. ────── Satire and Satyr. No. 7. Proceedings of Dr. Greenlaw's Seminary "C," 1927-8. The Johns Hopkins University Library.

45. ERSKINE, JOHN. The Virtue of Friendship in the *Faerie Queene*. PMLA XXX (1914). *Proc.,* xxii.

46. ────── Life, The Great Adventure: The story of the *Faerie Queene*. Delineator 110 (March, 1927). 29, 66, 69.
    Brief summary of FQ for popular reading.

47. ────── "The Faerie Queene." The Delight of Great Books. Indianapolis, 1928.
    Ch. IV: Repr. of preceding entry.

48. FAIRCHILD, HOXIE N. Edmund Spenser. Literary Digest International Book Rev. II (1924). 542-3.
    The complexity of elements which combine to give charm of FQ.

49. FLEMING, CHARLES F. Spenser's *Faerie Queene;* Sans Loy, Sans Foy, and Sans Joy. NQ, ser. xii. IV (1918). 71.
    Pronunciation of these names should indicate knighthood.

50. Fletcher, J. V. Some Observations on the Changing Style of the *Faerie Queene*. SP XXXI (1934). 152-9.

Demonstrates the poet's waning use of color. *Cf.* "Style and Diction," No. 19. *Rev.* YWES XV (1934). 215.

51. *French, P. W. A Commentary and questionnaire on *The Faerie Queene*. London, 1927.

52. Friedrich, W. G. Elfin. No. 38. Proceedings of Dr. Greenlaw's Seminary " C," 1926-7. The Johns Hopkins University Library.

53. ———— Note on *Faerie Queene,* I, i, 4-5. No. 28. *Loc. cit.*

54. ———— Note on *Faerie Queene,* I, x, 13. No. 31. *Loc. cit.*

55. ———— Notes on *Faerie Queene,* II, ix. No. 40. *Loc. cit.*, 1927-8.

56. ———— Spenser's " Cup of Gold with Wine and Water Fild." No. 26. *Loc. cit.*

57. Gentleman's Mag. V (1735). 660-1: Sp's description of Merlin; XXVIII (1758). 57-8; LXXI. i (1801). 117: Belge episodes historically interpreted; LXX. ii (1800). 1127-8: " Spenser's Allusions interesting to a Biographer "; LXXXII. ii (1812). 524: Quotes a letter of Baker to Strype, April 17, 1710, that Algrind is Grind-al inverted; XCVII. ii (1827). 403-5: Sp's genius and imagination; XCIX. i (1829). 42: Sp's hero lacks reality; n. s. I (1834). 476, by Thomas Green: Allegory destroys enjoyment of FQ.

58. Gibbon, John M. Melody and the Lyric from Chaucer to the Cavaliers. London, 1930.

87-8: Richard Carlton's four madrigals from FQ stanzas.

59. Gilbert, Allan H. Spenser's Cymocles. MLN XLVIII (1933). 230.

Cymocles, derived from καῦμα meaning *burning, glow,* esp. *burning heat of the sun,* suits the character. Name is usually derived from κῦμα, *a wave. Rev.* YWES XIV (1933). 228; Shakes. Jahr. 70 (1934). 166. *Cf. post,* No. 134.

60. GORDON, GEORGE. The Trojans in Britain. Essays and Studies by Members of the English Association. Collected by W. P. Ker. IX (1924). 9-30.

61. GRAY, M. M. The Influence of Spenser's Irish Experiences on *The Faerie Queene*. RES VI (1930). 413-28.
The influence of the Irish material on incident and background of FQ has been underestimated. *Rev.* YWES XI (1930). 198; Shakes. Jahr. 67 (1931). 117. *Cf. ante*, No. 29; *post*, Nos. 112, 124.

62. GREENLAW, EDWIN A. Spenser and British Imperialism. MP IX (1912).
Rev. Shakes. Jahr. 49 (1913). 182-3. Reprinted as " Spenser and the Party and Progress." Studies in Spenser's Historical Allegory, 1932.

63. ———— Spenser's Guyon. No. 17. Proceedings of Dr. Greenlaw's Seminary " C," 1927-8. The Johns Hopkins University Library.

64. ———— The Faerie Queene. Encyclopedia Americana. X, 708-10. Ed. 1929.

65. ———— Studies in Spenser's Historical Allegory. Monographs in Literary History, No. 2. Preface by Ray Heffner. The Johns Hopkins Press, 1932.
1. " The Matter of Britain" as subject-matter for Tudor historiographers and poets. Treatments of the theme aimed to establish Arthur's historicity and to relate the Tudor dynasty to the legendary hero. Two themes emerged from controversy. Sp uses one, the return of the Britons to power in the Tudor family. Shakespeare uses the other, the Lancaster-York story.
2. " Elizabethan Fact and Modern Fancy" traces to Dryden certain misconceptions and preconceptions in modern study of Sp's allegory. New method of study must determine contemporary theory and practice of historical allegory, and interpret FQ in light of these new findings. Illustrates a new method by a study of Sp's political intention in Bks. I, II. Bk. I is allegorical discussion of Elizabeth's first service to England—the re-establishment of religion. Bk. II discusses her second trial in struggle between political virtues and enemies of organized government.
3-4: Reprints of *Spenser and the Earl of Leicester*, and *Spenser and British Imperialism*.
Rev. TLS 31 (Sept. 22, 1932). 660. " The Spirit of Spenser "; MLN XLVIII (1933). 258-61, by M. Y. Hughes. Discusses Ch. 1; Lond. Merc. XXVII (1932). 85-7, by Yvonne French; Anglia Beibl. XLV (1934). 47-8, by Hans Marcus; Rev. ang.-amér. 10è. an. (1932-3). 147-8, by É. Legouis; Eng. Stud. XV (1933). 69-71,

by A. G. Van Kranendonk; YWES XIII (1932). 192-3. Regards
the passages in Rhodius, Plutarch, Pausanias, Arnobius, and Lucretius as less significant than Dr. Greenlaw thinks; RES X (1934).
350-3, by C. B. Millican. Discusses the Arthur problem in MHT
and VG; Archiv CLXVII (1935). 275-9, by A. Brandl.

66. GREER, SARA. The Tropes of Spenser's *Faery Queene*,
Book I. MS Material relating to E. Spenser by students
of the University of Chicago.
Copy in Newberry Library, presented by Dr. Carpenter.

67. GRIERSON, H. J. C. Cross Currents in English Literature. . . . The Messenger Lectures, Cornell University,
1926-7. London, 1929.
43-60: Sp's problem was to harmonize his three chief experiences:
i. his enthusiasm, gained at Cambridge, for the Renaissance; ii.
his Puritanism, also acquired at Cambridge; iii. his enjoyment of
the world at Court. As a serious effort to resolve these influences,
FQ fails. Because Sp is not most deeply touched by either the
thought or the temper of the Renaissance and Reformation, the
values of the FQ are Humanistic rather than Christian. See index.

68. GRUBB, MARION. A Brace of Villains. MLN L (1935).
168-9.
FQ V apparently circulating in MS *ca*. 1591.

69. HALLIWELL-PHILLIPPS, JAMES O. A Catalogue of Proc-
lamations, Broadsides, Ballads, and Poems . . . in The
Chetham Library, Manchester. London, 1851. Priv.
print.
166: "No. 1373. Two leaves containing part of an early copy
of Spenser's *Faerie Queen*, MS."

70. HARASZTI, ZOLTÁN. The Poet of Pure Fancy. More
Books (Bost. Pub. Libr. Bull.) VIII (1933). 213-22.
222: FQ is vehicle of Ariosto's greatest influence on Eng.
literature.

71. HARD, FREDERICK. Spenser's "Clothes of Arras and of
Toure." SP XXVII (1930). 162-85.
Sp's references to tapestries indicate his skill as a creative artist
in using materials from other than literary sources, but chiefly his
keen awareness of beauty in tapestries he had seen. (Many used
Ovidian materials didactically.) Tapestries seem closer to Sp's
pictorial concepts than do mere literary sources. *Cf.* FQ III, i,
34-9; III, xi, 28-46; Variorum III, App. viii. *Rev.* YWES XI
(1930). 197; Shakes. Jahr. 67 (1931). 118.

72. HARD, FREDERICK. Princelie Pallaces. Spenser and Elizabethan Architecture. Sewanee Rev. XLII (1934). 293-310.

Shows that the "stir of architectural interest in Elizabethan England" was great; it may be reflected in realistic descriptions of buildings in Sp's poetry. *Rev.* YWES XV (1934). 214.

73. HARMAN, EDWARD G. The "Impersonality" of Shakespeare. London, 1925.

App. IV: "Ralegh as Scudamore," p. 310.

74. HARTUNG, A. C. *Faerie Queene,* II, vii. No. 39. Proceedings of Dr. Greenlaw's Seminary "C," 1927-8. The Johns Hopkins University Library.

75. HEFFNER, RAY. Raleigh and Book III of the *Faerie Queene.* No. 18. Proceedings of Dr. Greenlaw's Seminary "C," 1926-7. The Johns Hopkins University Library.

76. —— False Una and False Florimell. Parallels between Bks. I and III. No number. Proceedings of Dr. Greenlaw's Seminary "C," 1926-7. *Loc. cit.*

77. —— The Earl of Essex in Elizabethan Literature. Diss., The Johns Hopkins University, 1928. Also Baltimore, 1934. Pp. 36.

78. —— Essex and Book Five of the *Faerie Queene.* ELH III (1936). 67-82.

FQ V, xi, 43-65 represents Essex (Artegall) as leader of the "forward school" and supports him in effort to force a progressive policy on Elizabeth and Burghley. *Cf.* Greenlaw, E. Studies in Spenser's Historical Allegory, ch. 4; also *post,* Nos. 80, 158.

79. —— Spenser's Allegory in Book I of the *Faerie Queene.* SP XXVII (1930). 142-61. *Cf.* PMLA XLIV (*Proc.,* 1929). xliii.

i. Una and the allegorical method of Bk. I may owe something to Elizabeth's coronation pageants; ii. Religion chosen as subject of Bk. I because Sp regarded it as Eliz.'s first problem and virtue; iii. Bk. I read by Sp's contemporaries as allegory of Eliz. and "her relation to the establishment of Pure Religion." *Rev.* YWES XI (1930). 197; Shakes. Jahr. 67 (1931). 118. *Cf. ante,* No. 65, ch. 2; Variorum I, App. ii, v, vi; "FQ, Sources," No. 40.

80. —— Essex, the Ideal Courtier. ELH I (1934). 7-36.

The living embodiment of Sp's hero, Bk. VI, is Essex. *Cf. post,* No. 156; Long, P. W. Engl. Stud. XLII (1910). 53-60. *Rev.* YWES XV (1934). 217.

81. HEISE, WILHELM. Die Gleichnisse in Edmund Spensers *Faerie Queene* und ihre Vorbilder.
    Rev. Shakes. Jahr. 39 (1903). 321-2, by W. Drechsler.

82. HOWARD, LEON. Elf, to wit, Quick. FQ II, x, 70. No. 10. Proceedings of Dr. Greenlaw's Seminary "C," 1928-9. The Johns Hopkins Univ. Library.

83. HUGHES, MERRITT Y. Spenser's Palmer. ELH II (1935). 151-64.
    FQ II: Palmer may stand in relation of an elder friend in whose company the hero constantly moves. *Cf.* "FQ, Sources," No. 123.

84. ———— Review of B. E. C. Davis's *Edmund Spenser: A Critical Study.* MLR XXVIII (1933). 513-5.

85. HUGHSON, R. English Poetic Allegory in the Sixteenth Century up to the *Faerie Queene.* M. A. Thesis, Columbia University, 1929.

86. JONES, H. S. V. A Spenser Handbook. New York, 1930. Chs. XIII-XX.

87. ———— Magnanimity in Spenser's Legend of Holiness. SP XXIX (1932). 200-6.
    Aristotelian high-mindedness has a Christian counterpart in magnanimity (a subdivision of fortitude) in the writings of scholastics. "High-mindedness" derived from *animus,* which means both *voluntas* and *fortitudo.* If Arthur is identified with both qualities, Bk. I may be compared with some Wit and Will moralities. Sp's concept of the importance of the will in moral life is made clear by a "medieval understanding of highmindedness." *Rev.* YWES XIII (1932). 194. *Cf. ante,* No. 6; "FQ, Sources," Nos. 90, 93.

88. JOYCE, P. W. Spenser's Irish Rivers. Repr. Littell's Living Age, 5th. ser. XXII (1878). 21-34.

89. JUDSON, A. C. Spenser's Theory of Courtesy. PMLA XLVII (1932). 122-36.
    Enumerates articles in Sp's creed of courtesy. Bk. VI fuses two conceptions of courtesy: one, that set up by books of the gentleman; the other, a knightly Christian ideal. The second is rather more emphasized in Bk. VI. *Rev.* YWES XIII (1932). 194. *Cf.* Crosland, Jessie. Italian Courtesy Books. MLR V (1910). 502-4. Of general interest as background; *post,* No. 92.

90. JUSSERAND, J. J. Edmond Spenser. Rev. de Paris, 1 May, 1903.
    This is identical with ch. in *Hist. litt. du Peuple Anglais,* 414 ff. *Rev.* of *Hist.* in Blackwood's Mag. CLXXVI (1904). 494 ff.; Spectator XCVIII (1907). 497, by T. Fisher Unwin.

91. KANE, ROBERT J. Tobacco in English Literature to 1700, with special Reference to the Authorship of the First Work Thereon. Summaries of Theses, Harvard University, 1929. 161-4.

> FQ III first allusion to tobacco in English poetry.

92. KELSO, RUTH. The Doctrine of the English Gentleman in the Sixteenth Century. Univ. of Illinois, Studies in Language and Literature XIV (1929). 1-288.

> Discusses Renaissance definitions of gentleman. General background for FQ, but no specific mention.

93. KIRKLAND, MRS. C. M. Spenser and the Faery Queen. *Rev.* Athenaeum. 1847. 956.

94. KNICKERBOCKER, W. S. A Student's Diagram of the Action, FQ I and II. PMLA XLV (*Proc.*, 1930). xxiv.

95. KNOWLTON, E. C. Genius as an Allegorical Figure. MLN XXXIX (1924). 89-95.

> Account of Genius as variously portrayed in works of Alan de Lille, Jean de Meun, Gower, Martin Franc, Jean Lemaire de Belges, Marot, etc. De Meun's characterization responsible for the shift in the place of Genius in French literature. *Cf.* CP XV (1920). 380 ff.

96. ———— The Genii of Spenser. SP XXV (1928). 439-56.

> Pagan and Christian views of Genius, disagreeing in case of specific genii, are in accord in setting up good and bad genii. Sp, familiar with these views, uses two genii in his allegory. One, false Genius (B. of Blis), is associated with "debasement of the creative functions in art and life"; the other, true Genius (G. of Adonis), is associated with "sound education in love and loving." *Rev.* YWES IX (1928). 173. *Cf. ante*, No. 95; *post*, No. 113.

97. KREINER, LILLIAN M. The Sixteenth Century Conception of an Educated Gentleman. M. A. Thesis, Columbia University, 1913.

98. LATHAM, MINOR WHITE. The Elizabethan Fairies. New York, 1930. Also Diss., Columbia University Library, 1930.

> 306: Sp's references to fairies. *Rev.* Jour. Amer. Folklore XLIV (1931). 223-4, by Louise Pound. Literary fairies had their heyday after publication of FQ and Shakespeare's MND. *Cf.* Leland, Mrs. Fannibelle. The "fairy" in English literature, with special reference to Spenser and Shakespeare. M. A. Thesis, Columbia Univ., 1908.

99. LAW, R. A. Tripartite Gaul in the Story of King Leir. Texas Studies in English IV (1924). 39-48.
Pt. II: Sp's "Celtica" identified as the "central division" of Gaul. *Rev.* YWES VI (1925). 169.

100. LAWSON, CHARLES F. The Allegory of the *Faerie Queene.* M. A. Thesis, Columbia University, 1904.

101. LEGOUIS, ÉMILE. Edmund Spenser. New York and London, 1926. Chs. 5-6.

102. Leisure Hour III (1854). 518-9. "The Poet Spenser."
Negligible.

103. LEMMI, C. W. Notes on the *Faerie Queene,* Book I. No. 2. Proceedings of Dr. Greenlaw's Seminary "C," 1926-7. The Johns Hopkins Univ. Library.

104. ——— Three Monsters in the *Faerie Queene.* No. 35. Proceedings . . . 1927-8. *Loc. cit.*

105. ——— Note on *Faerie Queene,* II, vii, 33. No. 36. Proceedings . . . *Loc. cit.*

106. ——— Note on *Faerie Queene,* II, vi. No. 38. Proceedings . . . *Loc. cit.*

107. ———Invocation to Calliope. No. 58. Proceedings . . . 1927. *Loc. cit.*
Cf. post, No. 140.

108. ——— The Angel in the *Faerie Queene,* II, viii. No number. Proceedings . . . 1930. *Loc. cit.*

109. ——— Britomart: The Embodiment of True Love. SP XXXI (1934). 133-39.
Britomart is Love, united with Plotinus's Earthly Venus. *Cf.* "FQ, Sources," Nos. 35, 79. *Rev.* YWES XV (1934). 216.

110. ——— The Episode of Mordant and Amavia, in FQ II, i. PQ XIII (1934). 292-5.
Does Sp here intend a refutation of the doctrine of spiritual purification by means of holy water? *Cf.* Lemmi, C. W. in PQ VII (1928). 220-3; VIII (1929). 270-87.

111. ——— The Serpent and the Eagle in Spenser and Shelley. MLN L (1935). 165-8.
FQ II, vi, 103 derived from Homer; may symbolize righteousness (the griffin).

8

112. LEWIS, C. S. Spenser's Irish Experiences and *The Faerie Queene.* RES VII (1931). 83-5.

The differences between Sp's and Boiardo's treatment of the "rabble attack" may be attributed to Sp's Irish experiences. *Cf. ante,* Nos. 29, 61; *post,* No. 124.

113. ——— Genius and Genius. RES XII (1936). 189-94.

FQ II, xii, 47 and III, vi, 31 seq. *Cf. ante,* Nos. 93, 94.

114. Lismore Papers. Ed. A. B. Grosart.

First series. III, 260-1: Identifies Scudamore with Sir John Scudamore; III, 274: On FQ IV, xi, 41.

115. Littell's Living Age XXXVIII (1853). 18-9.

FQ tedious.

116. LONG, P. W. Spenser's Sir Calidore. Engl. Stud. XLII (1910).

Rev. Shakes. Jahr. 47 (1911). 260.

117. MARSH, T. REESE. A Note on the Dedicatory Sonnets of Spenser. No. 6. Proceedings of Dr. Greenlaw's Seminary "C," 1926-7. The Johns Hopkins University Library.

118. McPEEK, JAMES A. S. The Influence of Catullus on English Literature to 1700. Summaries of Theses, Harvard University, 1932. 264-7.

Ch. I: Attributes the formal English tradition of Catullus to Philip Sidney. Sp mentioned among those who have taken themes directly or indirectly from Catullus. *Cf.* "FQ, Sources," No. 24.

119. Monthly Mag. VII (1799). 89: Coincidence of Sp and Racine (*Phedre's* sea monster and FQ II, xii); XVI (1803). 131-2: Cantabrigiana. No. 82. Spenser.

120. Monthly Rev. XC (1819). 403. Sp's style.

121. MORSE, H. K. Elizabethan Pageantry. A pictorial survey of Costume and its Commentators from *c.* 1560-1620. London, 1934. The Studio.

58: FQ cited below portrait of Elizabeth from collection of late Duke of Devonshire, Hardwick Hall.

122. *MOULTON, RICHARD G. Medieval Allegory. Spenser's Legend of Temperance, *Faerie Queene,* Book II. Oxford Summer Meeting, 1891. Sheffield, 1891.

A syllabus for study of Bk. II. A tabular "Analysis of Action of the FQ." [R. Heffner] *Cf.* Variorum II, App. ii, iii.

123. NEALE, J. E. Elizabeth and the Netherlands, 1586-7. EHR XLV (1930). 373-96.
Background of Sp's Belge episodes. No reference to Sp.

124. NEFF, MERLIN L. Spenser's Allegory of the Toll-Bridge. PQ XIII (1934). 159-67.
FQ V, ii, may reflect Sp's knowledge of graft in connection with Irish toll-bridges. Cf. ante, Nos. 29, 61, 112. Rev. YWES XV (1934). 217.

125. NEILL, J. KERBY. Abstract of a preliminary study of Mary Queen of Scots as Acrasia in Bk. II of the FQ. No number. Proceedings of Dr. Greenlaw's Seminary " C," 1930. The Johns Hopkins Univ. Library.

126. ——— Spenser's " Shamefastnesse," Faerie Queene, II, ix, 40-4. MLN XLIX (1934). 387-91.
Fundamental difference between Sp's virtue (an extreme passion, as popularly conceived of), and the Aristotelian mean. Rev. YWES XV (1934). 216.

127. ——— The Faerie Queene and the Mary Stuart Controversy. ELH II (1935). 192-214.
In Bks. 4-5 Duessa is Mary Stuart. Sp's attitude towards her is that of her enemies. Duessa's trial is " definitely linked with her appearance in Bk. 4." " One group of her sins, . . . is against temperance, the virtue of Book 2." Further studies of Acrasia and Radegund to follow. Cf. post, No. 163.

128. New Monthly Mag. LXV (1842). 331.
Quotes FQ on " Daunger."

129. New York Times, Book Rev., Dec. 1, 1935. P. 41, by Philip Brooks.
Note on S. S. and Ward E. Terry sale.

130. ——— April 26, 1936. P. 24.
FQ an early allusion to tobacco. Cf. ante, No. 91.

131. Nineteenth Cent. XIV (1883). 129.
Quotes FQ II, xii, 30.

132. North British Rev. XII (1849-50). 371.
Quotes Southey on Sp.

133. NOTCUTT, H. CLEMENT. The Faerie Queene and its Critics. Essays and Studies by Members of the English

Association. XII (1926). 63-85. Collected by John
Buchan.

Attempts to answer critics of structure of FQ. *Rev.* Proc. Eng.
Jour. Club, 1926-7, The Johns Hopkins University. 66-8, by C.
W. Lemmi; Univ. of California Chron. XXIX (1927). 221, by G.
Dundas Craig. *Cf. ante,* No. 33; *post,* No. 181, Chs. 1, 6.

134. Osgood, C. G. Comments on the Moral Allegory of the
Faerie Queene. MLN XLVI (1931). 502-7.

i. The reason for the substitution of temperance for continence;
ii. Cymocles built upon conception of κῦμα, *a wave*; iii. Sin-
cerity of Sp's moral purpose; iv. Maleger as "physical disease";
v. Sp's ability to portray character. *Cf. ante,* 59.

135. ——— The Voice of England. New York, 1935.

167-70: FQ, interpretation, sources, etc. General; good.

136. Osmond, Percy H. The Mystical Poets of the English
Church. London, 1919.

17-25: FQ's mysticism.

137. P., D. Queen Elizabeth: Real Persons in *The Faerie
Queene.* NQ, ser. iv. VII (1871). 176.

Elizabeth's "fair name" not really believed in by her contemporaries. *Cf.* Keightley, Thomas. *ibid.,* 49.

138. Padelford, F. M. Spenser's Arraignment of the Ana-
baptists. PMLA XXVIII (1913). *Proc.,* xiii.

139. ——— Political, Economic, and Social Views of Spenser. JEGP XIV (1915).

Rev. Shakes. Jahr. 59/60 (1924). 237-8.

140. ——— The Spiritual Allegory of *The Faerie Queene,*
Book One. JEGP XXII (1923). 1-17.

Interprets Bk. I. Notes Sp's indebtedness to Aristotle's *Ethics*
and to Protestant Christianity as seen in Calvin's *Institutes,* and
to idealism of Plato and his Italian followers. *Rev.* Shakes. Jahr.
62 (1926). 187; YWES IV (1923). 120. *Cf. ante,* Nos. 19-21.

141. ——— The Allegory of Chastity in *The Faerie Queene.*
SP XXI (1924). 367-81.

The plan and structure of the allegory of Bk. III. Sp's conception of chastity as a womanly virtue. [F. I. C. and A. P.] *Rev.*
YWES V (1924). 153-4; Shakes. Jahr. 63 (1927). 230.

142. ——— The Muse of the *Faerie Queene.* SP XXVII
(1930). 111-24.

Calliope is the Muse; Evidence: i. Sp's description of her in
TM; ii. classical writers concede her pre-eminence (Hesiod, Plu-

tarch, Virgil, Ovid); iii. Renaissance concept of epic as "primarily moral" and only secondarily historical. *Rev.* YWES XI (1930). 199-200; Shakes. Jahr. 67 (1931). 118. *Cf. ante,* Nos. 8, 107; "Sources, General," No. 21; "FQ, Sources," No. 120; Variorum, I, 506; "Teares of the Muses," No. 9.

143. Parker Society. The Remains of Archbishop Grindal. Cambridge, 1843.

> xiiin., xivn.: Sp's Algrind. Grindal's remarks must have been commonly known at the time, judging from Sp's familiarity with Grindal's views.

144. Parks, George B. The Order of Time in *The Faerie Queene.* Blueprint. Copy in Tudor and Stuart Club, Baltimore. Paper presented at Mod. Lang. Ass., 1929. *Cf.* PMLA XLIV (*Proc.,* 1929). xliii.

145. ——— Gloriana's Annual Feast. TLS 32 (June 29, 1933). 447.

> Cannot establish an annual chronology. *Rev.* YWES XIV (1933). 228. *Cf. post,* No. 182; "FQ, Sources," Nos. 107, 108.

146. Perkinson, Richard H. The Plot of the *Faerie Queene.* PMLA XLVIII (1933). 295-7, 299-301.

> *Rev.* YWES XIV (1933). 227-8. *Cf. ante,* No. 12.

147. Pons, M. . . . Apprécier l'art de Spenser d'après le second livre de la *Reine des Fées.* Rev. de l'Enseign. des Lang. Viv. 50è· an. (1933). 150-5.

148. Pott, Constance M. Francis St. Alban's "Fair Lady." Baconiana, 3rd. ser. V (1907). 190 ff.

> Sp possibly reflects new philosophy of Bacon.

149. Powell, Frederick Y. Some Words on Allegory in England. Privately printed Opuscula issued to Members of the Sette of Odd Volumes, XXXVIII, 15-8. (Copy in Library of Congress). [F. I. C. and A. P.] Chiswick, 1895.

> Allegorical elements in FQ which are also found in painters from Dürer to Angelo.

150. Proceedings of Dr. Greenlaw's Seminary "C," 1926-7. The Johns Hopkins University Library. No. 33.

> Note on *Faerie Queene* II, Proem 1-2.

151. Quarterly Rev. XXXVII (1828). 311. Sp "luxuriates" in forest description; LXIX (1842). 4. Quotes FQ I,

x, 17; CIII (1858). 56. Quotes FQ II, iv, 1 as an "article of faith" among gentlemen; CX (1861). 448. No terse or rapid narration in FQ; CLXXVIII (1894). 341. Sp's skill in first-hand description of animal life.

152. R., H. These Remarks on Spenser were transmitted to me by the Reverend Mr. J. Calton, of Marton, near Gainsborough, Lincolnshire. They were addressed to him by a Gentleman, his Friend, desiring his Judgment Concerning them, and permitting their being communicated to the Public through the Canal of our History. [Dated] May 22, 1742. The History of the Works of the Learned . . . 1742. London.

II, 209-22. Chiefly queries on diction, Bk. I.

153. READE, COMPTON. Memorial of Old Herefordshire. London, 1904.

176: Sp's immortalizing of Sir John Scudamore.

154. RENWICK, W. L. Edmund Spenser: An Essay. . . .
Ch. V: FQ.

155. Retrospective Rev. III (1821). 49.

Sp's skill in delineating moral pictures. Tasso in FQ.

156. REUNING, KARL. The Shepherd's Tale of the Powder Plot. Eine Spenser-Nachahmung. Beiträge zur Erforschung der Sprache und Kultur Englands und Nordamerikas. Bd. IV. H. 2. (1928). 113-54. Breslaw.

Text with notes and comments. Rev. Anglia Beibl. XL (1929). 238-9, by A. Eichler; YWES X (1929). 216.

157. RIDEOUT, THEODORE C. The Background of Reason and Sensuality in the Second Book of The Faerie Queene. No number. Proceedings of Dr. Greenlaw's Seminary "C," 1930. The Johns Hopkins Univ. Library.

158. ROWE, KENNETH. Sir Calidore: Essex or Sidney. SP XXVII (1930). 125-41.

Opposes Dr. Long's identification as Essex (Engl. Stud. XLII, 53), rejecting the evidence. Regards Sidney as prototype of Calidore. Rev. YWES XI (1930). 200; Shakes. Jahr. 67 (1931). 118. Cf. ante, Nos. 77, 78, 80.

159. RUSSELL, I. WILLIS. A Note on *Faerie Queene,* II, xii. No. 43. Proceedings of Dr. Greenlaw's Seminary " C," 1927-8. The Johns Hopkins Univ. Library.

160. ——— Spenser's Choice of Temperance for *Faerie Queene* II. No number. Proceedings of Dr. Greenlaw's Seminary " C," 1931. *Loc. cit.*

161. *SCHMID, CHRISTIAN H. Biographie der Dichter. Leipsig, 1769-70. 2 vols.
    II, 148-236: FQ criticism, etc. [F. I. C. and A. P.]

162. SCHOFIELD, W. H. Chivalry in English Literature. 142, 179.
    Cf. Shakes. Jahr. 48 (1912). 234; Anglia Beibl. XXX (1919). 158-61, by Th. Mühe; Rev. de Paris. July 1, 1911. 185 ff.

163. SCHULZE, IVAN L. Mary Stuart as Duessa. No. 39. Proceedings of Dr. Greenlaw's Seminary " C," 1926-7. The Johns Hopkins Univ. Library.

164. ——— The Witch and Her Beast. No. 6. Proceedings . . . 1928-9. *Loc. cit.*

165. SESSUMS, A. C. Note on *Faerie Queene,* I, iv, 23, 7. No. 49. Proceedings of Dr. Greenlaw's Seminary " C," 1926-7. *Loc. cit.*

166. ——— Note on *Faerie Queene,* II, viii, 34. No. 16. Proceedings . . . 1927-8. *Loc. cit.*

167. Shakespeare Jahrbuch 36 (1900). 102.
    Sp's botanical knowledge.

168. SHULL, VIRGINIA M. The Descriptive Background of *The Faerie Queene.* M. A. Thesis, Yale University, 1932.

169. SMITH, CHARLES G. Note on *Faerie Queene,* I, iv, 29, 1-5. No. 25. Proceedings of Dr. Greenlaw's Seminary " C," 1926-7. The Johns Hopkins Univ. Library.

170. ——— Note on *Faerie Queene,* I, xi, 28, 1-2. No. 29. Proceedings . . . *Loc. cit.*

171. ——— Note on *Faerie Queene,* I, Proem, 3, 1-2. No. 35. Proceedings . . . *Loc. cit.*

172. SMITH, CHARLES G. Note on Canto-Connection in the *Faerie Queene*. No. 20. Proceedings . . . 1927-8. *Loc. cit.*

173. ——— *Faerie Queene*, II, xi. No. 42. Proceedings . . . 1927-8. *Loc. cit.*

174. ——— Note on *Faerie Queene*, II, xii, 75, 6-9. No. 12. Proceedings . . . *Loc. cit.*

175. ——— Studies in the Fourth Book of the *Faerie Queene*. Diss., The Johns Hopkins University, 1930.

176. ——— Spenser's Theory of Friendship. PMLA XLIX (1934). 490-500.

> FQ IV conceives of friendship "as the operation in the world of man of a principle of cosmic love" derived from Lucretius. *Rev.* YWES XV (1934). 217; Shakes. Jahr. 71 (1935). 145. *Cf.* "FQ, Sources," Nos. 111-3.

177. ——— Spenser's Theory of Friendship. Pp. viii + 74. The Johns Hopkins Press, 1935. *Cf. ante*, No. 175.

178. SMITH, G. C. MOORE. Printed Books with Gabriel Harvey's Autograph or MS Notes. MLR, XXIX (1934). 68-70.

> 70: Note on FQ.

179. *SMITH, GEORGE WELLINGTON. Didacticism and Expressed Moralizing in *The Faerie Queene*. M. A. Thesis, University of Virginia, 1929.

180. SMITH, J. D. On Spenser's *Faery Queene*. Poet Lore X (1898). 492.

181. SPENS, JANET. Spenser's *Faerie Queene*: An Interpretation. London, 1934.

> Disregards much of the recent work on Sp's philosophy, especially by American scholars. Impressionistic. FQ intended to represent the seven deadly sins in eight books of eight cantos each. *Rev.* New Statesman and Nation IX, n. s. No. 203 (Jan. 12, 1935). 52, by K. John; Rev. ang.-amér. 12è. an. (1935). 429-30, by Émile Legouis; Quart. Rev. CCLXIV (1935). 181; TLS 33 (Dec. 13, 1934). 891; Life and Letters XI (1935). 475-7.

182. SPRAGUE, A. C. Gloriana's Annual Feast. TLS 32 (April 27, 1933). 295.

> "XII severall dayes" means annual feasts over period of 12 years. *Rev.* YWES XIV (1933). 228. *Cf. ante*, Nos. 144, 145; "FQ, Sources," Nos. 105-8.

183. STANGNATT, MABEL VIOLA. Blood Relationship in Spenser's *Faerie Queene*. M. A. Thesis, Columbia University, 1914.

184. STRATHMANN, ERNEST A. The Structure of Book II of the *Faerie Queene*. Paper read before the Mod. Lang. Ass., 1931. *Cf.* PMLA XLVI (*Proc.*, 1931). 1436.

185. STRONG, SIR ARCHIBALD. Four Studies. Adelaide, 1932.
"The Spirit of the Elizabethan Age." (Sp's devotion to the Queen.) *Rev.* TLS 32 (April 27, 1933). 291.

186. TILLYARD, E. M. W. Poetry Direct and Oblique. London, 1934.
28-32, 36: FQ.

187. Times Literary Supplement, London. 32 (June 8, 1933). 385-6. Ariosto.
Fundamental difference between Sp and Ariosto in aim and attitude toward evil.

188. Universal Mag. LXVIII (1781). 354 ff.: Warton on FQ; LXX (1782). 288-9: Sp's character (Warton); XCI (1792). 422-6: FQ and SC; XCIII (1793). 166.

189. VAN EFFEN, JUSTUS. "Dissertation sur la Poësie Angloise." Journal Litéraire. La Haye. 1717.
Cited by W. J. B. Pienaar. English Influences in Dutch Literature, 225.
IX, 188-9: "On trouve encore en Anglois une autre espéce de Poëme Epique plus ancien que celui de *Milton*: il est intitulé *the Fairy Queen*, la Reine des Fées; mais le fameux *Spencer*, qui en est Auteur, n'y a pas mis sans doute la derniere main. Ce sont proprement des piéces detachées d'un Poëme projetté, à qui les liaisons manquent encore; par consequent on ne sauroit juger si l'ordonnance en auroit été conforme aux regles de l'Epopée: tout ce qu'en peuvent dire ceux qui entendent le vieux langage de cette piéce, c'est que le but en est moral, les pensées très-Poëtiques, & qu'il y a des morceaux, qui peuvent aller de pair avec ce que tous les Auteurs ont fait de plus digne d'Admiration." Copy in Yale University Library.

190. Variorum Spenser. *Cf.* II, App. viii: The Castle of the Body; III, App. iv: The Masque of Cupid; II, App. i; IV, App. ii, on the date of composition.

191. WHITNEY, J. E. The Continued Allegory in the First Book of the *Faery Queene*. Trans. Am. Phil. Ass. XIX.
Rev. The Critic, n. s. XIII (1890). 232.

192. WILLIAMS, CHARLES. Reason and Beauty in the Poetic Mind. Oxford, 1933.
    51 ff.: Sp's fusion of beauty and reason in FQ. *Rev.* Commonweal XX (1934). 56. *Cf.* Havens, R. D. Thomas Warton and the Eighteenth-Century Dilemma. SP XXV (1928). 36-50.

193. WILLIAMS, MARY F. The Secondary Stress of Spenser's *Faerie Queene*, Book One. M. A. Thesis, The George Washington University, 1920.

194. WILSON, ELKIN C. The Idealization of Queen Elizabeth in the Poetry of her Age. Diss., Harvard University Summaries of Theses, 1934. Pp. 346-9.

195. WINGFIELD-STRATFORD, ESMÉ C. The History of English Patriotism. London, 1913. 2 vols.
    I, 220-5: Tudor toryism in FQ.

FAERIE QUEENE: CANTOS OF MUTABILITIE

See "Spenser and Platonism," Nos. 1-4, 11; "FQ, General," Nos. 61, 112; "FQ, Sources," Nos. 21, 24, 110-3; "Spenser's Philosophy," Nos. 1, 13-8.

1. ALBRIGHT, EVELYN M. Spenser's Reasons for Rejecting the *Cantos of Mutability*. SP XXV (1928). 93-127.
    Mutabilitie originally to be part of FQ (bk. on Irish affairs). Plan deliberately rejected because of severe criticism by Harvey and Cambridge friends. Much of the material incorporated in other of Sp's works (Bk. V, etc.). Date of *Mutabilitie's* composition, 1579-80 (evidence of Harvey's letter). *Rev.* YWES IX (1928). 172; Shakes. Jahr. 66 (1930). 239; Proc. Eng. Jour. Club, The Johns Hopkins University, 1928, by S. W. Stevenson. *Cf. post,* Nos. 2, 5, 6, 8, 15, 22, 24, 28.

2. ——— On the Dating of Spenser's *Mutability Cantos*. SP XXVI (1929). 482-98.
    Probable date is 1579-80 for composition of *Mutabilitie*. *Cf. post,* Nos. 4, 15, 22, 24, 28. *Rev.* YWES X (1929). 213-4.

3. ——— Spenser's Cosmic Philosophy and His Religion. PMLA XLIV (1929). 715-59.
    Sp's philosophy is Empedoclean rather than Lucretian. *Cf. post,* Nos. 15, 25, 30-3.

4. ——— Spenser's Connections with the Letters in Gabriel Harvey's *Letter-Book*. MP XXIX (1932). 411-36.
    432-6: Letter Four a reply to *Mutabilitie*. Date, 1579-80.

5. BELDEN, H. M. Alanus de Insulis, Giles Fletcher, and the *Mutabilitie Cantos*. SP XXVI (1929). 131-44.

Relation of *Christs Victorie in Heaven* to *Mutabilitie* and to Alanus's figure of Nature in *De Planctu Naturae*; 142-4: opposes Miss Albright's dating. Sp can not have written *Mutabilitie* before he went to Kilcolman, 1586. *Rev.* YWES X (1929). 213-4; Shakes. Jahr. 67 (1931). 117.

6. BENNETT, JOSEPHINE W. Spenser and Gabriel Harvey's *Letter-Book*. MP XXIX (1931). 163-86.

Mutabilitie dates from later than 1580 and Letter Four is not a reply to *Mutabilitie*. *Cf. ante,* Nos. 1, 4; *post,* Nos. 15, 22, 24, 28.

7. ———— Spenser's Venus and the Goddess Nature of the *Cantos of Mutabilitie*. SP XXX (1933). 160-92.

Sp's description of nature is Neo-Platonic; the philosophy of the cantos presents "a consistent and unified discussion" of the serious Platonic problem of the place of mutability in the plan. *Rev.* Shakes. Jahr. 70 (1934). 165; YWES XIV (1933). 227. *Cf. post,* Nos. 14, 15, and SP XVII (1920). 455.

8. BUSH, DOUGLAS. The Date of Spenser's *Cantos of Mutability*. PMLA XLV (1930). 954-7.

Mutabilitie dates from Sp's fuller maturity. *Rev.* YWES XI (1930). 199. *Cf. ante,* Nos. 1, 2, 4; *post,* Nos. 22, 24, 28.

9. ———— Mythology and the Renaissance Tradition . . . 1932.

117-23: Sources of mythology in *Mutabilitie*. *Cf.* "Sources, General," No. 26.

10. CUMMING, WILLIAM P. The Influence of Ovid's *Metamorphoses* on Spenser's *Mutabilitie Cantos*. SP XXVIII (1931). 241-56.

Sp's primary indebtedness is to Ovid; Dr. Greenlaw overestimates the Lucretian influence. Miss Albright's ascription of Sp's cosmic philosophy to Empedocles requires "several strictures." *Rev.* YWES XII (1931). 193. *Cf.* Greenlaw, E., in SP XVII (1920). 439 ff; *ante,* Nos. 3, 5; *post,* No. 30.

11. DAVIS, B. E. C. Edmund Spenser: A Critical Study.

226-30: Bruno's influence on *Mutabilitie*. *Cf.* also 212, 232-40.

12. DeLACY, HUGH. Astrology in the Poetry of Edmund Spenser. JEGP XXXIII (1934). 540-3.

13. FRIEDRICH, W. G. Spenser's Sapience and Christ. No. 8. Proceedings of Dr. Greenlaw's Seminary "C," 1927-8. The Johns Hopkins Univ. Library.

14. GREENLAW, EDWIN A. Some Old Religious Cults in Spenser. SP XX (1923). 216-43.

" Sp's philosophy of nature, esp. in the Cantos of *Mutability*. Its basis in Alanus de Insulis. Sp's interest in ancient cults, that of the Mater Deum (Cybele, etc.). Use of other sources, Lucretius, Virgil, Ovid, Apollonius, Rhodius, Plutarch, Natalis Comes, etc. Comparison with various passages in the FQ, etc. Importance of the ' body of philosophical poetry ' which all of these present. His conception of love as the ruling and redeeming force of the universe. . . . A study of the sage and serious Sp." [F. I. C. and A. P.] *Cf.* Meylan, E. F., in PMLA XLIX (*Proc.*, 1934). 1304.

15. ————— Spenser's *Mutabilitie.* PMLA XLV (1930). 684-703.

i. Answers Levinson. Canvasses possibility of Bruno's influence on Sp. It is as yet undemonstrated. ii. Answers Miss Albright by restating Lucretian influence on Sp. The critical problem of *Mutabilitie* is the interpretation of canto VIII. iii. *Mutabilitie* is late work. *Rev.* Shakes. Jahr. 67 (1931). 118. *Cf. ante,* Nos. 3, 5, 6; *post,* 16, 18.

16. HEFFNER, RAY. Review of Davis, B. E. C. *Edmund Spenser* . . . MLN L (1935). 192-5.

Lucretian influence in *Mutabilitie. Cf. ante,* Nos. 3, 5, 6, 14, 15; *post,* No. 18.

17. JONES, H. S. V. A Spenser Handbook.

Ch. XX: FQ, Mutabilitie Cantos.

18. LEVINSON, RONALD B. Spenser and Bruno. PMLA XLIII (1928). 675-81.

i. Resemblance of plea of Fortuna (*Spaccio*) and Mutability, and between *Spaccio* and VIII, 58 are further reasons for seeing Bruno's influence in *Mutabilitie.* ii. Bruno's influence on Sp is explanation of the apparent conflict between Sp's philosophy and the Lucretian scepticism. Opposes Greenlaw. *Cf. ante,* Nos. 14, 15, 16, and SP XVII (1920). 439 ff.

19. Littell's Liv. Age, 5th. ser. XXX (1880). 814-8. A Lost Poem by Edmund Spenser.

Cf. Carpenter, 165, S. Evans.

20. McINTYRE, J. LEWIS. Giordano Bruno. London, 1903.

33: *Mutabilitie* probably suggested by Bruno's *Spaccio. Cf. ante,* Nos. 14, 15, 16, 18.

21. PADELFORD, F. M. Further Discussion of Recent Spenser Studies. PMLA XLIV (*Proc.,* 1929). xliii.

22. PADELFORD, F. M. The *Cantos of Mutabilitie*: Further Considerations Bearing on the Date. PMLA XLV (1930). 704-11.

On the basis of certain prosodic and stylistic qualities the date of composition may be "subsequent even to the Legend of Courtesie." *Rev.* YWES XI (1930). 199; *cf.* Nos. 2, 6, 15; *post*, 24, 28.

23. PARMENTER, MARY. Bruno's Influence on Spenser's *Mutabilitie*. No. 36. Proceedings of Dr. Greenlaw's Seminary "C," 1928-9. The Johns Hopkins Univ. Library.

24. PURCELL, J. M. The Date of Spenser's *Mutabilitie* Cantos. PMLA L (1935). 914-7.

Applies stylistic test and finds cantos closer in style to FQ I-III than to later books. This method of dating *Mutabilitie* unsatisfactory. *Cf.* Albright, E. M., in SP XXVI (1929). 482 ff.; Bush, D., in PMLA XLV (1930). 954-7; Padelford, F. M., *ibid.*, 704 ff.; Variorum, II, App. i; *ante*, Nos. 1, 4, 6, 8, 15, 22; *post*, No. 28.

25. SAURAT, DENIS. Literature and Occult Tradition. New York, 1930.

163-238: Sp's philosophy in *Mutabilitie*, etc. Important.

26. SHERRICK, HAZEL L. A Study of Spenser's *Mutabilitie*. M. A. Thesis, University of Washington, 1925.

27. SMITH, CHARLES G. Source of Spenser's *Mutability*. No. 44. Proceedings of Dr. Greenlaw's Seminary "C," 1926-7. *Loc. cit.*

28. —— Spenser's Theory of Friendship. PMLA XLIX (1934). 490-500.

497 ff.: Resemblance of concord-discord theme of cantos and Bk. IV. Possibility of dating cantos "soon after 1590." *Cf. ante*, Nos. 1, 2, 6, 8, 15, 22, 24.

29. SPENS, JANET. Spenser's *Faerie Queene*: an Interpretation. London, 1934. Chs. I, II.

Rev. TLS 33 (Dec. 13, 1934). 891. On *Mutabilitie*.

30. STIRLING, BRENTS. The Concluding Stanzas of *Mutabilitie*. SP XXX (1933). 193-204.

The outcome of the debate in *Mutabilitie* owes much to Boethius's *De Consolatione Philosophiae*. Sp's first answers to Mutability are found in Boethius. So is the idea that Mutability, operating in a non-earthly sphere, "finds its master and refuge in God." No need of effort to trace sources, since Boethius was conventional in Sp's day. *Rev.* YWES XIV (1933). 227; Shakes. Jahr. 70 (1934). 165. *Cf. ante*, Nos. 3, 7, 10, 14, 15, 18; *post*, Nos. 31-4.

31. STIRLING, BRENTS. Spenser's Garden of Adonis and *Cantos of Mutabilitie*: A Reinterpretation. Diss., The University of Washington, 1934. *Cf. ante*, No. 10; Variorum III, App. iii.

32. ——— The Philosophy of Spenser's Garden of Adonis. PMLA XLIX (1934). 501-38.

33. ——— Two Notes on the Philosophy of *Mutabilitie*. MLN L (1935). 154-5.

    i. Verbal borrowings in *Mutabilitie* from Arthur Golding's translation of *Metamorphoses*. ii. Clarifies Boethian interpretation of *Mutabilitie* by showing that Sp's doctrine that "things achieve perfection and immutability by turning to themselves" may be taken as identical with concept presented three stanzas later, that "perfection and immutability are attained upon union with the Sabbaoth God." *Cf. Boethius, De Consolatione Phil.* Bk. IV, Prose 6; *ante*, Nos. 30-2.

34. TUVE, ROSEMOND. A Mediaeval Commonplace in Spenser's Cosmology. SP XXX (1933). 133-47.

    Quoting Chaucer's *Boethius*, and *Batman uppon Bartholome* (1582), shows a close relationship between Sp's thought and that of medieval period. *Rev.* YWES XIV (1933). 226; Shakes. Jahr. 70 (1934). 164. *Cf. ante*, Nos. 3, 30.

35. WILLIAMSON, GEORGE. Mutability, Decay, and Seventeenth-Century Melancholy. ELH II (1935). 121-50.

    Discusses the "metaphysical concept" which brought about the metaphysical shudder in Donne—the idea of the decay of the world. Sections II, III: Sp's *Mutabilitie* and its relation to this movement.

FAERIE QUEENE, SOURCES

See "Spenser and Sidney," Nos. 2, 4, 9, 12, 13, 21, 23, 26; "Editions," i-iii; "Spenser and Dante," Nos. 1, 4, 5, 7; "Spenser and Chaucer," Nos. 2, 3, 9, 10; "Spenser and Shakespeare," Nos. 4, 6; "FQ, General," Nos. 5, 6, 9, 20, 61, 65, 71, 72, 77-80, 95-6, 109, 111-2, 135, 140; "Spenser and Platonism," No. 3; "Mutabilitie," Nos. 14-5, 34; "Style, Diction," No. 21; "Addenda," Nos. 14-6.

1. *AINSWORTH, EDWARD G., JR. The *Orlando Furioso* in English Literature before 1640. Diss., Cornell University, 1929.

2. Ayres, H. M. The *Faerie Queene* and *Amis and Amiloun.* MLN XXIII (1908).
   Rev. Shakes. Jahr. 45 (1909). 228-9.

3. Baroway, Israel. The Imagery of Spenser and the *Song of Songs.* JEGP XXXIII (1934). 23-45.
   30-1, 35-7: The FQ's traces of Sp's reading of the *Song of Songs.*

4. Belden, H. M. Two Spenser Notes. MLN XLIV (1929). 526-31.
   i. Sp adapts classical material (Euripides, Plato, Ovid) for his treatment of the Florimell, Proteus, Helen episodes. ii. Britomart's nurse owes something to pseudo-Virgilian *Ciris.*

5. Bennett, Josephine W. Spenser's Hesiod. Amer. Jour. Phil. LII (April, May, June, 1931). 176-81.
   On evidence that FQ IV, xi, 48-51 is derived from Mombritius' translation of *Theogony,* assumes Sp's ignorance of Greek.

6. ———— Spenser's Garden of Adonis. PMLA XLVII (1932). 46-80.
   Allegory of the Garden of Adonis is based on a body of Platonic and Neo-Platonic conceptions of the universe "containing no elements of the Lucretian theory of origins." The Garden is an "otherworld paradise where Venus, the mother, or source of all forms, protects and enjoys Adonis, the father and generator of forms, in the process of acquiring the vital force necessary for "shaping their house of clay." *Rev.* YWES XIII (1932). 193; Shakes. Jahr. 69 (1933). 196. *Cf. post,* No. 116; "Mutabilitie," Nos. 14, 15; PMLA XLV, 684-95.

7. Berdan, John M. The Family of *The Faerie Queene.* Tudor and Stuart Club Lecture, Baltimore, 1924. The Johns Hopkins Alumni Mag. XII (1924). 267-87.
   Literary predecessors of FQ, chiefly *Orlando Furioso* and *La Spagna.*

8. Blackwood's Magazine LXXXVI (1859). 608-9, 626. Rev. of Tennyson's *Idylls.*
   Sp's Arthur draws very little from Arthurian tradition; CXVI (1874). 26-9: Compares Sp and Virgil, and Homer.

9. Blanchard, H. H. Spenser and Boiardo. PMLA XL (1925). 828-51.
   Study of parallels in *Orlando Innamorato* and FQ shows Sp had read Boiardo and that parts of this romance were in his mind when he created FQ. *Rev.* YWES VI (1925). 168; Shakes. Jahr. 63 (1927). 230-1.

10. BLANCHARD, H. H. Imitations from Tasso in the *Faerie Queene*. SP XXII (1925). 198-221.
   Continues Koeppel's study. Cites 21 parallels, many from *Rinaldo* (1562). *Cf.* Koeppel, E. Edmund Spenser's verhältniss zu Tasso. Anglia XI (1889). 341 ff.; Blanchard, H. H. Italian Influence on the *Faerie Queene*. Diss., Harvard University, 1921.

11. BRIE, FRIEDRICH. Shakespeare und die Impresa-Kunst seiner Zeit. Shakes. Jahr. 50 (1914). 9-30.
   17: FQ.

12. BRYCE, J. C. Spenser's "XII Morall Vertues." TLS 32 (Aug. 10, 1933). 537.
   Sp's Aristotelianism may come via Aegidius Columna Romanus, *De Regimine Principum, ca.* 1284. Sp may have known the ed. of 1494, printed at Seville. Aegidius' treatment of certain virtues is closer to Sp's than is Aristotle's. *Rev.* YWES XIV (1933). 228.

13. BUSH, DOUGLAS. Mythology and the Renaissance Tradition . . . 1932.
   Ch. V: Sp's use of mythology and his reading. See for FQ mythology.

14. CAIN, H. EDWARD. Spenser's "shield of faith." SAB X (1935). 163-6.
   The possible influence of certain coins inscribed "Scutum Fidei Proteget Eam." *Cf. post,* No. 96.

15. CAWLEY, ROBERT R. A Chaucerian Echo in Spenser. MLN XLI (1926). 313-4.
   Sp's House of Pride and Chaucer's *Hous of Fame,* 2141-2151. *Rev.* YWES VII (1926). 159.

16. COE, ADA H. Spenser and Ovid. CW XXII (1929). 91-2.
   Parallels between FQ I, i and *Metamorphoses* X, 86-105 (Wood of Errour). *Rev.* YWES X (1929). 216; *cf. post,* Nos. 18, 50.

17. COLEMAN, SISTER MARY EUGENE. Is Edmund Campion Guyon ? Proceedings of Dr. Greenlaw's Seminary "C," 1930. No number. The Johns Hopkins Univ. Library.

18. COOPER, LANE. Spenser and Ovid. CW XXII (1929). 166.
   Skeat, in 1894, pointed out relation of FQ and Ovid in Wood of Errour passage. *Cf. ante,* No. 16; *post,* No. 50. *Rev.* YWES X (1929). 216.

19. COVINGTON, F. F., JR. Spenser and Alexander Neckam. SP XXII (1925). 222-5.

Neckam's third *distinctio* of *De Laudibus Sapientiae* may have given a suggestion for Sp's Irish Rivers [FQ IV, xi]. Sp perhaps saw the original in MS, or in excerpts in Camden's *Britannia*. *Rev.* YWES VI (1925). 168-9.

20. CRANE, CLARA W. A Source for Spenser's Story of Timias and Belphebe. PMLA XLIII (1928). 635-44.

Violette, an old French romance, may be source of the messenger dove, FQ IV, viii, 3-12. *Rev.* YWES IX (1928). 172; Shakes. Jahr. 65 (1929). 225-6.

21. CUMMING, W. P. Ovid as a Source for Spenser's Monster-Spawning Mud Passages. MLN XLV (1930). 166-8.

Metamorphoses, I, 416-37; XV, 362-4, 375-8 suggested as sources for FQ I, i, 21; III, vi, 8, 3-9; VII, vii, 18. *Rev.* YWES XI (1930). 198-9. *Cf. post*, No. 64; "Mutabilitie," No. 32.

22. DAVIS, B. E. C. Edmund Spenser: A Critical Study.

Ch. IV: Romance; V: Allegory. *Cf.* also III: Humanism.

23. DENNIS, JOHN. The Grounds of Criticism in Poetry. The Select Works of John Dennis. London, 1718.

II, 453-4: FQ III, xi, 40 may derive from *Iliad*, 13.

24. DUCKETT, ELEANOR S. Catullus in English Poetry. Smith College Classical Studies. No. 6. Northampton, 1925.

131, 147: FQ II, xii, 74 ff. and *Carmen 62*; FQ VII, vii, 12 and *Carmen 64*, lines 1164: 304-6. *Cf.* "FQ, General," No. 118.

25. FAUST, GEORGE P. A Spenser Parallel. MLN XLIX (1934). 393.

FQ I, vii, 17 in two lines echoes *Sir Degare*. Sp must have read at least the sixteenth century version of it.

26. FLETCHER, JAS. M. J. Edmund Spenser and the Dorset Stour. NQ for Somerset and Dorset XXI (1934). 180-2.

FQ IV, xi, 32 may draw upon personal familiarity with Dorset Stour. Did Sp visit the Gorges family at Sturminster Marshall?

27. FOWLER, EARLE B. Spenser and the Courts of Love. PMLA XXXV (1920). *Proc.*, xii.

9

28. FOWLER, EARLE B. Spenser and the System of Courtly Love. Louisville, Ky., 1934.

While accepting the outward conventions of the courtly love system, Sp completely rejects its moral aspects, adhering to a philosophy based upon Platonic and Puritan concepts. *Rev.* YWES XV (1934). 213.

29. FRIEDRICH, W. G. Spenser's Tree of Life and the *Legend of the True History of the Cross.* No. 60. Proceedings of Dr. Greenlaw's Seminary " C," 1926-7. The Johns Hopkins University Library.

30. Gentleman's Mag. LXXXV (1815). ii. 2.

FQ mentions Egyptian Phao. Is this the Egyptian Phtha and where did Sp find the story?

31. GORDON, GEORGE. Virgil in English Poetry. (Warton Lecture on English Poetry). Proc. Brit. Acad. XVII. 39 ff. London, 1931.

47-8: Sp's debt to Virgil. *Cf. post,* Nos. 43, 44.

32. GREENLAW, EDWIN A. Two Notes on Spenser's Classical Sources. MLN XLI (1926). 323-6.

Hesiod (*Works and Days,* I, 287-92) as source of debate between Braggadochio and Belphoebe (FQ II, iii, 38). *Rev.* YWES VII (1926). 159.

33. ——— Una and Her Lamb. MLN XLII (1927). 515-6. Also No. 2. Proceedings of Dr. Greenlaw's Seminary " C," 1927-8. The Johns Hopkins University Library.

Sp here follows ancient legend of St. George rather than contriving a " subtle allegory of truth and innocence." *Rev.* YWES VIII (1927). 185. *Cf. post,* No. 93.

34. ——— Spenser's Guyon. No. 17. Proceedings of Dr. Greenlaw's Seminary " C," 1927-8. *Loc. cit.*

35. ——— Britomart at the House of Busirane. SP XXVI (1929). 117-30. *Cf.* Spenser and the Wagner Book. No. 8. Proceedings of Dr. Greenlaw's Seminary " C," 1926-7. The Johns Hopkins University Library.

Analogues between FQ III, xi-xii and *English Wagner Book* (Second Report), 1594, and *Amadis of Gaul* show Sp using the very old plot of Chateau Merveil of the Grail romances and giving new life to it without violating its original meaning. Resemblances between FQ III, xi, xii and *Arthur of Little Britain* (" probably the greatest single influence " on FQ). Sp's meaning in his treatment of the Chateau Merveil theme is to portray the Grail mysteries. His allegorical intent is to transform the castle of wonders and "its ritual to be dispelled" into a "representation of a love that is no true religion." *Rev.* YWES X (1929). 215; Shakes. Jahr. 67 (1931). 117. *Cf.* "FQ, Sources," No. 109.

36. HARRISON, T. P., JR. *The Faerie Queene* and the *Diana.* PQ IX (1930). 51-6.

Comparison of Montemayor's *Diana* and FQ, IV, vii ff. and VI, ix ff., indicates something of Sp's indebtedness to Spanish pastoral. *Rev.* YWES XI (1930). 198; Shakes. Jahr. 67 (1931). 117. *Cf. post,* No. 47.

37. —— Spenser and Boccaccio's *Olympia.* Univ. of Texas Studies in English XIV (1934). 5-30.

5-15, 19-30: FQ I, x and last two *Hymnes,* and *Olympia.* Boccaccio's emphasis upon the "ways of salvation in practical life" links him with Sp's thought, esp. in *Hymnes.* Sp may not have been unfamiliar with Boccaccio's *Bucolicum Carmen. Cf.* Winstanley, L. The Foure Hymnes. London, 1914.

38. HARTUNG, A. C. Cave of Mammon and St. Patrick's Purgatory. No. 32. Proceedings of Dr. Greenlaw's Seminary "C," 1927-8. The Johns Hopkins University Library.

39. HEFFNER, RAY. Parallel Passages in *Troilus* and Bk. V of the *Faerie Queene.* No. 8. Proceedings of Dr. Greenlaw's Seminary "C," 1925-6. The Johns Hopkins University Library.

40. HINTZ, HOWARD W. The Elizabethan Entertainment and *The Faerie Queene.* PQ XIV (1935). 83-90.

Pageantry as developed in entertainments presented on "progresses" is a vital influence on FQ (esp. I-III). Illustration of relation between these and literature by reference to *Robert Laneham's Letter,* 1575. *Cf.* "FQ, General," No. 79; *post,* Nos. 103, 105-8.

41. HUGHES, MERRITT Y. The Relation of the *Faerie Queene* to the *Nichomachean Ethics.* Paper read before the Mod. Lang. Ass., Pacific Coast Section, 1924. *Cf.* PMLA XXXIX (*Proc.,* 1924). lv. *Cf. post,* Nos. 45, 46.

42. —— Spenser's Debt to the Greek Romances. MP XXIII (1925). 67-76.

No evidence that Sp derived any episodes directly from the Greek romances. Four motifs in the story of Pastorella come ultimately from Longus or Heliodorus, but all of them had become literary commonplaces when Sp wrote. Possible to trace the influence of Heliodorus through Sidney to Sp's treatment of moral virtues. The fondness of Greek romancers for word-painting may have been a minor force which helped make FQ most pictorial of epics. *Rev.* YWES VI (1925). 168.

43. HUGHES, MERRITT Y. Virgilian Allegory and *The Faerie Queene.* PMLA XLIV (1929). 696-705. *Cf.* PMLA XLIII (*Proc.*, 1928). l.

Sp's Belphoebe is so conceived as to make it probable that Sp drew on the *Aeneid* (Venus) and the allegorical interpretations thereof. Interpreters to whom he seems indebted are Longus and Tasso.

44. ——— Virgil and Spenser. Univ. of California Pub. in English II, No. 3, 1929.

Pt. II. "The Epic and the Romance." The extent of Sp's debt to Virgil. *Rev.* YWES X (1929). 212-3; MLR XXV (1930). 244, by C. J. S.[isson]; CP XXV (1930). 96-7, by Paul Shorey; Rev. critique, 64è· an. (1930). 180-1, by A. Koszul; Literaturb. f. Germ. u. Rom. Phil. 52 (1931). 268-9, by Georg Bersch.

45. HULBERT, VIOLA B. Spenser's Twelve Moral Virtues "According to Aristotle and the Rest." Univ. of Chicago, Abstracts of Theses, Humanistic Series V (1928). 479-85.

Sp's knowledge of the *Nichomachean Ethics,* the virtues of which show little relation to Sp's except in number. *Cf. ante,* No. 41; *post,* Nos. 52, 53.

46. ——— A Possible Christian Source for Spenser's Temperance. SP XXVIII (1931). 184-210.

Aristotle's treatment of Temperance is not a satisfactory source for Bk. II. Rather, Sp agrees with the fine points of Christian treatments of temperance from the fathers to the present. Only a general interest in tracing sources. *Rev.* YWES XII (1931). 192. *Cf.* Padelford, F. M., in SP XVIII (1921). 334-46; DeMoss, W. F., in MP XVI (1918-9). 22-38 and 245-70; "FQ, General," Nos. 19-21.

47. HUME, MARTIN. Spanish Influences in Elizabethan Literature. Trans. Roy. Soc. of Literature, 2nd. ser. XXIX (1909). 1-35.

15 ff.: Sp influenced by Montemayor's *Diana* (chiefly in SC). *Cf. ante,* No. 36.

48. HUNTER, JOSEPH. Hallamshire. The History and Topography of the Parish of Sheffield. . . . London, 1869.

415-6: Sp perhaps took the name Una from "his own family" (the Althorpe Spencers). Sir Robert Tiptoft's wife was Una.

49. J., C. S. Spenser's Panope. NQ, ser. iv. VII (1871). 283.

Is there classical authority for Sp's figure of her?

50. JOHNSTON, MARY. Once More Spenser and Ovid. CW XXII (1929). 208.

Cites Catullus, 64: 288-91, for the "list of trees" tradition. Cf. ante, Nos. 16, 18.

51. ———— Parasites in Plautus and Spenser. CW XXVI (1933). 104.

FQ II, iii, 9, 2-9, parallels Terence's *Eunuchus*, 232-53, 255-64; FQ II, iii, 17, 7, echoes Plautus's *Miles Gloriosus*, 16-8, 25-30, 42-6, 52-3.

52. JONES, H. S. V. The *Faerie Queene* and the Medieval Aristotelian Tradition. JEGP XXV (1926). 283-98.

Ethics of the FQ have close contact with a line of ethical thought beginning with Aristotle and passing through the system of Thomas Aquinas. It closes with the Christian philosophy of Melanchthon. *Rev.* YWES VII (1926). 157-8; No. 12. Proceedings of Dr. Greenlaw's Seminary "C," 1926-7, by W. A. Darden. The Johns Hopkins University Library. *Cf. ante,* Nos. 45, 46.

53. ———— A Spenser Handbook.

Chs. XIII-XX: The Faerie Queene.

54. *KAPP, RUDOLF. Heilige und Heiligenlegenden in England. Studien z. 16 u. 17 Jahrhundert. Halle, 1934.

Rev. Shakes. Jahr. 70 (1934). 144. Sp's legend of St. George. *Cf. post,* Nos. 90, 93.

55. KOLLER, KATHRINE. Analogues to the debate between Guyon and Mammon. *Faerie Queene,* Bk. II, vii, xii. No number. Proceedings of Dr. Greenlaw's Seminary "C." The Johns Hopkins University Library.

56. LEGOUIS, ÉMILE. Edmund Spenser. New York and London, 1926.

Chs. V-VI.

57. LEMMI, C. W. Sources of the Dragon Error in *Faerie Queene*, I, i. No. 7. Proceedings of Dr. Greenlaw's Seminary "C," 1926-7. The Johns Hopkins University Library.

58. ——— The Episode of "Errour's Den" and the *Thebaid*. No. 19. Proceedings . . . 1926-7. *Loc. cit.*

59. ——— Sea-Monsters in *Faerie Queene*, II, xii, 23-25. No. 57. Proceedings . . . 1926-7. *Loc. cit.*

60. ——— The Sources of *Faerie Queene* I, v, 8. No. 9. Proceedings . . . 1926-7. *Loc. cit.*

61. ——— The Weeping Crocodile, *Faerie Queene* I, v, 18. No. 64. Proceedings . . . 1926-7. *Loc. cit.*

62. ——— The Savage Man in the *Faerie Queene*, IV, viii. No. 19. Proceedings . . . 1927-8. *Loc. cit.*

63. ——— The Sources of the Savage Man, *Faerie Queene* IV, viii. No. 61. Proceedings . . . 1926-7. *Loc. cit.*

64. ——— Monster-Spawning Nile-Mud in Spenser. MLN XLI (1926). 234-8.
     Source of this is chiefly Diodorus Siculus. *Rev.* YWES VII (1926). 159. *Cf. ante,* No. 21.

65. ——— Alain de Lille's *Complaint of Nature* and the *Faerie Queene*. No. 11. Proceedings . . . 1927-8. *Loc. cit.*

66. ——— Castle Joyous and the House of Busirane. No. 5. Proceedings . . . 1927-8. *Loc. cit.*

67. ——— Distribution of Mythological Material in the *Faerie Queene*. No. 29. Proceedings . . . 1927-8. *Loc. cit.*

68. ——— A Loan from Alanus and one from Conti (FQ II). No. 6. Proceedings . . . 1927-8. *Loc. cit.*

69. ——— The Influence of Trissino on the *Faerie Queene*. PQ VII (1928). 220-3.
     Extensive and important parallels between FQ and *L'Italia Liberata dai Gotti* (1547-8). *Cf. post,* Nos. 71, 72.

70. ——— Hudibras and the *Faerie Queene*. No. 35. Proceedings . . . 1928-9. *Loc. cit.*

71. LEMMI, C. W. Symbolism of the Classical Episodes in *The Faerie Queene*. PQ VIII (1929). 270-87. Also No. 66. Proceedings . . . 1926-7. *Loc. cit.*
    Sp's possible debt to Comes's *Mythologiae sive Explicationis Fabularum. Rev.* YWES XI (1930). 197. *Cf.* "FQ, General," Nos. 19-21; *post*, No. 71.

72. —————— Symbolism in *Faerie Queene*, II, xii. MLN L (1935). 161-5.
    Adds a few passages to those previously cited. *Cf. ante*, Nos. 69, 71.

73. LEVINSON, R. B. Spenser and Bruno. PMLA XLIII (1928). 675-81.

74. Literary Mag. and American Register V (Feb. 1806). 182-3. Copy in Yale University Library.
    " Spenser's Allegory of Una Explained." [Leon Howard]

75. LONG, WILLIAM. Stonehenge and its Barrows. Wiltshire Archaeological and Natural History Mag. XVI (1876). 188.
    FQ II, x, 66-7: On Stonehenge.

76. LOTSPEICH, H. G. Classical Mythology in the Poetry of Edmund Spenser. See " Sources in General," No. 26.

77. LOWES, J. L. Spenser and Gower. PMLA XXIX (1914). *Proc.*, xxix. *Cf. ibid.*, 388-452.

78. McMANAWAY, JAMES G. "Occasion" (*Faerie Queene*, II, iv, 4-5). MLN XLIX (1934). 391-3.
    Influence of contemporary sources—the Emblem books—on the unclassical figure here. *Rev.* YWES XV (1934). 216.

79. McMURPHY, SUSANNAH J. Spenser's Use of Ariosto for Allegory. Diss., University of Washington, 1923. Pub. in *University of Washington Publications in Language and Literature* II (1924). 1-54.
    Rev. YWES VI (1925). 168. *Cf.* I, App. iii; Variorum III, App. v; IV, App. iii.

80. MACFARLENE, JOHN. Antoine Vérard. Trans. Bibliographical Soc. 1896. IV, 11, 242; V (1899). 164.

81. MALTBY, JEANNETTE E. Spenser's Use of the Bible in the *Faerie Queene*, Books I and II. M. A. Thesis, University of Washington, 1926.

82. *MASCH, WERNER. Studien zum italienischen Einfluss in Spenser's *Faery Queene*. Diss., Hamburg, 1922.

83. MELDRUM, H. S. *The Pastime of Pleasure* by Stephen Hawes: A Probable Source of Spenser's *Faerie Queene*. M. A. Thesis, University of Washington, 1922.

84. MILLICAN, CHARLES BOWIE. Spenser and the Arthurian Legend. RES VI (1930). 167-74.
Sp influenced by the great popular interest in Arthurian legend during Elizabeth's reign. *Rev.* YWES XI (1930). 198; Shakes. Jahr. 66 (1930). 240. *Cf. post,* No. 85.

85. ——— Spenser and the Table Round: A Study in the Contemporaneous Background for Spenser's Use of the Arthurian Legend. Illustrated. Harvard Studies in Comparative Literature, VIII. *Cf.* Harvard Summaries of Theses, 1930. 205-7: " Studies in Spenser and Arthurian Legend."
A study of influences which shaped Sp's interest and knowledge. *Rev.* Bost. Transcript, May 25, 1932, Pt. IV, p. 3. " The Days of Spenser"; YWES XIII (1932). 190-1; Commonweal 16 (May 11, 1932). 56; Rev. ang.-amér. 10ᵉ· an. (1932-3). 148, by É. Legouis; TLS 31 (July 21, 1932). 521-2. " The Matter of Britain "; MLR XXVIII (1933). 291, by G. B.; MLN XLVIII (1933). 265-7, by R. F. Brinkley; PQ XII (1933). 411-2, by J. W. Ashton; Anglia Beibl. XLV (1934). 48-50, by Hans Marcus; Eng. Stud. XV (1933). 69-71, by A. G. Van Kranendonk; RES IX (1933). 326-7, by I. Gourvitch; JEGP XXXIII (1934). 475-7, by H. S. V. J.[ones]; Die Neueren Sprachen, 43rd. year (1935). 275-6, by Marie Schütt. *Cf.* Weiss, Adelaide M. Merlin in German Literature. Diss., Catholic University, 1933.

86. MILLS, LAURENS J. The Renascence Development in England of the Classical Ideas About Friendship. Summaries of Theses, University of Chicago, Humanistic Series IV (1925-6). 337-40.
Sp's virtue of friendship is Aristotelian. *Cf. ante,* Nos. 41, 42, 45, 46; *post,* Nos. 110-113; " FQ, General," No. 45.

87. NAYLOR, EDWARD W. The Poets and Music. London, 1928.
133-9: Sp's dozen passages on music seem to show familiarity with Cicero's *Somnium Scipionis*.

88. NEILL, J. KERBY. The Source of Spenser's Temperance. No number. Proceedings of Dr. Greenlaw's Seminary " C," 1931. The Johns Hopkins University Library.
Cf. ante, Nos. 45, 46.

89. NEILSON, WILLIAM A. The Origins and Sources of the *Court of Love.* Harvard University Studies and Notes in Philology and Literature VI. 1899. (Also, Diss., 1898.)

> 263-5: FQ III, xi and the *Court of Love.*

90. NIX, MARTHA J. A Study of the Influence of the Morality Plays on Edmund Spenser's *Faery Queene,* Book I. M. A. Thesis, University of Washington, 1925.

> *Cf. post,* No. 93; "FQ, General," Nos. 6, 87.

91. O'CONNOR, JAMES M. Spenser's Use of the St. George Legend, *The Fair Unknown,* and other medieval romance themes in Book I of the *Faerie Queene.* M. A. Thesis, University of Washington, 1926.

92. OSGOOD, CHARLES G. Spenser and the Enchanted Glass. Tudor and Stuart Club Lecture, 1930. The Johns Hopkins Alumni Mag. XIX (1930). 8-31.

> Sp without a clear-cut system of thought from Plato, Aristotle, Calvin, or the Middle Ages. FQ is mirror of Sp and the Elizabethan world.

93. PADELFORD, F. M. and MATTHEW O'CONNOR. Spenser's Use of the St. George Legend. SP XXIII (1926). 142-56.

> Probable sources of Sp's St. George material: Caxton's *Golden Legend,* the St. George homilies, lives of St. George by Mantuan, Barclay, Lydgate, and the etymologies in Caxton's prefatory comment on the *Life of St. George. Rev.* YWES VII (1926). 159; Shakes. Jahr. 65 (1929). 225. *Cf. ante,* Nos. 33, 54; *post,* No. 104; "FQ, General," No. 85.

94. PADELFORD, F. M. Spenser and *The Pilgrimage of the Life of Man.* SP XXVIII (1931). 211-8.

> Analogues between Guillaume de Guilevile's *Pilgrimage of the Life of Man* and FQ, SC (May and Sept.), and *Hymne of Heavenly Beauty. Rev.* YWES XII (1931). 193.

95. PETRIELLA, TEOFILO. La Novella di Britomarte nella Regina delle Fate di E. Spenser riportata alle sue fonti italiane. Salerno, 1913. Copy in Yale University Library.

96. PIENAAR, W. J. B. Arthur's Shield in the *Faerie Queene*. MP XXVI (1928). 63-8.

> Prototype of Arthur's shield in Eph. VI: 16, is the shield of faith. Van der Noot's *Theatre* . . . (1569) may have impressed on Sp "this imagery of sword and shield." *Rev.* Shakes. Jahr. 65 (1929). 225. *Cf. ante*, No. 14.

97. POPE, EMMA FIELD. The Reflection of Renaissance Criticism in Edmund Spenser's *Faerie Queene*. Abstracts of Theses, University of Chicago, Humanistic Series II (1923-4). 393-400. See "Diction," Nos. 21, 22.

98. PRIEST, HAROLD M. Tasso in English Literature, 1575-1675. Summaries of Dissertations, Northwestern University I (1933). 5-9. MS copy in Deering Library.

> Tasso's influence on FQ and *Amoretti*.

99. Quarterly Rev. XXV (1821).

> 511: FQ IV, xii, 17, 9, uses same figures as Euripides, *Herc. F.* 1039; *ibid.*, 432, 436: J. H. Hunt's translation of Tasso compared with Sp's Garden of Adonis passage.

100. QUEKETT, ARTHUR E. Spenser, *Faery Queene,* I, x, 58. NQ, ser. vi. IV (1881). 164.

> Identifies crystal tower as Elizabeth's palace of Shene (now Richmond). *Cf.* Kitchin, G. W., *Book I,* note on this passage.

101. RATHBORNE, ISABEL E. A New Source for Spenser's *Faerie Queene,* Book I. SP XXXIII (1936). 166-81.

> Concludes that (1) "the homily *Against Disobedience and wilful Rebellion* may well be a direct source for parts of the FQ, I, and throws considerable light on Sp's probable attitude toward the virtue of holiness and the religious basis of his encomium on the queen"; (2) the homily evidence "supports the belief that we are to look to Elizabethan conditions and habits of thought rather than to classical philosophy or even to continental Renaissance literature for the interpretation of Sp's allegory"; (3) it reinforces "belief in Sp's Anglican conservatism."

102. RICHTER, MARGARET R. Spenser's Use of Arthurian Romance. Stanford University, Abstracts of Dissertations II (1927). 119-24. Abstracted also in Stanford University Bull. ser. 5, No. 47. XII (1928).

> Extent and manner of Sp's use of Arthurian romance. Uses method of analogues.

103. SCHULZE, IVAN L. Elizabethan Chivalry, pageantry, and masque in Spenser. Diss., The Johns Hopkins University, 1930.

104. ——— The Maiden and Her Lamb, *Faerie Queene,* Book I. MLN XLVI (1931). 379-81.

> The frequent uses in the St. George legends of the maiden and her lamb appearing together. Impossible to designate a specific source. *Rev.* YWES XII (1931). 192. *Cf. ante,* Nos. 33, 90, 93.

105. ——— Spenser's Belge Episode and the Pageants for Leicester in the Low Countries, 1585-6. SP XXVIII (1931). 235-40.

> Certain of these pageants seem to have influenced Sp's Belge episode profoundly. Parallels given. *Rev.* YWES XII (1931). 193. *Cf.* " Sources, General," Nos. 37-8.

106. ——— Notes on Elizabethan Chivalry and *The Faerie Queene.* SP XXX (1933). 148-59.

> Elizabethan chivalry (court tournaments, etc.) must be regarded as much a source for Sp as are romances. Knights of Maidenhood passages may refer to activities of the Garter knights. *Rev.* YWES XIV (1933). 227; Shakes. Jahr. 70 (1934). 165. *Cf. ante,* No. 40.

107. ——— Elizabethan Chivalry and the Motif of the Faerie Queene's Annual Feast. Paper read before the Mod. Lang. Ass., 1933. *Cf.* PMLA XLVIII (*Proc.,* 1933). 1430; also *post.*

108. ——— Elizabethan Chivalry and the Faerie Queene's Annual Feast. MLN L (1935). 158-61.

> Resemblance between FQ chivalric descriptions and events at court. *Cf.* " FQ, General," Nos. 144, 145, 182.

109. SEDGWICK, W. B. Spencer [*sic*] and Ovid Again. CW XXII (1929). 184.

> FQ I, i, 8-9 derives from Ovid through Chaucer's borrowing from Joseph of Exeter's *Bellum Trojanum, ca.* 1190.

110. SMITH, CHARLES G. The Ethical Allegory of the Two Florimells. SP XXXI (1934). 140-51.

> The allegory of the two Florimells illustrates the degree to which Sp's work is permeated with Neo-Platonism. *Rev.* YWES XV (1934). 216. *Cf.* " FQ, General," No. 74.

111. ——— Spenser's Theory of Friendship. PMLA XLIX (1934). 490-500.

> FQ IV conception of friendship " as the operation in the world of man of a principle of cosmic love " is from Lucretius. *Cf. ante,*

No. 86; "Spenser and Puritanism," No. 1; Greenlaw, E., in SP XVII (1920). 439 ff. and SP XX (1923). 216 ff.; "FQ, General," No. 43.

112. SMITH, CHARLES G. Spenser's Theory of Friendship: An Elizabethan Commonplace. SP XXXII (1935). 158-69.

> i. Sp conceives of friendship as a unifying and harmonizing "principle of cosmic love operating in the world of man to promote concord." ii. "The parallels with a point of view analogous to Spenser's here for the first time brought forward must be considered as a part of the provenience of the Fourth Book of the FQ along with the data previously adduced by scholars." iii. Further evidence of importance of masques and pageants in Sp's literary environment. iv. Sp draws on a multiplicity of sources. v. Sp's political philosophy is essentially that of his "illustrious contemporaries," and their respective theories represent a common fund of ideas and reading. vi. Sp not concerned with "mere abstractions." He wrote "brilliant criticism of life." *Cf. ante,* No. 111; *post,* 113, 120; "FQ, General," No. 79.

113. ———— Sententious Theory in Spenser's Legend of Friendship. ELH II (1935). 165-91.

> Bk. IV shows that proverbial ideas have an integral place in Sp's conception of this virtue. He follows classical models and portrays ideal friendship between two persons only. Revival of proverbial wisdom in Ren. England was a diffused humanism. *Cf. ante,* Nos. 111, 112.

114. SMITH, ROLAND M. Una and Duessa. PMLA L (1935). 917-9.

> Sp drew these names from Ireland. Duessa would connote "wicked customs" or "evil usages."

115. ———— Spenser's Irish River Stories. PMLA L (1935). 1047-56.

> Sp "drew heavily on the topographical lore" he gleaned in Ireland.

116. STIRLING, BRENTS. The Philosophy of Spenser's "Garden of Adonis." PMLA XLIX (1934). 501-38.

> Fundamental concepts are Platonic, united with Ovid's philosophy of "turned shapes." Sp the popularizer of already popular material. *Rev.* Shakes. Jahr. 71 (1935). 145; YWES XV (1934). 216. *Cf.* Stirling, B. Spenser's "Garden of Adonis" and "Cantos of Mutabilitie": A Re-interpretation. Diss., Univ. of Washington, 1934; Variorum III, App. iii; Saurat, D. Literature and Occult Tradition, p. 184 ff.; Greenlaw, E. in SP XVII (1920); *ante,* No. 6; *post,* No. 120; "Spenser and Puritanism," No. 1.

117. TAYLOR, A. E. Spenser's Knowledge of Plato. MLR
XIX (1924). 208-10.
     FQ II, vii, 54 and IV, intro. stanza iii, are due to imperfect
     recollection of passages in Cicero's works. Doubts whether Sp
     knew Plato first-hand. [F. I. C. and A. P.] *Rev.* YWES V (1924).
     154-5.

118. THOMAS, HENRY. The Romance of Amadis of Gaul.
Trans. Bibliographical Soc. XI (1911). 251 ff.
     280: Masque of Cupid (FQ) and *Amadis of Gaul. Cf.* Southey,
     Robert. *Palmerin of England,* Preface, xliv, on Sp's knowledge of
     Amadis of Greece. Cf. Variorum, III, App. iv.

119. TUVE, ROSEMOND. The Red Crosse Knight and Medieval Demon Stories. PMLA XLIV (1929). 706-14.
     Earthly, rather than elfin, lineage of RCK is traced to affinities
     with romantic *enfances.* Sp's "unrealized literary heritage" seems
     to include the *Robert the Devil* legend, *Huon of Bordeaux, the Bel
     Inconnu,* and others. *Rev.* Proc. of Eng. Journ. Club, The Johns
     Hopkins University, 1929-30, by E. S. Shepard. *Cf. ante,* No. 93.

120. ———— Spenser and *The Zodiake of Life.* JEGP
XXXIV (1935). 1-19.
     Relationship of *Zod. of Life* (Googe's translation, 1565) and FQ.
     Sp's cosmological conception of love is similar to that in *Zod. of Life.*
     Googe's books may be one of stimuli propelling Sp to do his own
     cosmological treatment of love. *Zod. of Life* carries on tradition of
     "Christian 'astronomical' poetry." It presented its ideas with cer-
     tain approved devices such as "astronomical framework, didactic
     allegory, quests, dream-visions, gardens-of-love, and all the familiar
     devices of medieval romances." *Cf. ante,* Nos. 111, 112, 113, 116;
     "Spenser's Philosophy," Nos. 2, 4, 6, 14, 15, 17, 18.

121. UPCOTT, L. E. The Poets' Poet. TLS 29 (Mar. 6,
1930). 190.
     Tasso's Garden of Armida and Sp's Boure of Blis.

122. Variorum. I, App. iv; II, App. vii; III, App. ii, ix; IV,
App. v, vi. The Sources of Bks. I-IV.

123. WANN, LOUIS. The Rôle of Confidant(e) in the Renaissance Epic. Anglia LI (1927). 63-74.
     Sect. V: "The Confidant(e) in the Faery Queen." Studies rôle
     of Glauce and Palmer. *Cf.* "FQ, General," No. 81.

124. WELLS, WHITNEY. Spenser's Dragon. MLN XLI
(1926). 143-57.
     Vision of Tundale undoubtedly direct source of the Dragon, FQ I,
     xi. [A. P.] *Rev.* YWES VII (1926). 158; Shakes. Jahr. 62 (1926).
     187.

MINOR POEMS, COMPLAINTS, ETC.

See "Editions," i, v, for annotated texts; "Life, Miscellaneous," No. 22, iii.

1. DAVIS, B. E. C. The Text of Spenser's *Complaints.*
   MLR XX (1925). 18-24.
   Relation of quarto of 1591 and folio of 1611, especially the texts
   of RT and MHT. *Rev.* YWES VI (1925). 167.

2. FRIEDERICH, WERNER P. Spiritualismus und Sensualis-
   mus in der englischen Barocklyrik. Wiener Beiträge
   LVII (1932).
   See index for Sp. *Rev.* Archiv CLXVI (1934). 107-11, by Walter
   F. Schirmer.

3. FRIEDLAND, LOUIS S. Spenser's Minor Poems. Diss.,
   New York University, 1912.
   "Study of the Poems in connection with the literature of the
   French Renaissance, with chapters on Emblem poetry (with bibl.),
   on Sp's . . . metrics, *The Ruins, The Visions,* etc." [F. I. C. and
   A. P.]

4. GRIERSON, H. J. C. Cross-Currents in English Literature
   . . . (The Messenger Lectures, Cornell University,
   1926-7). London, 1929.
   40-3, and see index for Minor Poems.

5. New York Times, Book Rev., Oct. 28, 1934, p. 26. Note
   of sale of first edition of *Complaints* and *Foure Hymnes.*
   Sale of Dr. Roderick Terry's library.

6. PELTON, NELLIE F. The Minor Poems of Edmund Spenser. M. A. Thesis, The Johns Hopkins University,
   1918.

7. PIENAAR, W. J. B. Spenser's *Complaints.* TLS 23 (Dec.
   4, 1924). 825.
   Gives two line readings which fall back upon DuBellay, *Songe,*
   Sonnets XIV, V. These serve to reduce Koeppel's argument over
   the authorship of Sp's *Visions of Bellay, Visions of Petrarch,*
   Theatre of Worldlings. Cf. Koeppel, E. Engl. Stud. XV, XXVII.
   Rev. YWES V (1924). 158.

8. STEIN, HAROLD. Studies in Spenser's *Complaints.* Ox-
   ford, 1934. *Cf.* also Diss., Yale University Library.
   A comprehensive study of the poems. *Rev.* New York Herald-
   Tribune Books (Aug. 26, 1934). 13, by Samuel C. Chew; NQ
   CLXVII (1934). 232-3; MLR XXX (1935). 514-7, by W. L. Ren-

wick; Anglia Beibl. XLVI (1935). 45-8, by Rudolf Kapp; Rev. ang.-amér. 12ᵉ· an. (1935). 241, by É. Legouis; JEGP XXXIV (1935). 446-9, by H. S. V. Jones; TLS 34 (Aug. 8, 1935). 498; MLN LI (1936). 55-6, by E. A. Strathmann; YWES XV (1934). 218.

9. STRATHMANN, E. A. Note on Separate Publication of the *Complaints*. No. 32. Proceedings of Dr. Green-law's Seminary " C," 1928-9. The Johns Hopkins University Library.

AMORETTI

See " Parents and Family," No. 55; " Spenser's Marriage," Nos. 4, 10, 19; "Versification," Nos. 2, 6, 24, 35, 38.

1. *BALLIÈRE, PAUL. Poètes allemands et poètes anglais. Paris, 1927.

   187-91: Ed. Sp. A trans. into French of *Amoretti* 70, 75, 78, with brief intro. [F. I. C. and A. P.]

2. BAROWAY, ISRAEL. The Imagery of Spenser and the *Song of Songs*. JEGP XXXIII (1934). 23-45.

   29-30, 32-40: Evidence of Sp's reading of *Song of Songs*.

3. *BONDURANT, ———. The Sonnet Sequence as a Literary Form in English. M. A. Thesis, Columbia University, 1931.

4. CARPENTER, FREDERIC I. About two Sonnets "to the author" prefixed to Spenser's *Amoretti*. Repr. from MP XXII (1924).

5. ——— G. W. Senior and G. W. I. MP XXII (1924). 67-8.

   Suggests that " G. W. I." stands for " G. W. Junior." The two sonnets prefixed to *Amor.* may be ascribed to Geoffrey Whitney or to George Wilkins. [A. P.] *Rev.* YWES V (1924). 158-9.

6. CHALMERS, GEORGE. Supplemental Apology. 1799.

   Rev. Brit. Critic XV (1800). 128-34. Elizabeth is not the love celebrated; the sonnets were addressed to an Irish love.

7. CHURTON, EDWARD. Gongora. An Historical and Critical Essay on the Times of Philip III. and IV. of Spain. London, 1862. 2 vols.

   II, 295: Note on " Sonnet by Francisco de Torre " which is almost identical with *Amor.* 81. Suggests both Sp and de la Torre may have followed some Italian poet. *Cf. post*, No. 15.

8. DANNENBERG, FRIEDRICH. Shakespeares Sonette: Herkunst, Wesen, Deutung. Shakes. Jahr. 70 (1934). 37 ff.
41-2: Sp's sonnets.

9. GARROD, H. W. Spenser and Elizabeth Boyle. TLS 22 (May 10 and 24, 1923). 321, 355.
321: Cites passages in *Amor.* which may be read as plays upon name of Eliz. Boyle's first husband.

10. HALL, WILLIAM C. The Sonnet. Manchester Quart. XLVIII (1929). 262 ff.
275: The linked quatrains of *Amor.* traced to FQ stanza. *Cf.* 269-70, 278.

11. HARRISON, G. B. An Elizabethan Journal. London, 1928.
333: *Amor., Epithalamion,* and Sp's marriage noted. *Amor.* 54 quoted.

✝ 12. HUGHES, MERRITT Y. Spenser and the Greek Pastoral Triad. SP XX (1923). 184-215.
Influence of Renaissance intermediaries on *Amoretti.* Ultimate source in Theocritus, Bion, and Moschus. [F. I. C. and A. P.] *Rev.* Anglia Beibl. XXXIV (1923). 363-5, by S. B. Liljegren.

13. JONES, H. S. V. A Spenser Handbook.
Ch. XXV: Amoretti.

⟑ 14. KASTNER, L. E. Spenser's *Amoretti* and Desportes. MLR IV (1908).
Rev. Shakes. Jahr. 45 (1909). 288. *Cf. post,* No. 22.

15. *LEE, SIDNEY. London Times (June 24, 1904).
On *Amoretti* 81 and its source. *Cf. ante,* No. 7.

16. LEGOUIS, ÉMILE. Edmund Spenser. New York and London, 1926.
Ch. IV.

↱ 17. LITTLEDALE, H. A Note on Spenser's *Amoretti.* MLR VI (1911).
Rev. Shakes. Jahr. 48 (1912). 219.

↓ 18. LONG, P. W. Spenser and Lady Carey. MLR III (1908).
Rev. Shakes. Jahr. 45 (1909). 288. *Cf.* Strathmann, " Spenser's Circle," No. 5.

19. NOBLE, JAMES A. Sonnet in England. Contemp. Rev. XXXVIII (1880). 446-71.
Sp's sonnets lack grace and warmth.

20. PRIEST, HAROLD M. Tasso in English Literature, 1575-1675. Summaries of Ph. D. Dissertations, Northwestern University I (1933). 5-9.
Tasso's influence seen in *Amor.*, etc.

21. SCOTT, JANET G. The Sources of Spenser's *Amoretti.* MLR XXII (1927). 189-95.
Borrowing from Tasso in *Amor.* lxxii and lxxiii (Tasso, *Rime* 47 and 167). List of sources for individual sonnets. *Rev.* YWES VIII (1927). 186.

22. ——— Les Sonnets Élisabéthains.—Les Sources et L'Apport Personnel. (Bibliothèque de la Revue de Littérature Comparée, vol. 60.) Paris, 1929.
159-77: Sp and Tasso and Desportes; themes, technique, place of Sp. *Rev.* MLN XLV (1930). 328-9, by C. G. Osgood. *Cf.* " Versi-✗ fication," No. 16.

23. SEARS, STEPHEN F. The Sources of Spenser's *Amoretti.* M. A. Thesis, Columbia University, 1898.

24. SMITH, J. C. The Problem of Spenser's Sonnets. MLR ✗ V (1910).
Rev. Shakes. Jahr. 47 (1911). 261.

25. SPENS, JANET. Spenser's *Faerie Queene*: An Interpretation.
Ch. V: Amoretti.

ASTROPHEL

See " Editions," i, v, for annotated texts.

1. FRIEDRICH, W. G. The *Astrophell* elegies, a Collection of poems on the death of Sir Philip Sidney. Diss., The Johns Hopkins University, 1934.

2. ——— The Stella of Astrophel. ELH III (1936). 114-39.

3. HARRISON, T. P., JR. Spenser, Ronsard, and Bion. MLN XLIX (1934). 139-45.
Sp's " March " and *Astrophel* seem more closely related to Ronsard's *L'Amour oyseau* (1560) and *Adonis* (1563). Little or no trace of Sp's direct acquaintance with classical originals in Sp's poem. YWES XV (1934). 217.

4. JONES, H. S. V. A Spenser Handbook.
Ch. XXIII: Astrophel.

5. Monthly Packet, 3rd. ser. II (1881). 224 ff. Leicester in Holland.
230: Sp's *Astrophel* celebrates love of Sidney and Penelope.

6. PURCELL, JAMES M. Sidney's Stella. Oxford University Press, 1934.
58 ff.: Sp's *Astrophel* and its implications in regard to Sidney and Stella.

7. WEITZMANN, FRANCIS W. Notes on the Elizabethan "Elegie." PMLA L (1935). 435-43.
440: Sp first poet of note to apply "elegie" to chant of personal grief; 442: Sp listed by Meres as writing "elegie" or love plaint.

AXIOCHUS

1. FREYD, BERNARD. Spenser or Anthony Munday?—A Note on the *Axiochus*. PMLA L (1935). 903-8.
Argues for ascription of *Axiochus* to Anthony Munday. *Cf. post,* No. 4.

2. OSGOOD, C. G. Verse in Spenser's Prose. ELH I (1934). 4-5.

3. PADELFORD, F. M. One of Spenser's Lost Works Comes to Light. Paper read before the Mod. Lang. Ass., 1932. *Cf.* PMLA XLVII (*Proc.,* 1932). 1335; New York Times, Book Rev., Dec. 30, 1932. P. 13, col. 6. " Finds Spenser Book Missing Since 1758."

4. —— Spenser or Anthony Munday?—A Note on the *Axiochus*. PMLA L (1935). 908-13.
Replies to Freyd, *ante,* No. 1.

5. SPENSER, EDMUND. *Axiochus*. Ed. F. M. Padelford. The Johns Hopkins Press, 1934.
Cf. ante, p. 63 for reviews.

6. SYFORD, CONSTANCE M. On the *Axiochus* Translated by "Edw." Spenser. Paper read before the Mod. Lang. Ass., 1935. *Cf.* PMLA L (*Proc.,* 1936). 1359.

COLIN CLOUTS COME HOME AGAIN

See "Spenser and Raleigh," No. 8; "Editions," Nos. i, v;
"Versification," No. 41.

1. ALBRIGHT, EVELYN M. Spenser's Cosmic Philosophy
and His Religion. PMLA XLIV (1929). 715-59.
Lines 799-883 use material "akin" to Garden of Adonis, and employ similar treatment. Passage shows evidence Sp's cosmogony
derives from Empedocles. It is a "youthful" attempt at a "world
philosophy."

2. BAROWAY, ISRAEL. The Imagery of Spenser and the *Song
of Songs*. JEGP XXXIII (1934). 23-45.
38: Traces in CCCHA of Sp's reading of *Song of Songs*.

3. CHAMBERS, SIR E. K. The Elizabethan Stage. Oxford,
1923. 4 vols.
III, 207, 328: CCCHA and the work of contemporary writers
(Lodge and Alabaster).

4. CONWAY, EUSTACE. Anthony Munday and Other Essays.
New York, priv. print., 1927.
23 ff.: Identifies Palin as reference to Munday. *Cf.* 26-34.

5. GRAY, ARTHUR. Spenser's Aetion. TLS 34 (Jan. 24,
1935). 48.
Aetion is perhaps Marlowe. *Cf. post*, Nos. 17, 19, 22.

6. GREENLAW, EDWIN A. Two Notes on Spenser's Classical
Sources. MLN XLI (1926). 323-6.
Passage in Rhodius' *Argonautica* possible source of sea-passage in
CCCHA. *Rev.* YWES VII (1926). 159.

7. HANKINS, JOHN E. The "Harpalus" of Spenser's *Colin
Clout*. MLN XLIV (1929). 164-7.
Harpalus is George Turbervile; proof in his poem (pub. 1567) using
"Harpalus" as his name for himself. *Cf.* Koeppel, E. Anglia XIII
(1891). 42-71. *Rev.* Shakes. Jahr. 66 (1930). 239; YWES X (1929).
216.

8. HENLEY, PAULINE. Galathea and Neaera. TLS 32
(July 6, 1933). 464.
Accepts Professor Renwick's identification of Neaera. Suggests
that Galathea is Frances Howard, widowed Countess of Kildare.
Rev. YWES XIV (1933). 229. *Cf. post*, No. 18.

9. HEYWOOD, THOMAS. The Earls of Derby and the Verse
Writers and Poets of the Sixteenth and Seventeenth
Centuries. Chetham Soc., 1853. No. XXIX.
30, 32-5: Lord Strange as Amyntas of CCCHA.

10. HUNTER, JOSEPH. Chorus Vatum . . . B. M. Addit. MS
24,487.
fol. 29: Giles Fletcher = Palin; fol. 170: Matthew Roydon's *Elegy,
or Friend's Passion* . . . bound up with 1595 ed. CCCHA. *Cf.*
Library of Congress copy; fol. 115: Lord Strange and CCCHA.
MS 24,488 fol. 250ᵛ: R. Gentilis = Alcon; fol. 193: Fraunce is
Corydon in CCCHA.

11. JONES, H. S. V. A Spenser Handbook.
Ch. XXII: Colin Clouts Come Home Again.

12. KOLLER, KATHRINE. Scholarship in *Colin Clouts Come
Home Again.* Certain Aspects Reviewed. No number.
Proceedings of Dr. Greenlaw's Seminary "C," 1930.
The Johns Hopkins University Library.

13. ——— Studies in Spenser's *Colin Clouts Come Home
Again.* Diss., The Johns Hopkins University, 1932.

14. ——— Spenser and Ralegh. ELH I (1934). 37-60.
The undersong of CCCHA is Sp's friendship for Ralegh. Delay
in publishing CCCHA may have been due to attempt to aid Ralegh
recover favor at Court after the Throckmorton affair.

15. ——— Identifications in *Colin Clout's Come Home
Again.* MLN L (1935). 155-8.
17th c. marginal notes in a 1595 copy CCCHA show: i. an authen-
ticated Sp allusion in Sylvester's DuBartas (1605 ed., p. 272);
ii. the earliest record (1605-*ca.* 1650) of identification of people
mentioned in CCCHA; iii. these tally, with two exceptions, with
those of recent scholars; iv. the interest in Sidney and the strength
of the Stella-Lady Rich tradition. (*Cf.* "Astrophel," No. 5); v. the
marked popularity of certain of Sp's themes in CCCHA.

16. Lancashire Funeral Certificates. Ed. T. W. King and F.
R. Raines. Chetham Soc., 1869. LXXV.
68: Sp's reference to Lord Strange as Amyntas.

17. Maggs Brothers Catalogue No. 577, Pt. II. London,
1932.
141: Sp refers to Shakespeare as Aetion. *Cf. ante,* No. 5; *post,*
No. 22.

18. RENWICK, W. L. Spenser's Galathea and Neaera. TLS
28 (Mar. 14, 1929). 206-7.
Galathea = Lady Wallop; Neaera = Countess of Ormonde.

19. RENWICK, W. L. Spenser and Aetion. TLS 34 (Jan. 31, 1935). 62. *Cf. ante,* No. 5.

20. SANDISON, HELEN E. Spenser's Mansilia. TLS 26 (Sept. 8, 1927). 608.

> CCCHA I, 510, refers to Helena, Marchioness of Northampton, as Mansilia. Comments from her epitaph in Salisbury Cathedral and from Lansd. Roll 9 in B. M. support Sp's picture of her. The name may be derived from *Mansueta* or *Mansues.*

21. STRATHMANN, ERNEST A. Lady Carey and Spenser. ELH II (1935). 51-4.

> Lady Carey is Phyllis, not Charillis. CCCHA not a courtly poem. *Cf. post,* No. 23.

22. TILLOTSON, KATHLEEN. Spenser's Aetion. TLS 34 (Feb. 7, 1935). 76.

> Aetion, as praise of Drayton, fits in with other contemporary attitudes toward Drayton. *Cf. ante,* Nos. 5, 19.

23. WELPLY, W. H. Edmund Spenser . . . NQ, ser. xiv. VI (1932). 110.

> Identity of Phyllis, Charillis, and Amaryllis as daughters of Sir John Spencer. *Cf. ante,* No. 21.

24. ———— More Notes on Edmund Spenser. NQ, ser. xiv. IX (1933). 92-4, 111-6.

> vii: Thomas Stuteville's wife, niece of Lord North. Does CCCHA reference to her "place" mean her position at Court?

25. WILLIAMSON, GEORGE C. Lady Anne Clifford, Countess of Pembroke . . . 1590-1676. Her Letters and Work. Kendal, 1922.

> 61: CCCHA. *Cf. 63, 64, 96.* Negligible.

DAPHNAIDA

See "Editions," Nos. i, v for annotated texts; "FQ, Sources," No. 26; "Addenda," No. 14.

1. GREENLAW, EDWIN A. Rev. of Renwick's *Daphnaida.* MLN XLV (1930). 323-8.

2. HARRISON, G. B. An Elizabethan Journal. London, 1928.

> 97: Publication of *Daphnaida* noted.

3. HARRISON, T. P., JR. Spenser and Boccaccio's *Olympia*. Texas Studies in English XIV (1934). 5-30.

15-9: *Daphnaida* cast in mold of *Book of the Duchess*; use of Boccaccio's material. *Cf. post,* No. 8.

4. HUNTER, JOSEPH. Chorus Vatum . . . B. M. Addit. MS 24,488.

fol. 57 ff.: The Gorges family to whom Sp inscribed *Daphnaida*. Arthur Gorges = Alcyon; fol. 193: Corydon = Abraham Fraunce.

5. JONES, H. S. V. A Spenser Handbook.

Ch. XXI: Daphnaida.

6. SANDISON, HELEN E. Spenser's Alcyon: Arthur Gorges. Paper read before the Mod. Lang. Ass., 1927. *Cf.* PMLA XLII (*Proc.,* 1927). xl.

7. ——— Arthur Gorges, Spenser's Alcyon and Ralegh's Friend. PMLA XLIII (1928). 645-74.

A biographical study of Gorges and a list of his writings. *Rev.* Shakes. Jahr. 65 (1929). 226.

8. STARNES, DEWITT T. Bibliographical History of the Funeral Elegy in England from 1500 to 1638. Abstracts of Theses, University of Chicago, Humanistic Series I (1922-3). 399 ff.

404: Sp's *Daphnaida* influenced by Chaucer's *Book of the Duchess? Cf. ante,* No. 3.

9. WEITZMANN, FRANCIS W. Notes on the Elizabethan " Elegie." PMLA L (1935). 435-43.

440: Sp first poet of note to apply " elegie " to chant of personal grief; 442: Sp listed by Meres as writing " elegie " or love plaint.

EPITHALAMION

See " Editions," i, v; " Parents and Family," No. 55; "Amoretti," No. 11.

1. BAROWAY, ISRAEL. The Imagery of Spenser and the *Song of Songs*. JEGP XXXIII (1934). 31-2, 42-4.

Sp's reading of *S. of S.* traced in *Epithalamion.*

2. Blackwood's Mag. CXXIX (1881). 791-2. A Talk About Odes.

Epithalamion a " really Christian " poet's ode.

3. CLARKE, CHARLES and MARY COWDEN. Recollections of Writers. New York, 1878.

    125-6: Note on *Epithalamion*. [R. Heffner]

4. DUCKETT, ELEANOR S. Catullus in English Poetry. Smith College Classical Studies. No. 6. Northampton, Mass., 1925.

    109-13: *Epithalamion* parallels with *Carmen* 61. *Cf. post*, No. 9.

5. GRISMER, FRANK A. Spenser's *Epithalamion*. TLS 33 (April 26, 1934). 303.

    Stanza 1 and the envoy seem autobiographic. They constitute an envelop covering for entire poem, and were written perhaps as early as 1591. *Cf. post*, Nos. 6, 12; " Life, Miscellaneous," No. 59. *Rev.* YWES XV (1934). 218.

6. HAMER, DOUGLAS. Spenser's Marriage. RES VII (1931). 271-90.

    Cf. Eccles, M. TLS 30 (Dec. 31, 1931). 1053.

7. JONES, H. S. V. A Spenser Handbook.

    Ch. XXVII: Epithalamion.

8. LEGOUIS, ÉMILE. Edmund Spenser. New York and London, 1926.

    Ch. IV.

9. McPEEK, JAMES A. S. The Influence of Catullus on English Literature to 1700. Summaries of Theses, Harvard University, 1932. 264-7.

    Ch. II: The Epithalamia of Catullus and their influence on English Literature. Sp uses several Catullan motives, but is chiefly indebted to Marc-Claude de Buttet. *Cf. ante*, No. 4.

10. ———— The Major Sources of Spenser's *Epithalamion*. JEGP XXXV (1936). 183-213.

11. Manchester Quart. II (1883). 354. Rural Poetry of England, by George Milner.

    354-5: Sp most poetic of our " elder poets." Cites *Epithalamion*.

12. RENWICK, W. L. Spenser's *Epithalamion*. TLS 33 (May 3, 1934). 322.

    Explains the unity of the poem and envoy. *Cf. ante*, No. 5.

13. SPENS, JANET. Spenser's *Faerie Queene*: An Interpretation.

    Ch. V: Amoretti.

14. THALER, ALWIN. Shakspere and Spenser: the *Epithala-mion*. Paper read before the Mod. Lang. Ass., 1935. *Cf.* PMLA L (*Proc.*, 1935). 1359. Printed, SAB XI (1936). 33-40.

15. THOMPSON, FRANCIS. Works. Prose. Ed. W. Meynell. New York, 1913.
   III, 175: "Crashaw": *Epithalamion* is first appearance in English poetry of "ode of ardorous abandonment." [N. T. Weyand, S. J.]

FOUR HYMNS

See "Spenser and Platonism," No. 4; "Mutabilitie," No. 15; "Spenser's Philosophy," Nos. 6, 16-7; "FQ, Sources," Nos. 28-9, 92; "Addenda," No. 13.

1. ALBRIGHT, EVELYN M. Spenser's Cosmic Philosophy and His Religion. PMLA XLIV (1929). 715-59.
   Opposes Greenlaw, and finds Empedocles rather than Lucretius in the *Hymnes*. See esp. 739-40. *Cf.* Greenlaw, E. in SP XVII (1920). 320-59; *ibid.*, XX (1923). 216.

2. BENNETT, JOSEPHINE W. The Theme of Spenser's *Fowre Hymnes*. SP XXVIII (1931). 18-57.
   The *Hymnes* are a single structural unit, setting forth Platonic and Neo-Platonic love. The Platonism illustrated by reference to philosophical documents which the *Hymnes* most closely resemble— *Canzona dello Amore celeste & divino* of Benivieni and its *Commento* by Pico della Mirandola. *Hymnes* dated between "spring of 1595, and September 1596." *Rev.* YWES XII (1931). 192; Proc. Eng. Journal Club, Mar. 10, 1930-1, by Joseph B. Collins. The Johns Hopkins University. *Cf. post*, Nos. 5, 18; "Mutabilitie," No. 7.

3. ———— Spenser's *Fowre Hymnes*: Addenda. SP XXXII (1935). 131-57.
   i. Renaissance Christian Neo-Platonism is found in all four *Hymnes*. Sp follows Pico and Benivieni. *Hymnes* a single unit of exposition. ii. Sp revised first two (1578-80) to "fit the scheme" of four for publication in 1596. *Cf. ante*, No. 2.

4. BHATTACHERJE, M. Studies in Spenser.
   Ch. II, 19-38: Hymnes. See also discussion of Pico and Bruno.

5. COLLINS, JOSEPH B. Christian Mysticism in the Elizabethan Age. Diss., The Johns Hopkins University, 1933.

6. DAVIS, B. E. C. Edmund Spenser: A Critical Study.
Ch. IX: Hymnes. See also index.

7. DUSTOOR, P. E. Legends of Lucifer in Early English and in Milton. Anglia LIV (1930). 213-68.
226-8, 249-51: Sp's treatment of the expulsion.

8. FLETCHER, J. B. A Study of Renaissance Mysticism . . . PMLA XXVI (1911).
Rev. Shakes. Jahr. 48 (1912). 220.

9. FOWLER, E. B. The Problem of Spenser's *Fowre Hymnes*. Discussion by professors Hanford, Thompson, and Greenlaw. Mod. Lang. Ass., 1927. Cf. PMLA XLII (*Proc.*, 1927). xl.

10. FRIEDRICH, W. G. Christian Mysticism in Spenser's *Fowre Hymnes*. No. 65. Proceedings of Dr. Greenlaw's Seminary " C," 1926-7. The Johns Hopkins University Library.

11. HARRISON, T. P., JR. Spenser and Boccaccio's *Olympia*. Univ. of Texas Studies in English XIV (1934). 5-30.
5-15, 19-30: The last two *Hymnes* and the *Olympia*. Boccaccio's emphasis upon the "ways of salvation in practical life" link him with Sp's thought. Cf. Winstanley, L. The Foure Hymnes, London, 1916.

12. JONES, H. S. V. A Spenser Handbook.
Ch. XXVIII: The Fowre Hymnes.

13. LANDRUM, GRACE W. Spenser's Use of the Bible and his Alleged Puritanism. PMLA XLI (1926). 525 ff.

14. LEBEL, EUGENE C. Christian and medieval theology in Spenser's *Hymne of heavenly love* and *Hymne of heavenly beautie*. M. A. Thesis, University of Chicago, 1931.

15. LEE, R. W. Castiglione's Influence on Spenser's Early Hymns. PQ VII (1928). 65-77.
Detailed comparison of Sp's first two hymns and Castiglione (Hoby trans.) in 10 major items. Concludes that Sp constantly echoes Hoby's phraseology, but the hymns are nevertheless "individual poetic achievement." Significance of Castiglione's Platonism for Sp lies in worship of feminine beauty. Rev. Shakes. Jahr. 65 (1929). 225. Cf. ante, No. 2.

16. Lotspeich, H. G. Spenser's Urania. MLN L (1935). 144.

Sp's best treatment of theme of achieving knowledge of God by study of his works, in HHB 22-105. *Cf.* " Addenda," No. 10.

17. Newbolt, Sir Henry. Poetry and Time. (Warton Lecture on English Poetry.) Proc. Brit. Acad. VIII. London, 1918.

492: Hymne of Heavenly Beautie. Negligible.

18. Padelford, F. M. Spenser's *Fowre Hymnes*: A Resurvey. SP XXIX (1932). 207-32. *Cf.* PMLA XLVI (*Proc.*, 1931). 1435.

". . . is the Christian element in the last two hymns only coloring, with the basic conceptions unchanged," or " are the last two hymns basically Christian, with a mere coloring of Neo-Platonism? " Considers the last two basically Christian. Supports the view by reference to St. Augustine's *Confessions,* Benivieni's *Admonitions,* and the works of the Christian mystics. *Rev.* YWES XIII (1932). 194. *Cf. ante,* Nos. 2, 5; " FQ, General," No. 134; Padelford, F. M., in JEGP XIII (1914). 418-33.

19. ——— Spenser and *The Pilgrimage of the Life of Man.* SP XXVIII (1931). 211-8.

20. Quarterly Rev. LII (1834). 7, 13.

Style and versification, etc., in *Hymnes.*

21. Saurat, Denis. Les Idées Philosophiques de Spenser. Arsbok, 1924. Yearbook of the New Society of Letters at Lund. I, 251 ff.

Rev. YWES V (1924). 155. *Cf.* Saurat's Literature and Occult Tradition, 163-237.

22. ——— La " Sapience " de Spenser et la " Schekhina " de la Cabale. Revue de Littérature Comparée VI (1926). 5-15.

" The person termed Sapience in the second half of the *Hymn of Heavenly Beauty* was obtained from the Matron of the Cabalists." Parallel characteristics. [A. P.]

23. ——— Spenser and the Occult. New York, 1931. Translated from *La Littérature et l'Occultisme.* Paris, 1929.

Rev. New York Herald-Tribune Books (Feb. 22, 1931). 19. " Cabalistic." Sp's knowledge of the Cabala.

24. Shakespeare Jahrbuch 51 (1915). 222. *Cf.* Long, P. W. The Date of Spenser's Earlier Hymns. Engl. Stud. XLVII (1913).

25. SMITH, CHARLES G. Spenser's Theory of Friendship. PMLA XLIX (1934). 490-500.

493-5: The conception of love as a harmonizing and unifying force (Bk. IV and *Mutabilitie*) is present in the *Hymnes*.

26. SPENS, JANET. Spenser's *Faerie Queene*.

Ch. V: Amoretti.

27. STRATHMANN, ERNEST A. A Manuscript Copy of Spenser's *Hymnes*. MLN XLVIII (1933). 217-21.

Harleian MS 6910, *ca.* 1596, contains hitherto unrecorded copies of *Hymne in Honour of Beautie* and *Hymne of Heavenly Beautie*. *Rev.* YWES XIV (1933). 226.

28. *THOMPSON, NATHALIE Q. Spenser's Treatment of Love and Friendship Compared with Castiglione's. M. A. Thesis, University of Chicago, 1927.

29. TUVE, ROSEMOND. Spenser and the *Zodiake of Life*. JEGP XXXIV (1935). 1-19.

Relationship of *Zod. of Life* (Googe's translation, 1565) to Sp's work. Sp's cosmological conception of love in *Hymnes* is similar to that in *Zod. of Life*. *Cf. ante,* No. 25.

THE LETTERS

See "Spenser and Harvey," Nos. 1, 11; "Areopagus," No. 1; "Editions," vi, No. 33.

1. ALBRIGHT, EVELYN M. Spenser's Connections with the Letters in Gabriel Harvey's *Letter-Book*. MP XXIX (1932). 411-36.

The four letters are intended for Sp. Relation of letters to date of *Mutabilitie*. *Cf. post*, Nos. 2, 5.

2. BENNETT, JOSEPHINE W. Spenser and Gabriel Harvey's *Letter-Book*. MP XXIX (1931). 163-86.

Close study of the *Letter-Book* produces belief that of four so-called letters to Sp the first is "pure fiction" perhaps intended to be addressed to Sp; second is pure fiction which could hardly have been addressed to Sp; third, evidence shows, was intended for John Wood; fourth, "gives no evidence of the person to whom it was to have been, at least nominally, addressed." *Cf. ante,* No. 1. *Rev.* Shakes. Jahr. 68 (1932). 173.

3. BINKLEY, HAROLD C. Letter-Writing in English Literature. Summaries of Theses, Harvard University, 1926.
160-3.
Pt. II: Letter-writing as a Literary Form. Sp-Harvey letters.

4. CALDWELL, JAMES R. Dating a Spenser-Harvey Letter.
PMLA XLI (1926). 568-74.
On the first of the "two other very commendable letters." Date
of composition for first part is Oct. 5; for second part, Oct. 16.
[A. P.] Cf. post, No. 6.

5. GREENLAW, EDWIN A. Spenser's *Mutabilitie*. PMLA
XLV (1930). 695 ff.
The Letters do not refer to *Mutabilitie,* which is late work. Cf.
ante, No. 1.

6. HEWLETT, J. H. Interpreting a Spenser-Harvey Letter.
PMLA XLII (1927). 1060-5. Also No. 68 and No.
69. Proceedings of Dr. Greenlaw's Seminary "C,"
1926-7. The Johns Hopkins University Library.
Harvey's Letter of 23 Oct. 1579 is a travel letter, and shows
Harvey understood Sp to be writing seriously. Accepts Dr. Greenlaw's analysis of the difference in mood of Sp's letters of Oct. and
following April. Cf. ante, No. 4.

7. JONES, H. S. V. A Spenser Handbook.
Ch. XXXI: Letters.

8. MORRILL, BESSIE H. The Literary Letter in the Sixteenth
Century. M. A. Thesis, Columbia University, 1914.

9. PARMENTER, MARY. Colin Clout and Hobbinol: a reconsideration of the relationship of Edmund Spenser
and Gabriel Harvey. Diss., The Johns Hopkins University, 1933.

MOTHER HUBBERDS TALE

See "Editions," Nos. i, v; "Minor Poems, Complaints";
"Versification," Nos. 13, 40, 41; "Shepherd's Calendar," No.
56.

1. ALLEN, PERCY. Anne Cecil, Elizabeth & Oxford. Lon-
don, 1934.
Ch. VII: Mother Hubberds Tale. Interprets MHT in relation to
Alençon-Simier marriage plans and Earl of Oxford's troubles at

Court. Fox = Burghley; Ape = Alençon = Simier. *Rev.* TLS 33 (May 3, 1934). 321, 325. Something "new and strange" evolved from MHT in relation to trouble between Burghley's daughter and her husband, the Earl of Oxford.

2. Buyssens, E. Spenser's *Prosopopoia*, lines 241-2. NQ, ser. xiv. VIII (1933). 190.

On emendation and rhyme. *Rev.* YWES XIV (1933). 229. *Cf. post*, No. 11.

3. Catalogue of Additions to the Manuscripts of the British Museum. London, 1894.

34, 064: Extracts from Edmund Spenser and other English poets, fol. 27-40b. Fol. 33: Extract from MHT is wrongly said to be from *Ruins of Tyme*.

4. Edinburgh Rev. VIII (1806).

460-61: Quotes MHT.

5. Greenlaw, Edwin A. Spenser and the Earl of Leicester. Repr. as "Satire and Contemporary Allusion" in *Studies in Spenser's Historical Allegory.* 1932.

Rev. Shakes. Jahr. 47 (1911). 259-60; RES X (1934). 350-3, by C. B. Millican. *Cf. post*, No. 6.

6. Hard, Frederick. Spenser and Burghley. SP XXVIII (1931). 219-34.

MHT, 1171-1182, contains further criticism of Burghley. *Rev.* YWES XII (1931). 193. *Cf. ante*, No. 5.

7. Harris, Robert B. The Beast in English Satire from Spenser to John Gay. Summaries of Theses, Harvard University, 1932. 254-7.

Sp popularized the beast satire and endowed the *genre* with new materials and a wider range of satire, etc., which persisted for the next century. Some of works influenced by MHT.

8. Jones, H. S. V. A Spenser Handbook.

Ch. VIII: Mother Hubberds Tale.

9. Lawrence, C. E. The Personality of Spenser. Quart. Rev. CCXLIX (1927). 154-67.

Satire of MHT compared with Chaucer's satire.

10. Leible, Arthur B. Conventions of Animal Symbolism and Satire in Spenser's *Mother Hubberds Tale*. University of Chicago, Abstracts of Theses, Humanistic Series VIII (1929-30). 449-52.

Satire of rogues and clerics resembles SC; Sp probably following a satiric pattern popular in his time. MHT composed chiefly of conventional elements. Three tracts by Wm. Turner (hitherto neglected) help interpret MHT.

11. MABBOTT, THOMAS O. Spenser's *Prosopopoia,* lines 241-2. NQ, ser. xiv. VIII (1933). 62-3, 266-7.
Emendation of 241-2. Present imperfect rhyme may have resulted from dropping type. Sp's use of *m* and *n* assonance. *Rev.* YWES XIV (1933). 229. *Cf. ante,* No. 2.

12. MOHL, RUTH. The Three Estates in Medieval and Renaissance Literature. Columbia University Press, 1933.
227-9, 305-6, 329-30: MHT on the three estates.

13. NEALE, J. E. Queen Elizabeth. New York, 1934.
65: Quotes MHT 894-906 on Court conditions.

14. Notes and Queries CLXVII (1934). 232-3. Review of Harold Stein. Studies in Spenser's *Complaints.*
Upholds Stein's interpretation of MHT.

15. PREVITE-ORTON, C. W. Political Satire in English Poetry. Cambridge and New York, 1910.
48-54: Sp. Copies in Bost. Pub. Library and Princeton University Library.

16. RENWICK, W. L. The Complaints. Scholartis Press, 1928.
225-33: Mother Hubberds Tale.

17. RUSSELL, I. WILLIS. The Sources of Spenser's *Mother Hubberds Tale.* M. A. Thesis, The Johns Hopkins University, 1929.

18. ——— Some Notes on *Mother Hubberds Tale.* No. 11. Proceedings of Dr. Greenlaw's Seminary " C," 1928-9. The Johns Hopkins Univ. Library.

19. ——— Three Notes on Spenser's *Mother Hubberds Tale.* No. 19. Proceedings . . . *Loc. cit.*

20. ——— Allegory of *Mother Hubberds Tale.* No. 30. Proceedings . . . *Loc. cit.*

21. ——— Biblical Echoes in *Mother Hubberds Tale.* MLN XLIV (1929). 162-4.
Cites three Biblical echoes at variance with those suggested by Miss Landrum. *Cf.* " Spenser and Puritanism," No. 8.

22. WHIPPLE, T. K. Martial and the English Epigram. Univ. of California Pub. in Mod. Philol. X (1925). 279 ff.
325, 330: Sp's epigrams and MHT.

MUIOPOTMOS

See "Editions," i, v; "Minor Poems, Complaints"; "Life, Miscellaneous," No. 22.

1. ALLEN, PERCY. Anne Cecil, Elizabeth & Oxford. London, 1934.
Ch. VIII: "The Meaning of *Muiopotmos.*" Clarion = Earl of Oxford; Aragnoll = Burghley (Fox of MHT); Astery = Anne Cecil. Interpreted in relation to trouble between Anne Cecil and her husband, Oxford. *Rev.* TLS 33 (May 3, 1934). 321.

2. CLARK, EVA TURNER. Shakespeare's Plays in the Order of their Writing. . . . London, 1930.
649-53: *Muiopotmos* in relation to Oxford's fall. Clarion = Oxford. *Cf. post,* No. 3.

3. ——— Spenser's *Muiopotmos.* Hidden Allusions in Shakespeare's Plays. New York, 1931.
643-7: Clarion = Oxford. *Cf. ante,* No. 2.

4. DeLACY, HUGH. Astrology in the Poetry of Edmund Spenser. JEGP XXXIII (1934). 531-2.

5. DENKINGER, EMMA M. Spenser's *Muiopotmos* Again. PMLA XLVI (1931). 272-6.
Indicates errors in Lemmi's article in regard to the relations between Sidney and Penelope Devereux. Frances Walsingham as Stella obviates difficulties encountered by identifying Lady Rich and Stella, and suits CCCHA 532-6. *Cf. post,* Nos. 9, 10, 15, 19.

6. HULBERT, VIOLA B. A new interpretation of Spenser's *Muiopotmos.* SP XXV (1928). 128-48.
Weakness of the Raleigh-Essex interpretation. Suggests Sidney-Oxford quarrel of 1579. Sidney = Flie; Burghley = Spider. *Rev.* Shakes. Jahr. 66 (1930). 239-40; YWES IX (1928). 172. *Cf.* Lyon, Jessie. PMLA XXXI (1916). 90 ff; *ante,* Nos. 2, 3; *post,* No. 10.

7. JONES, H. S. V. A Spenser Handbook.
Ch. X: Muiopotmos.

8. LEMMI, C. W. The Allegorical Meaning of Spenser's *Muiopotmos.* PMLA XLV (1930). 732-48. Also No.

142   THE WORKS

23.   Proceedings of Dr. Greenlaw's Seminary "C,"
1928-9. The Johns Hopkins University Library.
Muiopotmos, like *Astrophel*, allegory of life and death of Sidney.
Clarion = Sidney; Aragnoll = Anjou; Venus = Elizabeth; Asterie
= Lettice Knolles; Sport and Play = La Mole and Simier. *Rev.*
YWES XI (1930). 200. Rejects the identifications; Shakes. Jahr.
68 (1932). 173; *ibid.*, 67 (1931). 117. *Cf. ante,* No. 5; *post,* Nos. 14,
18.

9.   LEMMI, C. W. Astery's Transformation in *Muiopotmos.*
PMLA L (1935). 913-4.
Astery's transformation probably derives from Lactantius' com-
ment on Statius.

10.   NADAL, T. W. Spenser's *Muiopotmos* in Relation to
Chaucer's *Sir Thopas.* . . . PMLA XXV (1910).
Rev. Shakes. Jahr. 47 (1911). 261.

11.   NELSON, LOUISE A. Muiopotmos. Calcutta Review, 3rd.
ser. XXXVII (1930). 333-41. [L. O. Hogan]
Interprets the poem in terms of the Raleigh-Essex quarrel. Resemblance of *Muiopotmos* to Chaucer's *Sir Thopas* and *Nun's
Priest's Tale.*

12.   PALGRAVE, FRANCIS T. Muiopotmos. Grosart's ed. Spenser. IV, lxx-lxxii.

13.   PEASE, ARTHUR S. Things without Honor. CP XXI
(1926). 27-42.
34n: *Muiopotmos* in relation to classical panegyric laudations.

14.   PURCELL, J. M. The Allegorical Meaning of Spenser's
Muiopotmos. PMLA XLVI (1931). 945-6.
Correction of Mr. Lemmi's article (*ante,* No. 8) in regard to
Penelope Devereux, Philip Sidney, and Lord Rich. *Rev.* Shakes.
Jahr. 68 (1932). 174. *Cf. ante,* No. 5.

15.   RATHBORNE, ISABEL E. Another Interpretation of *Muiopotmos.* PMLA XLIX (1934). 1050-68.
Muiopotmos may be a mock-heroic modelled on the *Batrachomy-
ochia* and in some ways a parody of FQ. *Rev.* YWES XV (1934).
218; Shakes. Jahr. 71 (1935). 146.

16.   Revue anglo-américaine 6ᵉ· an. (1928-9). 538-9.

17.   SMITH, REED. The Metamorphoses in *Muiopotmos.*
MLN XXVIII (1913).
Rev. Shakes. Jahr. 50 (1914). 146.

18. STRATHMANN, ERNEST A. Criticism of Spenser's *Muiopotmos*. No. 8. Proceedings of Dr. Greenlaw's Seminary " C," 1928-9. The Johns Hopkins University Library.

19. —— The Allegorical Meaning of Spenser's *Muiopotmos*. PMLA XLVI (1931). 940-5.

Answers and corrects Mr. Lemmi (PMLA XLV, 732-48). *Rev.* Shakes. Jahr. 68 (1932). 174.

20. —— Lady Carey and Spenser. ELH II (1935). 50, 55-7.

Lady Carey is not Aragnoll. *Muiopotmos* may allude to her needlework.

PROTHALAMION

See " Editions," i, v.

1. AFLALO, F. G. The Genius of the River. Quart. Rev. CCXIII (1910). 86.

2. MARSH, E. An Emendation in Spenser's *Prothalamium*. Lond. Merc. IX (1924). 300.

In concluding lines "brides" should read "birdes." [F. I. C. and A. P.]

3. JONES, H. S. V. A Spenser Handbook.

Ch. XXIX: Prothalamion.

4. Quarterly Rev. CCIX (1908). 371.

Supposed allusion to Inns of Court, *Proth.* 132-5.

THE RUINS OF ROME

See " Editions," i, v; " Minor Poems, Complaints."

1. JONES, H. S. V. A Spenser Handbook.

Ch. IX: The Ruines of Rome.

2. LOTSPEICH, H. G. Spenser's Urania. MLN L (1935). 141-6.

Sp's Urania owes to DuBartas' *Urania* the suggestion of a definitely religious element. She leads men to contemplation of the Heavenly Hierarchy and of God himself. This idea is unique in *Urania. Cf.* " Addenda," No. 10.

11

3. WEELER, PHILIP. Josuah Sylvesters Englische Überset-
zungen der Religiösen Epen des DuBartas. Diss., Tu-
bingen, 1902.

7: Sp (R. of R.) translation of DuBartas 104, 108.

THE RUINS OF TIME

See "Editions," i, v; "Minor Poems, Complaints."

1. CHETTLE, HENRY. *Cf.* "Criticism before 1651," No. 9.
2. JONES, H. S. V. A Spenser Handbook.

Ch. V: The Ruines of Time.

THE SHEPHERD'S CALENDAR

See "Life, Miscellaneous," Nos. 31, 47, 77; "Spenser's
Marriage," No. 18; "Editions," i, v, vii; "Language, Archaism," Nos. 6, 17, 29; "Diction, Style," No. 16; "Versification," Nos. 35, 44; "Addenda," No. 22.

1. ACHESON, ARTHUR. Shakespeare's Sonnet Story 1592-
1598. London, 1922.

6-7, 12-3: Rosalinde not Rose Daniel. Florio is Menalcas. This
supported by *All's Well,* I, i (Parolles).

2. ARBER, AGNES. Edmund Spenser and Lyte's *Nievve
Herball.* NQ CLX (1931). 345-7.

"April" may owe something to Henry Lyte's book. *Cf. post,* No.
33.

3. BANKS, THEODORE H. Spenser's Rosalind: A Conjec-
ture. Paper read before the Mod. Lang. Ass., 1935.
Cf. PMLA L (*Proc.,* 1935). 1359.

4. BASKERVILL, C. R. The Early Fame of the *Shepheards
Calender.* PMLA XXVIII (1913).

Rev. Shakes. Jahr. 50 (1914). 145.

5. Blackwood's Mag. I (1817). 484. Rosalind; CXVIII
(1875). 357-8. Elegies.

Moschus used in SC.

6. BOTTING, ROLAND B. The Composition of the *Shepheardes Calender.* PMLA L (1935). 423-34.

SC composed, in part, of poems of earlier date than the unifying ideas of the whole. These early poems, hastily revised, were supplemented by others for publication. Evidence of this includes: i. lack of perfect execution of unifying themes; ii. "other unmistakable evidences of haste" in both poetry and gloss.

7. BRADNER, LEICESTER. An Allusion to Bromley in the *Shepherds' Calendar*. MLN XLIX (1934). 443-5.

"July" 41-4, may refer to well in yard of Bishop of Rochester's residence at Bromley. Sp's change in name from St. Blaze to St. Bridget explained. Sp's connection with Bishop Young is given further support. *Cf. post*, Nos. 40, 62. *Rev.* YWES XV (1934). 217.

8. ———— The Latin Translations of Spenser's *Shepheardes Calender*. MP XXXIII (1935). 21-6.

Corrections in regard to the Dove and Bathurst translations. *Cf.* Carpenter, Ref. Guide, 195 and 201.

9. BRIE, FRIEDRICH. Shakespeare und die Impresa-Kunst seiner Zeit. Shakes. Jahr. 50 (1914). 9-30.

17: SC and FQ.

10. BRUNNER, K. Die Dialektwörter in Spensers *Shepherds Calender*. Archiv CXXXII (1914).

Rev. Shakes. Jahr. 51 (1915). 222.

11. BYROM, H. J. Edmund Spenser's First Printer, Hugh Singleton. The Library XIV, Pt. 2 (1933). 121-56.

Choice of Singleton "far from accidental." Circumstantial evidence shows Sp was linked with group opposing the Anjou marriage. Sp's possible connection with John Stubbe. *Rev.* YWES XIV (1933). 225.

12. CAMPBELL, JEANNETTE H. The Influence of *The Shepheards Calender* upon the formal pastoral of the period 1579-1602. M. A. Thesis, University of Chicago, 1928.

13. Catalogue of MSS in the Library of Gonville and Caius College, Cambridge.

II, 627: No. 595: *Cf.* Hunter, Joseph. Chorus Vatum . . . B. M. Addit. MS 24, 490 fol. 132: John Dove's *Poimenologia, quae vulgo calendarium Pastorum appellatur e versu Anglicano in Latinum traducta. Cf. ante*, p. 67.

14. CHAMBERS, SIR E. K. Sir Thomas Wyatt and Some Collected Studies. London, 1933.

Cf. "The English Pastoral" and *passim*.

15. CHAMBRUN, CLARA (Longworth) Comtesse de. Giovanni Florio. Paris, 1921.

31, 32: "Answers Grosart's objections to Halpin's theories that Rosalind is Rose Daniel, Florio's first wife and sister to Samuel Daniel, and Menalcas is Florio." [F. I. C. and A. P.]

16. CONWAY, EUSTACE. Anthony Munday and Other Essays. New York [Priv. print.], 1927.

23 ff.: Palinode refers to Anthony Munday. *Cf.* pp. 26-34; "Colin Clouts Come Home," No. 4.

17. COVINGTON, F. F., JR. An Early Seventeenth-Century Criticism of Spenser. MLN XLI (1926). 386-7.

Heywood and the 17th. c. popularity of SC.

18. CUNINGHAM, GRANVILLE C. Bacon and Edmund Spenser. Baconiana, 3rd. ser. V (1907). 153-77.

161: SC; 169: Rosalind.

19. ——— "Ignoto." Baconiana, 3rd. ser. XI (1913). 224 ff.

Relation of E. K. and anonymity of SC until 1611 to Bacon theory.

20. DARBISHIRE, HELEN. RES VIII (1932). 326-9.

21. DeLACY, HUGH. Astrology in the Poetry of Edmund Spenser. JEGP XXXIII (1934). 532-3.

22. DRAPER, J. W. The Glosses to Spenser's *Shepheardes Calendar*. JEGP XVIII (1919).

Rev. Shakes. Jahr. 59/60 (1924). 238.

23. DRYDEN, JOHN. Alexander's Feast, or the Power of Music.

Cf. Hunter, Joseph. Chorus Vatum . . . B. M. Addit. MS 24, 490, fol. 226ᵛ: Historical basis for Dryden's Ode in "Oct."

24. Edinburgh Rev. CXLIV (1876). 387 ff.

SC and Sidney. Negligible.

25. FLETCHER, J. B. Spenser and "E. K." MLN XV (1900).

Rev. Shakes. Jahr. 37 (1901). 272-3.

26. GRAY, THOMAS. See "Criticism after 1651," No. 59.

27. GREG, W. W. Pastoral Poetry and Pastoral Drama. London, 1906.

22: Summarizes several of Petrarch's eclogues to show the bitter attacks on ecclesiastical evils which are characteristic of Mantuan and are found in Sp.

28. GREENLAW, EDWIN A. The Shepheards Calendar.
PMLA XXVI (1911).
Rev. Shakes. Jahr. 48 (1914). 218-9.

29. HAINES, C. R. Timon: and other Emendations. TLS 23
(Mar. 6, 1924). 144.
3: Rosalinde an anagram; Menalcas is Florio.

30. HARINGTON, SIR JOHN. Nugae Antiquae. 1653. Ed.
Thomas Park. London, 1804.
II, 18 n: On "Algrind" as anagram. Quotes Upton.

31. HARRISON, T. P., JR. Spenser and the Earlier Pastoral
Elegy. Univ. of Texas Studies in English XIII (1933).
36-53.
Examines pastoral elements in all the elegiac pastoral poetry of
Sp for sources and common characteristics. The study investigates
E. K.'s "also divers other excellent both Italian and French Poetes,
whose foting this Author every where followeth." *Rev.* YWES XIV
(1933). 229.

32. ——— Spenser, Ronsard, and Bion. MLN XLIX
(1934). 139-45.
A source for SC "March." *Rev.* Shakes. Jahr. 71 (1935). 146.

33. HERBERT, A. S. "Chevisaunce." TLS 30 (Mar. 19,
1931). 234.
Identification of this flower ("April") as honey-suckle. *Cf. ante,*
No. 2.

34. HIGGINSON, J. J. Spenser's *Shepherd's Calender* in Relation to Contemporary Affairs. Columbia University,
1912.
Rev. Shakes. Jahr. 49 (1913). 261-2; Anglia Beibl. XXV (1914).
50-1, by H. T. Price; Athenaeum. 1912. II. 755.

35. HUGHES, MERRITT Y. Spenser and the Greek Pastoral
Triad. SP XX (1923). 184-215.
" Sp's debt to Theocritus, Bion, Moschus: their ' direct ' influence
negligible. Sp derives them through Ren. intermediaries with their
peculiar literary conventions. Influence of these on the SC
(' March ' and ' November ') . . . Comparison of the pastorals of
the Pléiade with SC." [F. I. C. and A. P.] *Rev.* Anglia Beibl.
XXXIV (1923). 363-5, by S. B. Liljegren.

36. ——— Virgil and Spenser. University of California
Pub. in English II, No. 3 (1929). 263-418.
Pt. I: *The Pastorals. Cf.* Bush, D. Mythology and the Renaissance
Tradition, 101-7.

37. HUNTER, JOSEPH. Chorus Vatum . . . B. M. Addit. MSS.

MS 24, 488, fol. 234; 24, 489, fol. 252ᵛ: E. K. is Edward Knight; MS 24, 489, fol. 86; 24, 490, fol. 132, 263: Bathurst's translation.

38. JONES, H. S. V. A Spenser Handbook.

Ch. III: The Shepheardes Calendar.

39. JUDSON, A. C. Review of Renwick's The Shepheardes Calendar. MLN XLVII (1932). 473-5.

Discusses the ecclesiastical sonnets.

40. ———— A Biographical Sketch of John Young, Bishop of Rochester, With Emphasis on his Relations with Edmund Spenser. Indiana University Studies XXI (1934). No. 103. 1-41. See esp. 20-4, 36-9.

Relation of SC to Sp's secretaryship under Young. Dido ("November") may be Susan Young; Lobbie = Bishop Young. Cf. Padelford, F. M. in PMLA XXXI (1916). 713 ff; ante, No. 7; post, No. 62; Legouis, É. Edmund Spenser. Paris, 1923, p. 41.

41. KLUGE, F. Spenser's Shepherd's Calendar und Mantuan's Eclogen. Anglia III (1880).

Rev. Amer. Jour. Philol. I (1880). 494—a summary.

42. KUERSTEINER, AGNES D. E. K. is Spenser. PMLA L (1935). 140-55.

43. LONG, P. W. Spenser's Rosalind. Anglia XXXI (1908).

Rev. Shakes. Jahr. 45 (1909). 287.

44. ———— The Name "Shepherds' Calendar." Archiv CXXXI (1913).

Rev. Shakes. Jahr. 51 (1915). 222.

45. Monthly Rev. CL (1839). 98-9. Quotes Hallam's Introduction to Literature of Europe, II, 190, on SC.

46. MUSTARD, W. P. E. K.'s Note on the Graces. MLN XLV (1930). 168-9.

Illustrations of the classical allusion in E. K.'s note on SC IV, 109.

47. NEWBOLT, SIR HENRY. "Some Poets and Their Scenery." Essays by Divers Hands. Being the Transactions of the Royal Society of Literature of the United Kingdom. New Series. V. Oxford, 1925. Ed. John Drinkwater.

130-2: Influence of Sicilian pastoral on Sp. Rev. TLS 24 (Sept. 3, 1925). 567.

48. NICHOLS, JOHN. The Progresses and Public Processions of Queen Elizabeth. London, 1823. 3 vols.
    III, 55-8: "Hobbinoll's Dittie in Prayse of Eliza Queene of the Sheepheards." (Webbe's imitation of this follows).

49. Notes and Queries, ser. iii. V (1864). 118-9. Bathurst's Latin translation.

50. PADELFORD, F. M. Spenser and *The Pilgrimage of the Life of Man.* SP XXVIII (1931). 216-7.
    Similarity of SC "May" and "September" to Lydgate's translation of *Pilgrimage.*

51. PANTLING, CONSTANCE. Poetic Wit. The Renaissance and Seventeenth Century. (From a lecture by T. S. Eliot at the British Institute). Rev. de l'Enseign. des Lang. Viv. 51ᵉ· an. (1934). 86-8, 134-5, 180-2.
    SC illustrates "pastoralism and petrarchianism and verbal floridity" and the "tendency towards a purely English idiom and a natural simplicity."

52. Parker Society. James Calfhill's Answer to John Martiall's Treatise of the Cross. Cambridge, 1846.
    47n, 52n: SC "March," 166, and "May," 309.

53. PARMENTER, MARY. Colin Clout and Hobbinoll: a reconsideration of the relationship of Edmund Spenser and Gabriel Harvey. Diss., The Johns Hopkins University, 1933.

54. PATTISON, BRUCE. The Roundelay in the August Eclogue of *The Shepheardes Calender.* RES IX (1933). 54-5.
    The rough diction may have source in contemporary tunes. *Rev.* YWES XIV (1933). 228.

55. PEARSON, A. F. SCOTT. Thomas Cartwright and Elizabethan Puritanism. Cambridge University Press, 1925.
    188-9: Thomalin in "July" is Cartwright.

56. PURDY, MARY M. Elizabethan Literary Treatments of the Proposed Marriages of Queen Elizabeth. Univ. of Pittsburgh Bull., Abstracts of Dissertations IV (1928). 147-53.
    Ch. VII: Sp and the Leicester marriage proposals (SC, FQ, MHT).

57. Reissert, O. Bemerkungen über Spenser's *Shepheards Calendar* und die frühere Bukolik. Anglia IX (1886).
    Rev. Amer. Jour. Philol. VIII (1887). 239-40.

58. Revue de l'Enseign. des Langues Vivantes 51è· an. (1934). 88-90.
    Quels genres littéraires définis sont employés par Spenser dans le Calendrier? *ibid.,* 462-3: Assignments for grammatical commentary on SC.

59. Royster, James F. E. K.'s " Elf < Guelph, Goblin < Ghibelline." MLN XLIII (1928). 249-52.
    E. K.'s fantastic etymology and evidence that it was repeated, with no reference to E. K., as late as 1671.

60. Smith, G. C. Moore. Spenser, *Shepherd's Calendar,* " November." MLR II (1907).
    Rev. Shakes. Jahr. 44 (1908). 284.

61. ——— MLR XXVI (1931). 456-9.

62. Stirling, Brents. Spenser and Thomas Watson, Bishop of Lincoln. PQ X (1931). 321-8.
    The Oak (" Feb.") identified as Thomas Watson, who, in Jan. 1578-9, was in the custody of John Young. *Cf. ante,* Nos. 7, 40.

63. Taylor, Rupert. The Political Prophecy in England. Diss., Columbia University, 1911.
    131-2: Sp.

64. Tillyard, E. M. W. Poetry Direct and Oblique. London, 1934.
    57-8: SC.

65. Times Literary Supplement. London. 30 (Feb. 5, 1931). 95.

66. Ward, B. M. The Seventeenth Earl of Oxford, 1550-1604. London, 1928.
    359-69: Pleasant Willy = Sidney; Gentle Spirit = Edw. deVere; see also index and appendix. Discusses identifications made by Malone, Bond, and E. K. Chambers. Rejects Lyly and Tarleton.

67. Welply, W. H. Spenser's Mistress Rosalind. NQ, ser. xiii. IX (1927). 389. *Cf. ibid.,* 350, by P. D. M.
    Cites Aubrey MS on Rosalind; suggests Sir Erasmus Dryden was cognizant of Sp's affairs, esp. the Chancery suit of Nov. 1596. Lady Dryden's pedigree may yield information about Rosalind's identity.

68. ——— Edmund Spenser. NQ, ser. xiv. VI (1932). 130-2.

69. WHITNEY, GEFFREY. Choice of Emblemes, 1586. Repr. in facs. Ed. Henry Green.

ix-x, xxiv, xxv, lxvi, 324-5: Sp's use of *Emblemes* in SC.

70. WILLIAMS, A. J. Baconiana, n. s. X (1902). 54-5.

71. WOODWARD, PARKER. Baconiana, 3rd. ser. IX (1911). 256 ff.

72. YATES, FRANCES A. John Florio. The Life of an Italian in Shakespeare's England. Cambridge University Press, 1934.

48-50: " Second Fruits " mentions Sp. On Rosalind, etc. See index.

TEARS OF THE MUSES

See " Editions," i, v; " Minor Poems, Complaints "; " Criticism before 1651," No. 33; " Spenser and Sidney," No. 18; " Addenda," No. 18.

1. CHAMBERS, SIR E. K. The Elizabethan Stage. London, 1923.

III, 412: Pleasant Willy = John Lyly, though Tarleton may be meant.

2. DAVIS, B. E. C. Our Pleasant Willy. NQ, ser. xii. XII (1923). 323-4.

" That Willy is not the same as ' that same gentle Spirit ' of I, 217; that ' Willy ' is Tarleton, and the ' same gentle Spirit ' is Lyly. The stanza a later interpolation. TM written *ca.* 1585. The interpolation, 1589." [F. I. C. and A. P.]

3. DAVISON, FRANCIS. A Poeticall Rhapsody. Ed. Hyder E. Rollins. Cambridge University Press, 1932.

II, 109 ff.: Willy in *Poet. Rhap.* is Sidney, but Sp's Willy is Richard Willey or Willes.

4. Gentleman's Mag. LXIX (1799). ii. 1067.

Is Willy the actor William Johnson. *Cf.* also, *ibid.,* # 4.

5. HEYWOOD, THOMAS. The Earls of Derby and the Verse Writers and Poets of the Sixteenth and Seventeenth Centuries. Chetham Soc. Pub., 1853. No. XXIX.

37-8: Sp's references to Lady Strange.

6. HOLLAND, H. H. Shakespeare, Oxford, and Elizabethan Times. London, 1933.

86, 208: TM (Willy) and *Venus and Adonis.* One of these is a paraphrase of the other.

7. JACKSON, B. G. Study of Spenser's *Tears of the Muses.*
M. A. Thesis, University of Washington, 1912.

8. JONES, H. S. V. A Spenser Handbook.
Ch. VI: Teares of the Muses.

9. LOTSPEICH, HENRY G. Spenser's Urania. MLN L
(1935). 141-6.
Sp's fusion, in Urania's lament, of astronomical themes (classical
element) and theological themes can be paralleled only in DuBartas'
Deuine Weeke and *Urania.* Sp is following the major contemporary
French poet in making the fusion. *Cf.* "FQ, General," Nos. 8, 142;
"FQ, Sources," No. 120; "Addenda," No. 10.

10. NICHOLSON, BR. A Literary Craze. NQ, ser. vi. XI
(1885). 252; *ibid.,* 158, by A. Hall.
Pleasant Willy = Lyly.

11. PADELFORD, F. M. The Muse of the *Faerie Queene.* SP
XXVII (1930). 111-24.

12. STIRLING, BRENTS. Terpsichore's Lament and "Pleasant
Willie." JEGP XXX (1931). 556-62.
Terpsichore's lament arraigns the jig, of which Tarleton was
prime exponent. Tarleton and "Pleasant Willie," then, are anti-
thetical. These considerations remove one difficulty in assigning TM
to Sp's early period.

13. STOTSENBURG, JOHN H. Sidney's Shake-speare Sonnets.
Baconiana, old ser. I (1892). 53 ff.
58-9: Sp and Sidney in TM. *Cf.* also p. 54.

14. TWITCHETT, E. G. London Merc. XX (1929). 633.

15. WARD, B. M. The Seventeenth Earl of Oxford. London,
1928.
267-8: Sidney = Pleasant Willy; Oxford = Gentle Spirit; 364-7:
Rejects Tarleton identification. *Rev.* MLN XLIV (1929). 202-3,
by E. G.[reenlaw].

16. WILLIAMS, A. J. Baconiana, n. s. X (1902). 101.

THEATRE OF WORLDLINGS

See "Visions of Petrarch"; "Editions," i, v; "Minor
Poems, Complaints"; Spenser's Circle," No. 32.

1. FLETCHER, J. B. Spenser's Earliest Translations. JEGP
XIII (1914).
Rev. Shakes. Jahr. 51 (1915). 222.

2. FRIEDLAND, LOUIS S. Spenser's Earliest Translations. JEGP XII (1913).
Rev. Shakes. Jahr. 50 (1914). 145.

3. GALLAND, RENÉ. Un Poète Errant de la Renaissance, Jean van der Noot et l'Angleterre. Rev. de Litt. comparée II (1922). 337-50.
"A study of Noot's life, based on Vermeylen. Doubts Sp's authorship of the sonnets. Thinks Noot stimulated Sp's interest in pictures (Emblems). Probable influence of Noot's epic, l'Olympiade, on Sp. Parallelism. 'Spenser done l'impression d'être inépuisable comme une force de la nature.'" [F. I. C. and A. P.]

4. HUNTER, JOSEPH. Chorus Vatum . . . B. M. Addit. MS 24,489.
Fol. 109 ff.: Van der Noot and Sp. Cf. ante, No. 3; post, Nos. 5, 6.

5. PIENAAR, W. J. B. Edmund Spenser and Jonker van der Noot. Eng. Stud. VIII (1926). 33-44, 67-76.
Relation of Sp and Noot in production of Theatre and Noot's influence on Sp. French the working basis of the translation; Italian and Dutch versions consulted. Theatre a landmark in national literature; its influence on Sp's later work. [A. P.]

6. ———— Spenser's Complaints. TLS 23 (Dec. 4, 1924). 825.

7. SISSON, CHARLES J. Grafton and the London Grey Friars. The Library, 4th. ser. XI (1930-1). 121-49.
131-2: John Vandernote, physician, is author of the treatise on the plague, printed 1569. He died in 1555. This is probably not the poet. Cf. ante, No. 4.

THE VIEW OF IRELAND

See "Life, Miscellaneous," Nos. 20, 22, 37, 60; "Spenser and Sidney," No. 10; "Editions," i, No. 20 and v, No. 32; "Apocrypha," No. 9; "Style, Diction," Nos. 18, 23; "Addenda," No. 17.

1. A Statute of the Fortieth Year of King Edward III . . . Ed. James Hardiman for the Irish Archaeological Society. Dublin, 1843.
115n: Sp's project of reforming the "mere Irish" mentioned.

2. *Advertisement for Ireland, being a description of the State of Ireland in the reign of James I. Dublin Soc. of Antiquaries, 1923. [A. P.]

3. Ancient Irish Histories. The Works of Spenser, Campion, Hanmer, and Marleburrough. Dublin, 1809.
Vol. I: Sp's *Veue.*

4. Anti-Jacobin Rev. XXII (1805). 310; XXIV (1806). 134.
Quotations from the *Veue.*

5. Athenaeum. 1869. I. 58. Letter from J. P. Collier about text used for his edition of *Veue.*

6. BAUER, R. Die Iren und irischen Verhaltnisse der Elizabethanischen Zeit in der Darstellung von Edm. Spenser und der " Calenders of the Carew Papers." Diss., Halle, 1924 [?].
Rev. YWES VI (1925). 169.

7. BELLOC, HILAIRE. A Shorter History of England. New York, 1934.
341: Sp.

8. Blackwood's Mag. XXXI (1832). 379 ff: Sp's *Veue,* etc.; CXXVIII (1880). 244.
" Irish Distress and its Origin," quotes *Veue*, saying it has " held good down to the present day."

9. BUCHANAN, GEORGE. " Rerum Scoticarum Historia." Opera Omnia. Edinburgh, 1715. Vol. I.
See Carpenter, Ref. Guide, 207 for note.

10. Catalogue of MSS in Trinity Coll., Dublin. Ed. T. K. Abbott. Dublin, 1900.
No. 589: " Eudoxus and Irenaeus " fol. Chart. s. xvi. " Dialogue betweene Eudoxus and Irenaeus on the History of Ireland, 1596." *Cf.* Carpenter, Ref. Guide, 208: " Spenser " does not occur in the index. But see " Eudoxus."

11. Catalogi Cod. MSS Bibl. Bodl., Partis Quintae. Oxon., 1862.
No. B. 478. MS *V. of I.* carries this note; and the names of former owners.
" olim possedit " Johannes Panton, Lincoln; postea Ricardus Basnett.
Note: " Mr. Collings, I pray enter this copie for Mathew Lownes to be prynted when he doe bringe other attoryte. Thomas Man."

Photostat copy of this MS among *Rotographs of Manuscripts and Rare Printed Books. Modern Language Association.* Deposited at the Library of Congress. # 250.

12. CLINCHE, BRYAN J. The First Century of Religious Persecution in Ireland. Amer. Cath. Quart. Rev. X (1885). 269 ff.

   278: Sp quoted as " eye-witness " of Irish condition.

13. COLE, GEORGE W. Bibliographical Pitfalls—Linked Books. Papers of Bibl. Society of America XVIII (1924). 12-30.

   Bacon's *The Use of the Law* and Sp's *Veue.* Discusses *Veue,* published along with Campion, Hanmer, etc. [A. P.]

14. COLGAN, NATHANIEL. The Shamrock in Literature: A Critical Chronology. Roy. Soc. Antiq. Ire., 5th. ser. VIII (1896). 211 ff.

   218: *Veue* refers to shamrocks (water-cresses?). *Cf. post,* No. 24.

15. COLLIER, J. P. (ed.). Trevelyan Papers. A. D. 1446-1643. Camden Soc., 1863.

   Vol. 84: Papers from and about Ireland during and just after Sp's time. Chiefly for Sir Arthur Chichester.

16. COVINGTON, F. F., JR. Spenser in Ireland. Diss., Yale University, 1924.

17. ——— Spenser's Use of Irish History in the *View of the Present State of Ireland.* Texas Studies in English IV (1924). 5-38.

   Sp's knowledge of Irish history; his chief sources; his point of view (always English); his reliance upon memory for Irish history. *Rev.* YWES VI (1925). 168.

18. Devereux Papers with Richard Broughton's Memoranda (1575-1601). Camden Miscellany XIII. Ed. Henry E. Malden. London, 1923.

   viii: The universality of Sp's assumption (FQ and *Veue*) that Irish rebels were enemies of " cause of God."

19. Dublin Rev. X (1841). 218, 222-3. The Wants of Ireland.

   Quotes *Veue.*

20. Dunlop, R. The Plantation of Munster, 1584-1589. EHR III (1888). 250-69.

" The basic account. That it was suggested by Perrot's Report, 1582. Started at favorable time when Munster was largely depopulated and its lands forfeited by rebellion, but its prospects thwarted by the frequent pardons in subsequent years involving many titles in litigation; the undertakers were left to fight the Irish claims. A Commission on titles, 1588, was ruthless against the Irish . . . and so the scheme proved a failure. The early survey was incompetent. The various plans ill conceived and poorly supported . . . Sp's comment on the Plantation (*V. of I.*)." [F. I. C. and A. P.]

21. ——— Ireland Under the Commonwealth. Manchester, 1913. 2 vols.

I, lix: Sp. [F. I. C. and A. P.]

22. ——— An Unpublished Survey of the Plantation of Munster in 1622. Roy. Soc. Antiq. Ire. LIV (1924). 128-46.

Excerpts from B. Mus. Sloane MS 4756, fol. 80 sqq., dating after 1622 (May 12) when James I appointed a commission for the survey. 143-4: The Seignory of Kilcolman in 1622. Refers to the condition of Sp's property and describes the new house, etc.

23. Edinburgh Rev. X (1807). 41; XLI (1824-5). 405; LXXXVII (1848). 319-20.

Quotations from the *Veue*.

24. Frazer, W. The Shamrock: its History. Roy. Soc. Antiq. Ire., 5th. ser. IV (1894). 132.

Sp's references to shamrocks. *Cf. ante*, No. 14.

25. General Catalogue of Books in all Languages, Arts and Sciences, that have been printed in Ireland, and published in Dublin, from the year 1700, to the Present Time. Dublin, 1791.

69: " Spencer's View of the State of Ireland. 12mo."

26. Gentleman's Mag. LXIX ii (1799). 1067.

What is Sp's animal " garron," in *Veue*?

27. Gottfried, Rudolf B. A Veue of the Presente State of Ireland, by Edmund Spenser. Diss., Yale University, 1935.

28. ——— Spenser's Ireland Dialogue. TLS 35 (Feb. 8, 1936). 116.

Connection of the *Veue* with some contemporary notes on Ireland.

29. HENLEY, PAULINE. Spenser in Ireland. Cork, 1928.
Ch. VII: Sp and Political Thought. *Rev.* TLS 27 (1928). 422.

30. HERBERT, SIR WILLIAM. Croftus: sive de Hibernia Liber. Pr. from MS. Ed. W. E. Buckley. Roxburghe Club, 1887.
"In Latin, by one of the 'undertakers' *c*. 1583. A description of Ireland, sketch of history, on traits of Irish, outline of policy, etc. 37 ff. Urges 'colonization of parts of Ireland,' gives reasons why previous attempts have failed. . . . Some points of argument like *V. of I*." [F. I. C. and A. P.]

31. HORE, HERBERT F. Extracts from the Irish Correspondence in H. M. State Paper Office. Kilkenny Arch. Soc., n. s. II (1858-9). 331 ff.
Documents relating to 1558-72. [R. Heffner]

32. HULL, ELEANOR. A History of Ireland and Her People to the Close of the Tudor Period. London, 1926.
Index: References to Sp's years in Ireland.

33. HUNTER, JOSEPH. Chorus Vatum . . . B. M. Addit. MS 24,490.
Fol. 25: In Cott. Titus B. XII. No. 129 are folio leaves said to be in the hand of Sir Philip Sidney "which undoubtedly they may be though the letter is larger and taller" than Sidney's usual hand. Quotes a portion of a treatise which may be Sp's. [It is Sidney's.] *Cf. post*, No. 57.

34. JENKINS, CLAUDE. The Church and Religion in the Age of Shakespeare. Lecture delivered at University Coll., London, Oct. 28, 1929. History, n. s. XV (1930-1). 199-211.
210: Refers to Dean Church on Sp's treatment of State of Ireland.

35. JONES, H. S. V. Spenser's Defense of Lord Grey.
Rev. EHR XXXVI (1921). 306, by F. J. R.; Archiv CXLVII (1924). 148; The Nation (N. Y.) CX (1920). 555-6, by Preserved Smith; Sewanee Rev. XXIX (1921). 252-3, by L. W. F.

36. ———— A Spenser Handbook.
Ch. XXX: View of Ireland.

37. JOYCE, P. W. An illustrated History of Ireland. London, 1919.
128, 226, 230: Sp. Negligible.

38. KEATING, GEOFFREY (*ca.* 1570-1650). History of Ireland. Address to Reader. Facs. and translation given. Facsimiles of National Manuscripts of Ireland. Ed. John T. Gilbert. London, 1884. Pt. IV, ii.
Plate LXXIII B. Keating lists Sp among historians who have tried to vilify Ireland.

39. *KEYES, EVA B. Spenser and his Political Philosophy. In MS material relating to Spenser, by students of the University of Chicago.
Copy in Newberry Library, presented by Dr. Carpenter.

40. Kilkenny Arch. Soc., n. s. I (1856-7). 94 ff. Extracts from the Irish Correspondence in H. M. State Papers Office.
100: Sp's " contemporary vilification " of O'Byrne.

41. LONGFIELD, ADA. Anglo-Irish Trade in the Sixteenth Century as illustrated by the English Customs Accounts and Port Books. Proc. Roy. Irish Acad. XXXVI. C. (1924). 317 ff.
324-5: Cites *Veue* on Irish clothing.

42. Maps of Ireland. Six sixteenth century MS maps of Ireland. Photostat reproductions from copies in B. M. and Trinity College, Dublin. Copies in Newberry Library, presented by Dr. Carpenter.
1. Irelande . . . collected surueied by Baptista Boazio . . . engraved by Renolde Elstrack. Lond., Sudbury, 1578. Trin. Coll., Dublin.
2. Prouence of Munster . . . by Francis Jobson. MS on paper, 1589. Trin. Coll., Dublin.
3. Map of Ireland. MS on paper, 1570-2. B. M.
4. Map of Ireland. MS on paper, 1570-2. B. M.
5. Hibernia . . . engraved by Bolognino Zaltieri. In his *Britanniae Insulae . . . Nova Descriptio . . .* Venice, 1565. B. M. *Cf.* Carpenter, Ref. Guide, 213.
6. Map of the County of Cork. In colors on vellum. By Francis Jobson, *ca.* 1589. Trin. Coll., Dublin.

43. McGOVERN, J. B. Irish Book Lover II (1910-1). 59. Promise of O'Donovan's review of *Veue.*

44. MARTIN, WILLIAM CLIFF. The Date and Purpose of Spenser's *Veue.* PMLA XLVII (1932). 137-43.
Date of the *Veue* is mid-summer, 1596. " One noble person " is Essex rather than Drake [Grosart's suggestion]. Purpose is to

win himself favor at Court. His plans "are drawn almost wholly
from contemporary proposals and estimates." *Rev.* YWES XIII
(1932). 194; Shakes. Jahr. 69 (1933). 197.

45. MAXWELL, CONSTANTIA E. Irish History from Contemporary Sources, 1509-1610. London, 1923.
250-2: Sp's *Briefe Note of Ireland.*

46. MERRILL, ELIZABETH. The Dialogue in English Literature.
37-8, 64: Sp's use of the form.

47. MEZGER, FRITZ. Der Ire in der englischen Literatur bis
zum Anfang des 19 Jahrhunderts. Leipsig, 1929.
(Palaestra CLXIX).
37-43: Veue. *Rev.* Eng. Stud. XIII (1931). 150-1, by A. G.
Van Hamel.

48. North British Rev. VII (1847). 538. Quotes *Veue.*

49. O'RAHILLY, THOMAS F. Irish Poets, Historians, and
Judges in English Documents, 1538-1615. Proc. Roy.
Irish Acad. XXXVI. C. (1922). 86-120.
86: Cites *Veue.*

50. O'SCINGIN, JAMES. Statement written for Sir Edw.
Fyton, Pres. of Connacht, by Brehon on Old Irish Law,
1571. Facsimiles of the National Manuscripts in Ireland. Ed. John T. Gilbert. London, 1882. Pt. IV, i.
xxix-xxx: Quotes *Veue* on Irish custom of " Caenn Coguis."

51. PERROTT, SIR JAMES. The Chronicle of Ireland, 1584-
1608. Ed. Herbert Wood. Dublin (The Stationers'
Office), 1933.
Refers to many of Sp's circle, though not to Sp. See index.

52. PRAZ, MARIO. Machiavelli and the Elizabethans. Proc.
Brit. Acad. XIV. London, 1928.
56: Sp's use of Machiavelli in the *Veue.*

53. Quarterly Rev. XXXVIII (1828). 54, 535-6. Quotes
Veue.

54. RENWICK, W. L. Review of F. R. Johnson, A Critical
Bibliography . . . MLR XXIX (1934). 448.
Ware's exemplar of the *Veue* was not the MS in Trin. Coll.,
Dublin.

12

55. RICH, BARNABE. Greenes Newes both from Heauen and Hell, by B. R. Repr. from original edition, by R. B. McKerrow. Stratford, 1922.

56. S., H. K. St. J. Author's Errors. Spenser. NQ, ser. xi. V (1912). 248; 358, by A. R. Bayley.

Sp's confusion of Lionel, Duke of Clarence, and George, brother of Edward IV.

57. SIDNEY, SIR PHILIP. Discourse on Irish Affairs. Cotton MS Titus Bxii. No. 129. Printed in Sidney's *Defense of Poetry*. . . . Ed. A. Feuillerat. Cambridge University Press, 1923. Pp. 46-50.

" A defense of Sir H. Sidney's policy in Ireland, 1577-8. A fragment. For the criticism of Sidney to which this is an answer see Cott. MS Titus B x, 115 ff." [F. I. C. and A. P.] *Cf. ante,* No. 33.

58. STAFFORD, T. Pacata Hibernia. Ireland appeased and reduced, or an historie of the late Warres of Ireland, especially within the province of Mounster, under the Government of Sir George Carew, Knight, then Lord President of that province, and afterwards Lord Carew of Clopton, and Earle of Totnes, etc., wherein the Siedge of Kinsale, the Defeat of the Earle of Tyrone and his Armie, the Expulsion and sending home of Don Juan de Aguila, the Spanish Generall, with his forces, etc., are related, *with fine oval portrait of Queen Eliza- beth, Hondius's map of Mounster, folding plates of battles, Cahir Castle taken by Earl of Essex,* 1599, *Glin Castle, Limerick, The Cittie of Limerick, Youghal, Corke,* etc. Printed by Aug. Mathews for Robert Mil- bourne, 1633. [R. Heffner] See *Short Title Catalogue.*

59. THEOBALD, BERTRAM G. Francis Bacon Concealed and Revealed. London, 1930.

46: The *Veue* is another piece of camouflage of Bacon's identity.

60. WARE, SIR JAMES. . . . De Hibernia et Antiquitatibus Ejus . . . (1633). Ed. by Samuel Hartlib. A Collec- tion of Tracts and Treatises . . . illustrative of . . . Ireland. London, 1860.

I, 187: Sp and the *Veue*.

61. WESTROPP, THOMAS J. Promontory Forts in the County Kerry. Roy. Soc. Antiq. Ire. XL (1910). 179 ff.

193-204: Account of Smerwick; 196-8: Sp's defense of Lord Grey.

62. ———— President's Address. Proc. Roy. Soc. Antiq. Ire. XLVI (1916-7). 1 ff.

4: Refers to "more or less trustworthy essays by Edmund Spenser, Edmund Campion, and Meredith Hanmer . . ."

63. ———— A Commonplace Book Relating to Ireland. Roy. Soc. Antiq. Ire. XXIX (1899). 429.

244: Refers to Sir Richard Cox's description of Co. Cork.

64. WILSON, PHILIP. The Writings of Sir James Ware and The Forgeries of Robert Ware. Trans. Bibl. Soc. XV (1917). 83 ff.

84: Mentions Ware's publication of *Veue*, 1633.

VIRGIL'S GNAT

See "Editions," i, v; "Minor Poems, Complaints."

1. FRANK, TENNEY. Vergil; A Biography. New York, 1922.

Ch. III: The Culex. A discussion of the poem which Sp translates.

2. HUGHES, MERRITT Y. Virgil and Spenser. Univ. of California Pub. in English II, No. 3 (1929).

309-14: Virgil's Gnat. An Interchapter. Sp's treatment of the Latin text. *Cf. ante,* No. 1.

3. JONES, H. S. V. A Spenser Handbook.

Ch. VII: Virgil's Gnat.

4. LOTSPEICH, HENRY G. Spenser's *Virgil's Gnat* and the Latin Original. ELH II (1935). 235-41.

5. LOWELL, D. O. S. and C. KNAPP. Vergilianism. CW XXVIII (1934). 41 ff.

43-4: The Culex. Sp's versification of this at VG 313-28.

6. MILLICAN, C. B. RES X (1934). 350-3.

7. RUSSELL, I. WILLIS. Spenser's *Virgil's Gnat* and the Earl of Leicester. No. 17. Proceedings of Dr. Greenlaw's Seminary " C," 1928-9. The Johns Hopkins University.

THE VISIONS OF BELLAY

See " Editions," i, v; " Minor Poems, Complaints," esp. No. 7; " Life, Miscellaneous," No. 22.

1. Amer. Journal of Philology XXIII (1902). 464.
   Reports Koeppel's and Fletcher's notes.

2. JONES, H. S. V. A Spenser Handbook.
   Ch. XII: The Visions of Bellay.

3. Quarterly Rev. XXXIV (1826). 316n.
   Sp's version of Bellay's
     " Rome de Rome est le seul monument "
   is better than the original.

THE VISIONS OF PETRARCH

See " Editions," i, v; " Minor Poems, Complaints," esp. No. 7; " Life, Miscellaneous," No. 22.

1. JONES, H. S. V. A Spenser Handbook.
   Ch. XII: The Visions of Petrarch.

2. JUSSERAND, J. J. Spenser's *Visions of Petrarch*. Athenaeum 1902.
   Rev. Shakes. Jahr. 39 (1903). 326.

VISIONS OF THE WORLD'S VANITY

See " Editions," i, v; " Minor Poems, Complaints."

1. JONES, H. S. V. A Spenser Handbook.
   Ch. XI: Visions of the World's Vanitie.

III.
CRITICISM, INFLUENCE, ALLUSIONS

III. CRITICISM, INFLUENCE, ALLUSIONS

In General

See "Editions," esp. i, ii, iii, v, for editorial and reviewers' comments; "Criticism before 1651"; "Criticism after 1651"; "Addenda," Nos. 19-20.

1. BOUCHIER, JONATHAN. Spenser. NQ, ser. iv. XII (1873). 206.
   Spenser ranks below Shakespeare and Milton.

2. BOHME, TRAUGOTT. Spensers literarisches Nachleben bis zu Shelley. Berlin, 1911.
   Last chapter the same as in Berlin Diss., 1909, "Spensers Einfluss auf Shelley." *Rev.* Engl. Stud. XLIV (1912). 403-8, by F. Brie; Shakes. Jahr. 48 (1912). 348-9.

3. BRADNER, LEICESTER. The Use of Spenser in the Propaganda of the Commonwealth Period. Paper read before the Mod. Lang. Ass., 1932. *Cf.* PMLA XLVII (*Proc.*, 1932). 1335.

4. BRINKLEY, ROBERTA F. The Commonwealth Adaptation of Spenser's Political Allegory. Paper read before the Mod. Lang. Ass., 1932. *Cf.* PMLA XLVII (*Proc.*, 1932). 1335.

5. ———— Arthurian Legend in the Seventeenth Century. Johns Hopkins Monographs in Literary History. No. 3. The Johns Hopkins Press, 1932.
   151-64: Sp as source for 17th. c. Arthurian epic (Blackmore's completion of Sp's plan by portrayal of Arthur's political virtues). *Rev.* Rev. ang.-amér. 10ᵉ· an. (1932-3). 145-8, by É. Legouis; TLS 31 (July 21, 1932). 521-2. *The Matter of Britain*; MLN XLVIII (1933). 267-8, by J. J. Parry; Eng. Stud. XV (1933). 69-71, by A. G. Van Kranendonk; RES X (1934). 101-2, by C. B. Millican; Anglia Beibl. XLV (1934). 50-2, by Hans Marcus.

6. BUSH, DOUGLAS. Some Allusions to Spenser. MLN XLII (1927). 314-6.
   Allusions from 1592-1801.

7. *CARPENTER, FREDERIC I. Survey of the Renaissance. Lecture on Spenser. n. d. MS, University of Chicago Library.

163

8. CORY, H. E. The Critics of Edmund Spenser. Univ. of California, 1911.
   Rev. Shakes. Jahr. 49 (1913). 219; Athenaeum. 1911. II. 156.

9. ———— Spenser, the School of the Fletchers, and Milton. Univ. of California, Pub. in Mod. Philol. II (1910-2).

10. DOTTIN, PAUL. La Littérature Anglaise. Paris, 1931.
    34-7: Sp.

11. GRANT, A. J. Ariosto. History, n. s. XX (1935). 18-28.
    24: Sp one of great imaginative writers of 16th. c.

12. HARRIS, R. B. The Beast in English Satire from Spenser to John Gay. Summaries of Theses, Harvard University, 1932. 254-7.
    Sp's influence on beast satire (MHT).

13. HARRISON, CHARLES T. The Ancient Atomists and English Humanism of the Seventeenth Century. Summaries of Theses, Harvard University, 1932. 257-9.
    Sp's influence on 17th c. poets. Sp first who gave an English verse translation of Lucretius.

14. HUNTER JOSEPH. Chorus Vatum . . . B. M. Addit. MSS.
    MS 24,487: fol. 4, 11, 27ᵛ-8, 29, 49, 59, 71, 73, 74, 81, 119, 158, 165, 187, 223, 243.
    MS 24,488: fol. 105ᵛ, 131, 133, 135, 143, 210, 250, 254.
    MS 24,489: fol. 31, 52, 62, 85, 86, 179, 298.
    MS 24,490: fol. 84, 132, 139, 188, 226, 254, 256ᵛ, 263.
    MS 24,491: fol. 31, 45, 58, 136, 257.

15. LAWRENCE, C. E. The Poet's Poet. Bookman (London) 72 (1927). 261-2.
    Sp's influence on the great poets down to Keats.

16. MAAR, HARKO GERIT DE. Elizabethan Romance in the Eighteenth Century. Zalt-Bommel, 1924.
    Chs. II, III, IV, V, VII and App. II, III: List of Spenser imitations, 1595-1785. Not a complete list. See *Allusion Book,* forthcoming.

17. MORTON, E. P. The Spenserian Stanza before 1700. MP IV (1907).
    Rev. Shakes. Jahr. 44 (1908). 284.

18. Osgood, C. G. The Voice of England. New York, 1935.
See index "Spenser" for Sp's influence in English literature.
163-70: Sp sketch and criticism.

19. Patterson, R. F. (ed.). Six Centuries of English
Literature. London, 1933.
I: Chaucer to Spenser. Intro. by W. L. Renwick. *Rev.* TLS 32
(July 6, 1933). 460, 466.

20. Pienaar, W. J. B. English Influences in Dutch Literature and Justus van Effen as Intermediary. Cambridge
University Press, 1929.
ix, 10, 11: Van der Noodt and Sp; 225: Van Effen on Sp.

21. Reschke, Hedwig. Die Spenserstanze bei den Spensernachahmern des Neunzehnten Jahrhundert.
Rev. Engl. Stud. 53 (1919-20). 430-2, by Walther Fischer.

22. Revue de l'Enseign. des Lang. Viv. 51è· an. (1934).
60-4.
Lyrical fervor of 16th. c. must be sought in Sp. A general discussion of Renaissance figures and attitudes.

23. Sélincourt, Hugh de. The Successors of Spenser.
Cambridge History of English Literature. IV, ch. IX.

24. Sharp, Robert L. The Revolt Against the Metaphysical
Poetry. A Study in the Development of Neo-Classicism
in England. Summaries of Theses, Harvard University, 1932. 278-81.
The active strains emerging from the 16th. c. and affecting the 17th.
Best expressed in Spenserianism, which opposed "extravagance,
obscurity, and roughness."

25. *Shevyrev, S. P. Istoriya poezii. Moskva, 1835.

26. Spurgeon, Caroline F. E. Five Centuries of Chaucer
Criticism and Allusion. London, 1925. 3 vols.
Many allusions to Sp. See index.

27. Walker, Hugh. The Revelation of England Through
her Poetry. (Warton Lecture on English Poetry).
Proc. Brit. Acad. VIII. London, 1917.
181 ff.: Sp. Not important.

28. White, Harold O. Plagiarism and Imitation During
the English Renaissance. Cambridge, Mass., 1935.
96-7: Sp's imitative methods. Quotes E. K. and *Letters*. See
index. *Rev.* MLN LI (1936). 198-9, by Douglas Bush.

CRITICISM BEFORE 1651

See " Spenser and Shakespeare," Nos. 6, 9, 11, 14; " Addenda," Nos. 39-43.

1. BEAUMONT, FRANCIS.

> *Cf.* Baldwin, T. W. The Three Francis Beaumonts. MLN XXXIX (1924). 505-7.
> Francis Beaumont, Master of Charterhouse, is the man whose praise of Sp is referred to in Carpenter, Ref. Guide, 231.

2. BENSLY, EDWARD. The Name "Hudibras." NQ 168 (Mar. 2, 1935). 160.

> Notes Zachary Grey's suggestion that Butler took the name from FQ II, ii, 17.

3. BOLTON, EDMUND. *Hypercritica. Oxford, 1722.

> *Cf.* Hunter, Joseph. Chorus Vatum . . . B. M. Addit. MS 24,487, fol. 4.
> *Nero Caesar, or Monarchie Depraved. An Historicall Worke. . . . By the Translator of Lucius Florus. London . . . 1624. [E. A. Strathmann] 161: Sp's placing the battle between Boadicea and the Romans on the river Severn. *Cf.* Hunter, Joseph. Chorus Vatum . . . B. M. Addit. MS 24,490, fol. 470.

4. BROWNE, WILLIAM.

> *Cf.* Barber, Cora L. Spenser's Influence on William Browne. M. A. Thesis, Columbia University, 1905; Retrospective Rev. II (1820). 149, 151, 156, 171, 184: The *Pastorals* and Sp.; Durkee, Cora L. *Britannia's Pastorals* as a Spenserian Imitation. M. A. Thesis, Yale University, 1926.

5. CAREW, THOMAS. Poems. Ed. with memoir by W. Carew Hazlitt. Roxburghe Library, 1870. "A Rapture," p. 65. [J. G. McManaway]

6. Catalogue of the Pamphlets, Books, Newspapers, and Manuscripts Relating to the Civil War, the Commonwealth, and Restoration, collected by George Thomason, 1640-1661. London, 1908.

> I, 655: [July 27] "The Faerie Leveller; or, King Charles his Leveller described in Queene Elizabeth's dayes. By Edmond Spenser in his unparaleld Poeme, entituled The Faerie Queene. [Stanzas 29-54, Bk. V, canto ii]. Printed just levell anens the Saints Army. (July 27). E. 454. (23)." *Cf.* Carpenter, Ref. Guide, 237.

7. Catalogue of the Fifty Manuscripts & Printed Books Bequeathed to the British Museum by Alfred H. Huth. Ed. F. G. Kenyon. London, 1912.

> 45: Smith's *Chloris* dedicated to Sp.

8. CHALKHILL, JOHN. Thealma and Clearchus. . . . London, 1683.

   Cf. Hunter, Joseph. Chorus Vatum . . . B. M. Addit. MS 24,487, fol. 27ᵛ-8; Retrospective Rev. IV (1821). 230-1, 231n.

9. CHETTLE, HENRY.

   Cf. Jenkins, Harold. The Life and Work of Henry Chettle. London, 1934. 51: Chettle's reference to *R. of Time,* 222-4.

10. CHURCHYARD, THOMAS.

    Cf. Brydges, Sir Egerton. Censura Literaria (1807). IV, 366: *A Praise of Poetrie*; *ibid.,* (1806). II, 308: *The Challenge.*

11. COVINGTON, F. F., JR. An Early Seventeenth-Century Criticism of Spenser. MLN XLI (1926). 386-7.

    Rev. YWES VII (1926). 160. Thos. Heywood and the popularity of SC.

12. DANIEL, SAMUEL. Tethys Festival: or the Queenes Wake . . . 1610. Somers' Tracts, James I. London, 1809.

    II, 191: "The deviser [S. Daniel] appears to have had his eye upon the marriage of Thames and Isis, in the Faery Queen, . . ."

13. DAVENANT, SIR WILLIAM.

    Cf. Harbage, Alfred. Sir William Davenant. Univ. of Pennsylvania Press, 1935. 132-133, 197: Davenant's mention of Sp.

14. DAVISON, FRANCIS. A Poetical Rhapsody, 1602-1621. Ed. Hyder E. Rollins. Cambridge, Mass., 1931-2.

    See index, " Spenser," " Colin," " Cuddie," " Thenot," "Wrenock," etc. *Cf.* Reyher, Paul. Les Masques Anglais (1512-1640). Paris, 1909. 148, 148n: Sp and the masque. *Cf.* "FQ, General," No. 2.

15. DESAINLIENS, CLAUDIUS. Campo di Fior, or else the Flourie Field of Foure Languages . . . London, 1583. Prefixed to this is a verse beginning, " Although my Floure be waxt a wethered weede . . ." which seems an echo of SC VI, 109.

    Copy in Folger Shakespeare Library. Cited by Yates, Frances. John Florio . . . Cambridge, 1934. 49n.

16. DIGBY, SIR KENELM. (1603-65). A Discourse concerning Edmund Spenser.

    Cf. Harleian MS 4153 [Catalogue, 1808. III, 120], which describes the Discourse as " incomplete." *Cf.* also Harleian MS 7375. *Cf.* Bligh, E. W. Sir Kenelm Digby and his Venetia. London,

1932. 277-80 gives a transcription of this Discourse, B. M. Addit. MS 41,846.

Sir Kenelm Digby's Remarks on Spencer's Fairy Queene. Dated " from a board my ship the Eagle the 13th. of June, 1628." 26 leaves. (Cat. Harleian MSS. 1808. III, 528.)

Cf. Halliwell-Phillipps, James O. A Brief Description of the Ancient and Modern Manuscripts Preserved in the Public Library, Plymouth. London, 1853. 24, No. cxxvi: A letter from Sir " Kenelme Digby to my hon. frend Sir Edward Esterling, alias Stradling, abord his shipp, on Spenser's Faerie Queene. Fol." *Cf.* also, Thomas Thorpe's Bibliotheca Manuscripta. Catalogue of Ancient and Modern Manuscripts . . . Recently Purchased from the Libraries of His Royal Highness the late Duke of Sussex, the late B. H. Bright, Esq., Dr. Southey, the late poet laureate, and Sir Charles Bagot. London, 1844. No. 193: MS of Sir Kenelme Digby's Letter to Sir Edward Stradling, upon Spenser's Faerie Queene, whom the writer calls the English Virgil, *twenty-four pages, folio,* 1622.

Cf. also, Wurtsbaugh, Jewel. Digby's Criticism of Spenser. RES XI (1935). 192-5. Gives a summary and quotations from Digby's two critical notes; Variorum, II, App. xi.

17. DONNE, JOHN.

> *Cf.* Friederich, Werner P. Spiritualismus und Sensualismus in der englischen Barocklyrik. Wiener Beiträge, 1932. LVII. 197: Sp and Donne contrasted.

18. DRAYTON, MICHAEL. *Legends. " To the Reader." In Poems,* 1619.

> [312]: Sp first to use " legend " for verse instead of prose; the suitability of the term. [L. F. Ball] *Cf.* Drayton's *Works.* Ed. J. William Hebel. 1932. II, 382.
>
> *Poems.* London, 1605. " To the Reader." Speaks of Sp as using " cantos " in the Italian fashion. *Cf.* Merten, Maria. Michael Drayton's *Poly-olbion* im Rahmen der englischen Renaissance. Diss., Oranienburg, 1934. Ch. III: " Drayton and Spenser."

19. FLETCHER, GILES (the elder).

> *Cf.* Hunter, Joseph. Chorus Vatum . . . B. M. Addit. MS 24,487: fol. 73, 74.

20. ———— (the younger).

> *Cf.* Belden, H. M. Alanus de Insulis, Giles Fletcher, and the *Mutabilitie Cantos.* SP XXVI (1929). 131-4. Resemblance of *Christs Victorie in Heaven* to *Mutabilitie.* Fletcher probably saw *Mutabilitie* in folio of 1609 and owed his knowledge of Alanus's *De Planctu Naturae* to Sp's reference (VII, vii, 9, 6, 9).

21. FLETCHER, PHINEAS. De Literis Antiquo Britanniae. 1633.

> *Cf.* Hunter, Joseph. Chorus Vatum . . . B. M. Addit. MS 24,487: fol. 81; Waibel, Karl. Phineas Fletchers " Purple

Island " in ihrer Abhängigkeit von Spensers " Faerie Queene."
Engl. Stud. LVIII (1924). 321-67; Shakes. Jahr. 63 (1927). 231;
Boas, F. S. TLS 22 (Mar. 29, 1923). 216; Bush, Douglas. My-
thology and the Renaissance Tradition, 165-71.

22. GRAVES, T. S. Some Chaucer Allusions, 1561-1700. SP
XX (1923). 469-78.

> 473-5: Sp allusions.

23. Greenes Funeralls, 1594.

> *Cf.* Crawford, Charles. Greenes Funeralls. SP extra ser. I
> (1929). 1-39.
> 7: FQ stanzas (1590) signed " Ignoto." Also, *passim.*

24. GREENLAW, EDWIN. A Note on Spenser and Chapman.
No. 4. Proceedings of Dr. Greenlaw's Seminary " C,"
1925-6. The Johns Hopkins Univ. Library.

25. GRUBB, MARION. A Brace of Villains. MLN L (1935).
168-9.

> *Arden of Feversham* (1592) seems to derive description of one of
> its villains from FQ V. If so, FQ V was circulating in MS at
> least four years before publication.

26. GUILLIM, JOHN. A Display of Heraldrie . . . London,
1611.

> Sect. III, Ch. 17, p. 150: "*Toades* and *Frogs* doe communicate
> this naturall property, that when they sit, they hold their heads
> steady and without motion: which stately action, *Spencer* in his
> *Shepheards Calender* calleth the *Lording* of *Frogs.* . . ." Also,
> *ibid.,* Sect. VI, Ch. 5, p. 266 for another reference to same phrase
> from Sp.

27. GUILPIN, EDW. Skialetheia. 1598.

> *Cf.* Collier, J. P. Miscellaneous Tracts, No. 4. Shakespeare
> Association Facsimiles, No. 2, 1931, " Satyre vi." Also, Hunter,
> Joseph. Chorus Vatum . . . B. M. Addit. MS 24,487, fol. 223.

28. HABINGTON, WILLIAM. Castara. 1634.

> *Cf.* Hunter, Joseph. Chorus Vatum . . . B. M. Addit. MS
> 24,488, fol. 254.

29. HANCOCKE, GEORGE . . . to his frende J.[ohn] L.[ane].
Douce MS 170. (Also Ashmolean MS 53.) Ed. F. J.
Furnivall for the Chaucer Society in *John Lane's Con-
tinuation of Chaucer's Squire's Tale*, 1888, 1890. n. s.
23. *Cf.* Carpenter, Ref. Guide, 242; *post,* No. 35.

> 8: Sp's comment in FQ IV, ii, 31-5.

30. HARLEIAN MSS.

No. 5353, fol. 2. *Cf.* John Manningham's Diary. Camden Soc., 1868, p. 2 for this. [R. Heffner]; No. 6910. *Cf.* Hunter, Joseph. Chorus Vatum . . . B. M. Addit. MS 24,490, fol. 139: the presence of Sp items is noted in this collection; No. 677, item 25: *Mother Hubbardes Tale* in a 16th. c. hand. The catalogue ascribes the poem to Edmund Spenser. [R. Heffner]

31. HEFFNER, RAY. Some Spenser Allusions. No. 62. Proceedings of Dr. Greenlaw's Seminary "C," 1926-7. The Johns Hopkins University Library.

32. HEPWITH, JOHN. The Calidonian Forrest. 1641.

Borrows diction, general style, and Jove-intervention episode from MHT. *Cf.* Hudson, Hoyt H. John Hepwith's Spenserian Satire upon Buckingham: with some Jacobean Analogues. Huntington Library Bulletin, No. 6, 1934, 40-1, 51-4.

33. HEYWOOD, THOMAS. Hierarchie of the Blessed Angells. 1635. [F. F. Covington]

249-50: Sp and TM, SC, CCCHA. [Copies in Wrenn Library, Univ. of Texas, and in Library of Congress.] For text, *cf.* MLN XLI (1926). 386-7.

34. JEFFERY, VIOLET M. John Lyly and the Italian Renaissance. Paris, 1929.

92: Sp's influence. *Rev.* Anglia Beibl. 44 (1933). 45-56, by H. Glunz. 51: Sp and Lyly.

35. LANE, JOHN. Triton's Trumpet. 1621.

Cf. B. M. Roy. MS 17. B xv, 1621. [R. Heffner]; Trin. Coll.. Dublin, MS O. ii. 68; Hunter, Joseph. Chorus Vatum . . . B. M. Addit. MS 24,488, fol. 143, and MS 24,489, fol. 85; Carpenter, Ref. Guide 242-3, lists this under both Lane and Lloyd. Both are Lane's. [R. Heffner]

Corrected Historie of Guy of Warwick. 1621. *Cf.* Hunter, Joseph. Chorus Vatum . . . B. M. Addit. MS 24,489, fol. 85.

Spenser's Squiers Tale which hath been loste . . . now brought to light. Douce MS 170 (1615); Ashmolean MS M 8. 53 [R. Heffner]. *Cf.* Chaucer Soc. Pub., n. s., vol. 23. 1888, 1890. Ed. Furnivall; Emerson, Francis W. The Spenser in John Lane's Chaucer. SP XXIX (1932). 406-8. *Rev.* YWES XIII (1932). 194.

36. Locrine. 1595.

Cf. Shakes. Jahr. 38 (1902). 297-8; Sir E. K. Chambers. The Elizabethan Stage. 1923. IV, 27.

37. *LLOYD, LODOWICK.

Cf. Owen, Edward. "Lodowick Lloyd." North Wales Guardian, Feb. 4-April 15, 1931. *Rev.* Rev. celtique XLVIII (1931). 447. Mentions Sp's friendship with Lloyd.

38. MARLOWE, CHRISTOPHER.

Cf. Eccles, Mark. Christopher Marlowe in London. Harvard University Press, 1934. See index; Eliot, T. S. Elizabethan Essays. London, 1934. " Christopher Marlowe." 24-7: Sp's influence on lyric passages in Marlowe; Robertson, J. M. Marlowe, A Conspectus. London, 1931. 41: Cites parallels, Tamberlaine II, IV, iv, and FQ I, vii, 32 sq., etc. See also 7, 160, 168 for Sp and Marlowe.

39. MCVICKER, ALBERTA. Spenser's Literary Reputation from 1579-1650. MS material relating to E. Spenser by students of the University of Chicago. Copy in Newberry Library, presented by Dr. Carpenter.

40. MERES, FRANCIS.

Cf. Francis Meres's Treatise " Poetrie." A Critical Edition. Ed. Don Cameron Allen. Univ. of Illinois Studies in Lang. and Lit. XVI (1933). Nos. 3-4. See index. *Rev.* MP XXXIII (1935). 195-7, by C. R. Baskervill.

41. MILTON, JOHN.

Bense, J. F. " Meliboeus Old " in Milton's *Comus.* Neophilologus I (1916). 62-4. *Comus* 824-57 refers to Spenser as Meliboeus.

Bush, Douglas. Mythology and the Renaissance Tradition. 294-7. Sp and Milton. Also ch. XV.

Hanford, James H. A Milton Handbook. New York, 1933. See index.

Hunter, Joseph. Chorus Vatum . . . B. M. Addit. MS 24,490, fol. 188. FQ influence on PL.

Variorum Spenser, II, App. v: " Spenser and Milton."

Emerson, Francis W. Why Milton Uses " Cambuscan " and " Camball." MLN XLVII (1932). 153-4.

Tillyard, E. M. W. Milton. London, 1930. App. H. Spenser's Influence on Milton. *Cf.* Greenlaw, E. in SP XIV and XVII; also Cory, H. E. Spenser, The School of the Fletchers, and Milton.

French, J. Milton. Milton as a Historian. PMLA L (1935). 469-79. 472-3: Sp.

Gray, F. Campbell. Milton's Counterpoint. Sewanee Rev. XLIII (1935). 134-45. *Passim,* Sp.

Miller, Joseph R., Jr. Spenser's Influence on Milton's Prose and Poetry. MS study, Univ. of Virginia, 1929.

*Hurd, Richard (Bishop of Worcester). Spenser and Milton. In English Critical Essays of the 16th, 17th, and 18th Centuries. Ed. Edmund D. Jones. 1922. Pp. 370-3. [L. O. Hogan]

*King, William. Milton's Epistola ad Pollionem. 1738. London. " Mother Hubberds Tale." On the interpretation thereof. [Leicester Bradner] *Cf.* Milton's Epistle to Pollio. Translated from the Latin, London, 1740, p. 13.

Osgood, C. G. *Lycidas,* ll. 130, 131. RES I (1925). 339-40. FQ echoed.

Tatlock, J. S. P. Milton's Sin and Death. MLN XXI (1906). 239-40. FQ I, i, 14-5 and III, vii, 47-8 possible sources.

Taylor, George C. Milton's Use of DuBartas. Harvard University Press, 1934. Sp as intermediary between DuBartas and Milton. *Cf.* Greenlaw, E. in SP XIV and XVII. *Rev.* MLR XXXI (1936). 84-5, by B. A. Wright.

Schöffler, Herbert. Protestantismus und Literatur. Leipsig, 1922. 71-86: Das Wiedererwachen Spensers und Miltons.

42. Monthly Packet, 3rd. ser. I (1881). 531. Babington's Plot.

Alludes to Sp.

43. MORE, HENRY.

Cf. Philosophical Poems of Henry More. Ed. Geoffrey Bullough. Manchester University Press, 1931. Intro., *passim* for Sp; The Complete Poems. Ed. A. B. Grosart. 1878. Chertsey Worthies' Library. Priv. print. Most of More's work is in Spenserian stanza. See intro., *passim*; Hunter, Joseph. Chorus Vatum . . . B. M. Addit. MS 24,490, fol. 235 f. Sp's influence on Henry More; Conway Letters. Ed. Marjorie Nicholson. New Haven, 1930. See index, " More " and " Sp " and 40, 42.

44. NASHE, THOMAS. To the Gentlemen Students of both Universities.

Cf. Brydges, Censura Literaria, VII, 152-69. 167: Comparison of Sp and some foreign writers.

45. NICCOLS, RICHARD. The Cuckow. 1607.

Imitates Sp's language, style, esp. FQ III and MHT. The Beggar's Ape. 1627, written *ca.* 1610. Imitates MHT, retaining Fox-Ape as chief characters and keeping them very much as they are in Sp. *Cf.* Hudson, Hoyt H. John Hepwith's Spenserian Satire on Buckingham: with some Jacobean Analogues. Huntington Library Bulletin, No. 6 (1934). 62-9.

46. PEIRCE, MARJORIE. The Allusions to Spenser up to 1650. M. A. Thesis, University of Chicago, 1927.

47. SHEPPARD, SAMUEL. The Faerie King, Fashioning Love and Honour. 1646.

Photostat in Tudor and Stuart Club Library. *Cf.* Hunter, Joseph. Chorus Vatum . . . B. M. Addit. MS 24,487, fol. 11ᵛ, 69ᵛ; Brinkley, R. F. Arthurian Legend . . . 111-3.

48. Spenser Group. Spenser Allusions. PMLA XLVIII (1933). 623-8.

Cf. YWES XIV (1933). 226.

49. TILLEY, M. P. The Comedy *Lingua* and *The Faerie Queene.* MLN XLII (1927). 150-7.

Study of source of *Lingua* (1607). Main action traced to FQ II, ix, xi, xii. [A. P.] *Rev.* YWES VIII (1927). 186.

50. WEBBE, WILLIAM. A Discourse of English Poetrie. 1586.
   Cf. Hunter, Joseph. Chorus Vatum . . . B. M. Addit. MS 24,487, ✓
   fol. 49.

CRITICISM AFTER 1651

See " Addenda," Nos. 21-7, 44-9.

1. An Essay on the Poets. London, 1712.
   12-3 : Sp.

2. Anthologia Hibernica. Dublin. I (June, 1793). 448;
   II (Sept. 1793). 168. Poetical Balance.
   A tabular analysis. Sp compared, on a wide range of qualities,
   with poets from Homer to Pope.

3. ARMISTEAD, EDWIN. Spenser and the Daisy. NQ, ser. iii.
   VII (1865). 33.
   Quotes Alexander Smith's Dreamthorp . . . 1863. Prothalamion
   31, refers to English daisy.

4. ARMSTRONG, JOHN. An Imitation of Spenser. Written at
   Mr. Thomson's Desire, to be inserted into the Castle of
   Indolence. Chalmers' English Poets. XVI, 543.

5. ASCOLI, GEORGES. La Grande-Bretagne Devant l'Opinion
   Française au XVIIᵉ· Siècle. Paris, 1930. 2 vols.
   II, 121 : Cites translation of Sir William Temple, Oeuvres Mêlées,
   1693, II, 303-4. Probably first reference to Sp in France.
   II, 120 : Refers to Guy Miège, l'Etat Présent de la Grande-Bretagne. Amsterdam, 1708, II, 54: mentions Sp [H. C. Lancaster];
   also Baillet, Adrien. 1685-6. Jugements des Savants, IV, 397.

6. Athenian Mercury, July 11, 1691.
   Cf. Spurgeon, C. F. E. Five Hundred Years . . . 1925, I, 263, for
   text.

7. BARTON, BERNARD. Poetic Vigils. London, 1824.
   126: Flowers. Allusion to FQ.

8. BEDELL, WILLIAM. The Shepherd's Tale of the Powder
   Plot. Eine Spenser-Nachahmung. Ed. Karl Reuning.
   Beiträge zur Erforschung der Sprache und Kultur Englands und Nordamerikas. IV, hf. 2. Breslaw, 1928.
   113-54: Text, notes, some commentary. Rev. Anglia Beibl. XL
   (1929). 238-9, by A. Eichler; YWES X (1929). 216.

9. BEER, N. A History of British Socialism. London, 1929.
   46-7 : Sp as an anti-communist and anti-democratic.

13

174   CRITICISM, INFLUENCE, ALLUSIONS

10. BENCHOFF, H. J. The Political Element in Spenser's Poetry. M. A. Thesis, Columbia University, 1904.

11. BENSLY, EDWARD. Literary Queries: Tennyson, Spenser. NQ, ser. xiv. II (April 19, 1930). 319.
No. 2: Pope's delight in reading FQ. Cf. ibid., 279, by S.

12. BESTOR, A. E., JR. Emerson's Adaptation of a Line from Spenser. MLN XLIX (1934). 265-7.
Emerson's wide reading of Sp and its influence on his work.

13. BILDERDIJK, WILLEM. (1756-1831) "De Dichter aan zijne bruid." Nieuwe Dichtschakeering II. Rotterdam, 1819. See Dichtwerken, Haarlem, 1856. X, 172. An imitation of Sp. Cf. Smit, Johan. Bilderdijk et la France. Paris, 1929. 199: Sp's influence on Bilderdijk.

14. BLACKMORE, SIR RICHARD.
Cf. Brinkley, Roberta F. Sir Richard Blackmore's Arthurian Epics. No number. Proceedings of Dr. Greenlaw's Seminary "C," 1929-30. ibid., Blackmore's Portrayal of Spenser. MLN XLVI (1931). 313-6; ibid., Arthurian Legend in the Seventeenth Century. Baltimore, 1932. 151-64.

15. BOLD, HENRY. Verses, prefixed to Cartwright's Comedies, 1651.
Cf. Hunter, Jos. Chorus Vatum . . . B. M. Addit. MS 24,489, fol. 31.

16. BOLWELL, ROBERT. The Pastoral Element in Spenser's Poetry. Western Reserve Bull. XIX (1916). 17-27.

17. BOTTA, ANNE C. LYNCH. Handbook of Universal Literature. Boston, 1902.
450-2, 481-2: Sp.

18. BOUCHIER, JONATHAN. Poetic Parallels: Spenser, Shelley. NQ, ser. viii. VIII (1895). 304.
FQ V, iii, 1, and Lines Written Among the Euganean Hills, "Many a green isle needs. . . ."

19. BOYLE, HON. R.
Cf. Carpenter, Ref. Guide, 254. Both "Remarks" are Jortin's q. v.

20. *BOWLES, WILLIAM LISLE. The Works of Pope. London, 1806. "The Poetical Character of Pope."
Contrasts Pope and Spenser.

21. BRIE, FRIEDRICH. Imperialistische strömungen in der englischen literatur. Halle, 1928.
      28 ff.: Sp's imperialism.

22. British Quart. Rev. XIV (1819). 362.
      Sp lacks vigor and coherence; *ibid.*, XLII (1865). 29-47. A general appreciative essay.

23. BRODRIBB, C. W. An Epigram of Spenser. NQ, ser. xi. V (1912). 269.

24. BROWN, JOHN. John Bunyan. . . . Revised by Frank M. Harrison. London, 1928.
      Ch. XII: The Place of *Pilgrim's Progress* in Literature, *passim* for Sp.

25. BRYDGES, SIR EGERTON. Censura Literaria.
      V, 404: Sp working under great hardships in Ireland.

26. ――― *Ibid.,* VII, 93: Quotes anonymous comment ON BOOKS, No. XXII. 1808.
      Early nineteenth century attitude toward Sp and Milton.

27. BURGES, SIR JAMES BLAND. Richard the First, a Poem: in Eighteen Books. London, 1801. 2 vols.
      Uses Spenserian stanza. *Rev.* Monthly Rev. large ser. XXXVII (1802). 287-91; Brit. Critic XVII (1801). 221-9.

28. BURTON, ROBERT.
      Cf. Hughes, M. Y. Burton on Spenser. PMLA XLI (1926). 545-67. *Rev.* Shakes. Jahr. 64 (1928). 218-9; YWES VII (1926). 160; No. 14. Proceedings of Dr. Greenlaw's Seminary " C," 1926-7, by Frederick Hard.

29. BUSH, DOUGLAS. Mythology and the Renaissance Tradition.
      Cf. index for Sp's influence up to 1680.

30. CAMOENS, LUIS DE. The Lusiad of Camoens translated into English Spenserian verse by Robert Ffrench Duff. London, 1880.
      viii, xl, xlv: Spenserian verse.

31. CAMP, CHARLES W. The Artisan in Elizabethan Literature. New York, 1923.
      50-1: Sp's artisans.

32. CAMPBELL, J. H. The Influence of the *Shepheards Calendar. Cf.* " Shepherd's Calender," No. 12.

33. CARY, HENRY FRANCIS. Memoir . . . London, 1847. 2 vols.

I, 42: Letter of May 7, 1792: On Sp's admiration of the Italians. *Cf.* I, 112, 136.

34. CHEMIN, CAMILLE. Dans les sentiers de la Renaissance Anglaise. Rev. de l'Enseign. des Lang. Viv. 42è· an. (1925). 397.

35. CHURTON, EDWARD. Gongora. An Historical and Critical Essay on the Times of Philip III. and IV. of Spain. With Translations. London, 1862. 2 vols.

II, 138, 295: Remarks on relation of *Amoretti* 81 and de la Torre's *Sonnet* 23.

36. COLERIDGE, SAMUEL TAYLOR. Table Talk.

Rev. Quart. Rev. LIII (1835). 84-5, 89-91. Sp's influence and mental quality. *Cf.* Thompson, Francis. " Coleridge " in Works, ed. W. Meynell. New York, 1913. III, 182: Sp's influence on Coleridge. [N. T. Weyand, S. J.]; NQ, ser. vi. VIII (1883). 206, by F. Haverfield. Resemblance of FQ IV, iv, 1-2 and *Christabel*, pt. ii. "Alas! they had been friends in youth. . . ."

37. COLLIER, J. P. Poetical Decameron.

I, 61, 95-6, 170, 183-4.

38. COLLINS, WILLIAM.

Cf. The Poems of William Collins. Ed. Edmund Blunden. The Haslewood Books. Chiswick Press, 1929. 82-3, 167, 168, 171, 173: Sp. *Cf.* Falls, Cyril. The Poetry of William Collins. Nineteenth Cen. LXXXVIII (1920). 826.

39. CORY, H. E. Edmund Spenser: A Critical Study. Univ. of California Press.

Rev. Nation (N. Y.) CVI (1918). 739. [A. P.]; Lit. Zentralbl. LXXIV (1923). 419, by M. L.

40. COURTHOPE, WILLIAM J. The Genius of Spenser; an English prize essay read in the theatre, Oxford, June 17, 1868. London, 1868.

41. CRAIK, GEORGE L. Spenser and His Poetry.

Rev. West. Rev., n. s. XXXI (1867). 133-50.

42. [CROXALL, SAMUEL.] An Original Canto of Spenser . . . now made public by Nestor Ironside, Esq. 1713. Facs. repr., 1912.

Rev. Anglia Beibl. XXXI (1920). 15-6, by Bernhard Fehr.

43. DAVIS, B. E. C. Edmund Spenser: A Critical Study. Cambridge University Press, 1933.

Rev. Criterion XII (1932-3). 701-3, by W. L. Renwick; YWES XIII (1932). 191; TLS 32 (Sept. 28, 1933). 637-8. *The New Poet*; Spectator CLI (Aug. 4, 1933). 165-6, by Seán O'Faoláin; New York Times, Book Rev., July 30, 1933, p. 2, by P. M. Jack; MLR XXVIII (1933). 511-5, by M. Y. Hughes. An important review; New Statesman and Nation V n. s. (1933). 362-4, by Lawrence Stapleton; Quart. Rev. CCLX (1933). 364-5; Lond. Merc. XXVIII (1933). 566, by John Sparrow; NQ, ser. xiv. VIII (1933). 287-8; Observer, Mar. 5, 1933, by F. S. Boas; Oxford Mag. Apr. 27, 1933. 581, by J. S.; The Cambridge Bull. LXXII (1933). 12; Eng. Stud. XVI (1934). 112-4, by A. G. Van Kranendonk; RES X (1934). 462-4, by Douglas Hamer; MLN L (1935). 192-5, by Ray Heffner; Anglia Beibl. XLVI (1935). 37-43, by Rudolf Kapp.

44. DOUGHTY, CHARLES M. The Dawn of Britain. London, 1906.

VI, 242: Sp near the Muses.

45. DRYDEN, JOHN. Alexander's Feast.

Cf. Hunter, Joseph. Chorus Vatum . . . B. M. Addit. MS 24,490, fol. 226. A gloss in E. K.'s " October " notes gives historical basis for Dryden's account of the feast.

46. DUNBAR, HELEN F. Symbolism in Medieval Thought and its Consummation in the *Divine Comedy.* Yale University Press, 1929.

500: "Allegory versus Personification." Sp. [C. D. Baker]

47. Edinburgh Rev. XXXIII (1820). 315. Pope on reading Sp; *ibid.,* XLII (1825).

52-3. Sp steeped in romance. Compared with Rubens.

48. FANSHAWE, [SIR] RICHARD. The Lusiad, or Portugals Historicall Poem: Written in the Portingall Language by Luis de Camoens; and now newly put into English by Richard Fanshawe, Esq. London, 1655. " The Translator's Postscript," sig. b2^v:

" For (to name no more) the *Greek* HOMER, the *Latin* VIRGIL, *our* SPENCER, and even the *Italian* TASSO (who had a *true*, a great, and no obsolete story, to work upon) are in effect wholly fabulous. . . ."

49. FAWKES, FRANCIS. The Idylliums of Theocritus. 1767. In Chalmers' *English Poets*, XX.

156: " Preface to Fawkes' Theocritus." Unsuitability of Sp's style for translation of Theocritus. Cites in proof FQ III, vi, 11-2.

50. FLETCHER, JEFFERSON B. Literature of the Italian Renaissance. New York, 1934.

51. FOXLEY, CHARLES. Verse Translations from Lucretius. Cambridge University Press, 1933.

    vi: Use of Sp stanza. *Rev.* CR XLVIII (1934). 75, by Cyril Bailey.

52. FREE, JOHN. Poems on Several Occasions . . . London, 1757. "An Historical and Critical Account of the Origin and Peculiar Nature of English Poetry."

    xxviii: Sp's FQ uses "mixed Heroick style."

53. FULLER, RONALD. Literary Craftsmanship and Appreciation. London, 1934.

    66, 266, 273: SC, FQ.

54. GALLUP, Mrs. ELIZABETH W. The Bilateral Cypher of Francis Bacon. London, 1899. Also Baconiana, n. s. IX (1901). 77 ff.

    83-4: SC and E. K. and Bacon.

55. Gentleman's Mag. II (1732). 786.

    FQ stanzas tire the ear and limit Sp's reputation; *ibid.,* XIX (1749). 66: FQ use of "leech" to mean "physician."

56. *GLEN, WILLIAM. The Lonely Isle, a South Sea Island Tale. [London?], 1816.

    Uses Sp stanza.

57. GOLDER, HAROLD. Bunyan and Spenser. PMLA XLV (1930). 216-37.

    Sp's influence on Bunyan must be regarded as problematical.

58. ——— Bunyan's Giant Despair. JEGP XXX (1931). 360-78.

    In this instance the debt to Sp is traced through "old wives' tales" rather than to any evident reading of Sp.

59. GRAY, THOMAS. *Cf.* "Metrum. Observations on English Metre." The Works of Thomas Gray. Ed. Edmund Gosse. New York, 1885. 4 vols.

    I, 340-1: Sp's use of decasyllabic measure in SC "August." *Cf.* Nicholls, Norton. "Reminiscences of Grey." 1805. Letters of Thomas Grey. Ed. D. C. Tovey. London, 1904. II, 275-92: Gray's fondness for Sp. [F. I. C. and A. P.]

60. GREENLAW, EDWIN A. Outline of English Thought in the 16th. Century. No. 1. Proceedings of Dr. Greenlaw's Seminary " C," 1925-6. The Johns Hopkins University Library.

61. ———— Recent Spenser Studies. Paper read before the Mod. Lang. Ass., 1929. *Cf.* PMLA XLIV (*Proc.*, 1929). xliii.

62. GWYNN, STEPHEN L. Spenser. In Masters of English Literature. New York and London, 1904. Pp. 44-5. [L. O. Hogan]

63. HAAS, CORNELIUS E. DE. Nature and the Country in English Poetry of the First Half of the Eighteenth Century. Amsterdam, 1928.
    255-8: Sp's influence on rural poetry 1700-1750. General, slight.

64. HACKET, BP. Verses on Spenser, *ca.* 1670. *Cf.* Repr. European Mag. XIII (1788). 237; Athenaeum. 1883. I. 247.

65. HALES, J. W. Folia Litteraria. London, 1893.
    259-60: 18th. century sympathized with Sp's moralizing genius and enjoyed imitating him.

66. ———— Poet's Poet. In Modern English Essays. Ed. E. Rhys. London, 1922. [L. O. Hogan]
    II, 241-6: Sp an inspiration to subsequent poets. A good appreciative essay.

67. HARMAN, E. G. Edmund Spenser and the Impersonations of Francis Bacon.
    Rev. Spectator CXII (1914). 919; *Cf.* Squire, J. C. Books in General, First Series. 1919-21. " The Mantle of Sir Edwin," 68-73: Regards the Bacon identification of Sp as preposterous.

68. HARRIS, ROBERT B. The Beast in English Satire from Spenser to John Gay. Summaries of Theses, Harvard University, 1932. 254-7.
    Influence of MHT.

69. HARRISON, T. P., JR. Spenser and Shelley's *Adonais*. University of Texas Studies in English XIII (1933). 54-63.
    Parallels showing that most of Shelley's debt is to *Astrophel* and SC.

70. HART, JOHN S. Spenser and the *Faerie Queene*. Philadelphia, 1854.

71. HAYWARD, THOMAS. The British Muse. Preface by William Oldys. London, 1738.
    I, xvi, xvii, xxii: Quotations from Sp.

72. HEBER, REGINALD. "Morte d'Arthur. A Fragment." Life of Reginald Heber . . . by his Widow . . . New York, 1830. 2 vols.
    II, 485-525: Three cantos in Sp stanza.

73. ———— *Ibid.*, I, 8 and note: Sp one of Heber's favorite poets.

74. HEYLYN, PETER. Cosmographie in foure Bookes . . . London, 1652. Printed for Henry Seile. [F. R. Johnson]
    "An Appendix to the former work," 196, No. 4: Nature of Fairyland in Sp.

75. HODGSON, JAMES T. Memoir of the Rev. Francis Hodgson. London, 1878. 2 vols.
    I, 60: Gifford's comment on Sp, and Sp's versification.

76. HOWELL, JAMES. Londoniopolis. 1657. Cited in SP XX (1923). 477.

77. *HURD, RICHARD (Bishop of Worcester). Faerie Queene. Repr. in English Critical Essays of the 16th, 17th, and 18th Centuries. Ed. Edmund D. Jones. 1922. Pp. 373-80. [L. O. Hogan]

Chatto + Windus / London ed. p 57 78. HUXLEY, ALDOUS. Jesting Pilate. New York, 1926.
    71: The emptiness and tediousness of Sp's art.

79. IRVING, WASHINGTON. The Sketch-Book of Geoffrey Crayon. (London, 1820, first ed.) New York, 1863. 164.

80. IRVING, WILLIAM H. An Imitation of the *Faerie Queene*. MLN XLIII (1928). 80.
    In regard to a Canto of the *Faerie Queene*. Bodl. Godw. Pamph. 1668, dated 1739. *Cf.* Gentleman's Mag. IX (1739). 276.

81. JONES, H. S. V. A Spenser Handbook. New York, 1930.
    Rev. YWES XI (1930). 195-6; Pittsburgh Monthly Bull. 36 (1931). 37; Springfield Republican, Feb. 9, 1931. P. 6, col. vii; New

York Evening Post, Mar. 28, 1931, Sect. IV, p. 8; MLR XXVI
(1931). 496, by E. C. B.; MLN XLVI (1931). 560-1, by F. M.
Padelford; JEGP XXX (1931). 423-4, by J. W. Draper; TLS 30
(Feb. 12, 1931). 118; Rev. ang.-amér. 10è· an. (1932-3). 146-7, by
É. Legouis; RES VIII (1932). 94-5, by Douglas Hamer; Shakes.
Jahr. 69 (1933). 197.

82. Journal Britannique, par M. Maty (à la Haye). V (May,
1751). 104-5.

Imitations of Sp listed: i. Thompson's *Castle of Indolence;* ii.
Progrès de l'Envie, à la manière de Spenser; iii. *Education a Poem
in Two Cantos written in imitation of the stile and manner of
Spenser's Faery Queen,* by Gilbert West, Esq. London, 1751.

83. KEATS, JOHN.

Cf. Bushnell, Nelson S. The Style of the Spenserian Stanzas, Sonnets, and Odes of Keats. Summaries of Theses, Harvard University,
1928. 121-4: Ch. I: Spenserian stanza, as used by Keats, very
different from original form of Sp.

Gwin, H. H. The Influence on Keats of Spenser, Milton, and
Shakespeare. M. A. Thesis, University of Virginia, 1928.

Finney, C. L. Keats's Philosophy of Beauty: An Interpretation
of the Allegory of *Endymion* in the light of the Neo-Platonism of
Spenser. PQ V (1926). 1-19. Citations, showing fundamental influence of Sp's philosophy on Keats.

Hales, J. W. Folia Litteraria. London, 1893. 302: Sp's effect on
Keats.

The Letters of John Keats. Ed. Maurice B. Forman. Oxford University Press, 1931. 2 vols. *Cf.* I, 5, 21; II, 350, 396, 414, 493, 532.

The Poetical Works of John Keats. Ed. H. Buxton Forman. New
York, 1895. I, 122-3 n: *Endymion* II, 380 compared with Sp's FQ
III, vi, 44-7.

Wright, Herbert G. The Date of Keats's Spenserian Stanza. TLS
29 (May 29, 1930). 458. *Cf.* "Addenda," No. 28.

84. KOLLER, KATHRINE. Identifications in *Colin Clout's Come
Home Again.* MLN L (1935). 155-8. See No. i.

85. KOEPPEL, EMIL. John Day's *Peregrinatio Scholastica* in
ihrem Verhältnis zu Spenser, Chaucer und den '"Gesta
Romanorum." Die Neueren Sprachen. Festschrift Wilhelm Viëtor. 1910. Marburg. 1-13.

5 ff.: Sp's influence.

86. LAMB, CHARLES.

Cf. The Works of Charles Lamb. Ed. E. V. Lucas. 1905. Vol. VI,
"Letters," 37. Letter to Coleridge, July 7, 1796, verses "To The
Poet Cowper."

Johnson, Edith C. Lamb Always Elia. London, 1935. 81, 82, 134:
Lamb's allusions to Sp.

182   CRITICISM, INFLUENCE, ALLUSIONS

French, J. Milton. Lamb and Spenser. SP XXX (1933). 205-7.
Shows Sp's influence on Lamb over a period of thirty years.
Hard, Frederick. Lamb on Spenser. SP XXVIII (1931). 656-70.
Also in Royster Memorial Studies. University of North Carolina,
1931. 124-38: Lamb's allusions to Sp. Rev. Anglia Beibl. XLIV
(1933). 242.
Lamb and Spenser Again. SP XXX (1933). 533-4.
Lucas, E. V. Recollections of Charles Lamb. (From a Con-
temporary Manuscript). Lond. Merc. XXXI (1934). 146-51. 147:
Lamb's love of Spenser.

87. Landor, W. S. Citation and examination of W. Shakespeare . . . to which is added a Conference of Master
Edmund Spenser . . . with the Earl of Essex touching
the state of Ireland, A. D., 1595. London, 1834. [R.
Heffner] See 249 ff.

88. Law, Robert A. Holinshed as Source of Henry V and
King Lear. Univ. of Texas Studies in English XIV
(1934). 38-44.
41: Shakespeare used Sp's Lear story.

89. Legouis, Émile. Edmund Spenser. (Les Grands Écri-
vains Étrangers.) Paris, 1923.
Pt. I: The life. Pt. II: The Works. Rev. Rev. de l'Université de
Bruxelles, No. 3, 1924. 268-80, by Paul de Reul; Rev. de Litt. Comp.
IV (1924). 365; Rev. de l'Enseign. des Lang. Viv. 41è·an. (1924).
145-57, by F. Delattre; TLS 23 (Jan. 24, 1924). 45-6, by George
Saintsbury. A French Critic of Spenser. An interesting and rich
essay; Anglia Beibl. XXXV (1924). 355-6, by S. B. Liljegren;
YWES V (1924). 155-6 and IV (1923). 123-4; Litteris I (1924).
15-8, by G. Saintsbury; Bull. Bibl. et Pedagogique du Musée belge
XXX (1926). 44-7, by V. Bohet; Bookman (Lond.) 72 (1927). 261-
2, by C. E. Lawrence.

90. ———— Edmund Spenser. New York and London, 1926.
Six lectures delivered in 1922 at The Johns Hopkins University.
Rev. New Statesman XXVIII (1926). 278; TLS 25 (Nov. 4,
1926). 773; Bull. Bibl. et Pedagogique du Musée belge XXX
(1926). 44-7, by Bohet; SAQ XXVI (1927). 209-11, by P. F.
B.; Commonweal V (Feb. 2, 1927). 360, by Paul Crowley; Univ.
of Cal. Chron. XXIX (1927). 222-5, by M. Y. Hughes; Nation
and Athenaeum XL (1927). 515; Quart. Rev. CCXLIX (1927).
154-67, by C. E. Lawrence. The Personality of Spenser; YWES
VIII (1927). 184; Nation (N. Y.) CXXIV (1927). 192.

91. ———— and Louis Cazamian. A History of English
Literature. Translated from the French by Helen Doug-

Lewis, C. S: allegory of Love, chapter on Spenser. Certainly among most important C20 Spenser criticism. etc.

las Irvine. New York, 1926. 2 vols. Frequently reprinted.

I, 173-85: Spenser.

92. LEMMI, C. W. The Serpent and the Eagle in Spenser and Shelley. MLN L (1935). 165-8. *Cf.* "Shepherd's Calendar," No. 31.

93. LLOYD, ROBERT. The Connoisseur. No. 67. May 8, 1755. In Chalmers' *British Essayists.* 1807. XXXI, 4.

Sp's "impenetrable cloud" of allegory.

94. London Times Literary Supplement 21 (Mar. 2, 1922). Leading article. *Pierre de Ronsard.*

Comparison of Sp and Ronsard. Sp excelled in epic and ode and in moral purity; Ronsard excelled in sonnet, chanson, odette, and rhymed epigram.

95. McGILL, WINIFRED. A Study of the Spirit of Edmund Spenser. M. A. Thesis, University of Washington, 1924.

96. MARSHALL, RODERICK. Italy in English Literature, 1755-1815. New York, 1934.

218: Cary's admiration of Sp. *Cf. ante,* No. 33; 312: Gurney's imitation of Sp stanza in translation, *ca.* 1808, of *Orlando Furioso*; 306: *Memoirs of Lorenzo da Ponte, ca.* 1800, refers to Sp.

97. MELVILLE, HERMAN. 1851. Moby Dick. Boston, 1922.

539: "Etymology: Extracts" quotes FQ. *Cf.* Howard, Leon. Melville and Spenser—A Note on Criticism. MLN XLVI (1931). 291-2. *The Encantadas* and FQ.

Thomas, Russell. Melville's Use of Some Sources in *The Encantadas.* Amer. Lit. III (1931-2). 432-56. Some 24 quotations from Sp.

98. MICKLE, W. J. The Concubine: A Poem in Two Cantos. In the manner of Spenser. 1767.

Rev. Critical Rev. XXIII (1767). 398-9. On the Sp stanza.

99. ———— The Lusiad, or, Discovery of India. An Epic Poem Translated from the Original Portugese of Luis de Camoëns. London, 1776.

See "Dissertation on the Lusiad and Observations on Epic Poetry" for Sp. In 1793 ed., ccxciii, ccxcix, cccxxxiii and *passim.*

100. ———— Poems. In the British Poets. Chiswick, 1822. LXVI.

Biographic and critical sketch, by R. A. Davenport, discusses *passim* influence of Sp on Mickle.

101. NETHERCOT, ARTHUR H. Abraham Cowley, The Muses'
Hannibal. Oxford University Press, 1931. See index
for Sp.

102. NICHOLSON, MARJORIE (ed.). The Conway Letters.
New Haven, 1930.
173, 192n: Sp's influence on the philosophical romance *Bentivolio
and Urania*, 1660, by N[athaniel] I[ngleo].

103. OLDYS, WILLIAM. *Cf. ante*, No. 71.

104. PARNELL, THOMAS. An Essay on the Different Stiles of
Poetry. 1713.
A⁴ recto. *Cf.* Chalmers' *English Poets*, IX, 413 n. [J. G. Mc-
Manaway]

105. PECK, WALTER E. The Poet's Poet. TLS 24 (Jan. 1,
1925). 9.
Shelley was the first to whom the phrase was applied, but Lamb
was the first to apply it to Sp (1846).

106. PLUME, DR. Pocket book of Writing. 1680. Essex Rev.
XIV (1905). 14. [E. Greenlaw]

107. Poet Lore X (1898). 492, by J. D. Smith. A sonnet on
Sp's manner and subject.

108. PONTE, LORENZO DA. Denkwürdigkeiten des Venezianers.
Ed. Gustav Gugitz. Dresden, [1924]. 3 vols.
III, 33: Based on 2nd. ed. of Da Ponte's *Memoir* (1829-30).

109. POTTER, ROBERT. A Farewell Hymn to the Country. Attempted in the manner of Spenser's *Epithalamion*. London, 1749.
16-7: Sp. *Cf.* also The Poetical Register and Repository of Fugi-
tive Poetry for 1804. London, 1806. 405-16.

110. POTTS, ABBIE FINDLAY. The Spenserian and Miltonic
Influence in Wordsworth's *Ode* and *Rainbow*. SP
XXIX (1932). 607-16.
Sp's wedding songs influence these poems.

111. POWYS, JOHN COWPER. A Glastonbury Romance. New
York, 1932.
203, 252: Sp allusions.

112. ——— Autobiography. New York, 1934. Pp. 298.

113. Prefaces, Dedications, Epistles. Selected from Early Books, 1540-1701. Preface signed "W. C. H." Printed for private circulation, 1874.

114. PRIDEAUX, MATHIAS. An Easy and Compendious Introduction for Reading all sorts of Histories. Sixth ed. Oxford, 1682.

> 379: ". . . Spencers Fairy Queen . . . may pass with singular commendations for Moral Romances, being nothing else but Poetical Ethicke, that with apt contrivance, and winning Language, inform Morality . . ."

115. *PURCELL, HENRY. The Fairy Queen: An Opera, 1692. Introduction by Dennis Arundell. Cambridge University Press, 1931 (also, 1903).

> Text from *Midsummer Night's Dream. Rev.* MLN XLVII (1932). 207-8, by H.[azelton] S.[pencer]; The Cambridge Bulletin LXVIII (1931). 2.

116. Quarterly Rev. CCVI (1907). 49, by R. E. Prothero.

> Pope's age "improved" Sp; XXIII (1820). 429, 433: Pope vindicated on charge of "traducing" Sp.

117. QUILLER-COUCH, SIR ARTHUR. The Poet as Citizen and Other Papers. Cambridge University Press, 1934.

> 203: It is erroneous to regard Sp as a courtly poet.

118. RAY, JOHN. A Collection of English Words not generally used. 1691. [E. Greenlaw]

> 85: Spenser's words.

119. RENWICK, W. L. Edmund Spenser: An Essay on Renaissance Poetry. London, 1925.

> "Re-creation of background and thought" in which Sp worked. Emphasis on theories, literary ideas, etc. *Rev.* TLS 24 (April 30, 1925). 296. *Edmund Spenser;* Lond. Merc. XII (1925). 549, by D. S. Mirsky; Lit. Rev. V (New York Even. Post) June 27, 1925, p. 5. "*S. O. S.*" Call to Aid in Rescuing Spenser . . . by J. T. Shipley; Nation (N. Y.) CXXI (July 8, 1925). 77; Bookman (Lond.) LXVIII (1925). 267-8, by R. L. M.; Nation and Athenaeum XXXVII (April 25, 1925). 107, by Richard Aldington. *Spenser and the Italians.* Sp's place between Pléiade and Italian poets on one hand, and Keats and Pope on the other; New Statesman XXV (May 30, 1925). 202-4; JEGP XXV (1926). 273-5, by H. S. V. Jones; YWES VI (1925). 166-7; PQ VI (1927). 221-2, by F. M. Padelford.

120. RENWICK, W. L. Edmund Spenser. In The Great Tudors. Ed. Katharine Garvin. London, 1935. Pp. 521-36.
Rev. New York Times, Book Rev., Jan. 19, 1936, p. 12, by Katherine Woods.

121. Retrospective Rev. IX (1824). 291.
Sp " continually " borrows from Ariosto.

122. RINAKER, CLARISSA. Thomas Warton's Observations on the Fairy Queen of Spenser. Univ. of Illinois Stud. in Lang. and Lit. II (1916). 36-58.
7 : " Observations on the Faerie Queene of Spenser."
Rev. Athenaeum, October, 1916. 468. Cf. MacClintock, William D. Joseph Warton's Essay on Pope. Chapel Hill, 1933.

123. SANDISON, HELEN E. Three Spenser Allusions. MLN XLIV (1929). 159-62.
17th. c. references. Rev. YWES X (1929). 216.

124. *SCHMID, CHRISTIAN H. Biographie der Dichter. Leipsig, 1769-70. 2 vols.
II, 234-6: Sp's influence. [F. I. C. and A. P.]

125. SCHELLING, FELIX. English Literature during the Lifetime of Shakespeare.
Rev. Shakes. Jahr. 48 (1912). 291-2.

126. SÉLINCOURT, E. DE. Oxford Lectures on Poetry. Oxford University Press, 1934.
V : " Spenser." Nature of pictorial and musical aspects of Sp's poetry and the contribution of these qualities to his charm in narrative. Sp as story-teller uses the sentimental manner (as defined by Schiller) ; shows himself a lover of beauty, a believer in man's nobility, and a connoisseur of human emotion. Rev. YWES XV (1934). 14; MLR XXX (1935). 239-40, by L. C. Martin.

127. SHENSTONE, WILLIAM. The Schoolmistress. In Imitation of Spenser. Works of Shenstone, 1777, I, 320 ff.

128. *Singer, . . . Sir Calidore, the Knight of Courtesy: Reflections submitted to all Christian Gentlemen. London, 1892. [R. Heffner]

129. SMITH, ALEXANDER. "Sydney Dobell." Last Leaves. 1868. Quoted in Spurgeon, Five Hundred Years . . . II, pt. III, 34.
179: Sp the fountain-head of poetry that appeals to those who like romantic, didactic, allegorical, intense poetry. Cf. Lond. Quart. Rev. XXXI (1868-9). 142 ff.

130. SOREL, CHARLES. The Extravagant Shepherd: or, The History of the Shepherd Lysis. An Anti-Romance; written originally in *French,* and now made *English.* London . . . by *T. Newcomb* for *Thomas Heath* . . . 1654. Ded. signed " John Davies." *Cf.* " The Translator to the Reader," sig. aᵛ:

> " The *indecorum* of Homers gods, the fault in *Virgils* Chronology, *Tasso* making *Christians* speak like *Heathens, Spencers* confusion, and different choice of names, are things never to be forgiven." Entire passage excellent neo-classic criticism of romance and pastoral. Important. [J. G. McManaway]

131. SOUTHEY, ROBERT. Lay of the Laureate.

> *Rev.* Brit. Crit. L (1816). 41-2. Quotes the allusions to Sp. *Cf.* Casson, T. E. Robert Southey. Manchester Quart. LII (1933). 38-56. 47: Sp stanza in Southey's *Tale of Paraguay.*

132. SPENS, JANET. Spenser's *Faerie Queene.* London, 1934.

> *Passim* for Sp's influence on Milton, Shelley, Wordsworth, etc.

133. STEPHEN, SIR LESLIE. English Literature and Society in the Eighteenth Century. London, 1931.

> See Lectures I, IV, V for Sp in the 18th. century.

134. STEWART, RANDALL. Hawthorne's Debt to Spenser. Paper read before the Mod. Lang. Ass., 1930. *Cf.* PMLA XLV (*Proc.,* 1930). xxv.

135. ——— Hawthorne and *The Faerie Queene.* PQ XII (1933). 196-206.

> Sp's influence on Hawthorne's characterization and the contrivance of situation. *Rev.* Shakes. Jahr. 70 (1934). 165.

136. STOLL, E. E. Poets and Playwrights: Shakespeare, Jonson, Spenser, Milton. University of Minnesota Press, 1930.

> Ch. VI: Spenser. Spenser's early Renaissance romanticism is indebted to the classics, the Italians, and the new spirit of his own world. His style, unlike his structure and his plot, is deeply classical. *Rev.* New York Times, Book Rev., Aug. 31, 1930, p. 12, by S. A. Coblentz; YWES XI (1930). 197; MLN XLVI (1931). 125-6, by H. Spencer; MLR XXVI (1931). 473, by Allardyce Nicoll; Univ. of Cal. Chron. XXXIII (1931). 476-8, by M. Y. Hughes; Anglia Beibl. XLIII (1932). 371, by S. B. Liljegren; Shakes. Jahr. 69 (1933). 172, by Wolfgang Keller; JEGP XXXIII (1934). 130-2, by Warner G. Rice.

137. [THOMAS, Mrs. ELIZABETH.] Poems on Several Occasions, By a Lady. London, 1726.

68-76: "A Pindarick Ode in Imitation of Spencer's Divine Love, inscribed to Mrs. Katherine Bridgeman." "Unfinish'd."

138. THOMPSON, FRANCIS. The Works of Francis Thompson. Prose. London, 1913. "The Poets' Poet."

III, 140 ff.

139. THOMPSON, WILLIAM. Sicknesse. A Poem. Three Books. London, 1745.

I, 18 and "Notes" 43: Dates beginning of English poetry from Sp, who, better than any other, was acquainted with "the very life and being of poetry." Also II, 99 and notes, 103.

140. THOMSON, JAMES. The Castle of Indolence. An Allegorical Poem Written in Imitation of Spenser. London, 1748.

Cf. "Advertisement" prefixed to List of Obsolete Words. Sp's diction. Cf. Brooks, Philip. Notes on Rare Books. New York Times, Book Rev., June 16, 1935. p. 21: Thomson's popularizing of Sp stanza; Morel, Leon. James Thomson. Paris, 1895. See 224-9, 377, 626-34: Sp's influence on Thomson.

141. TIGHE, Mrs. HENRY. Psyche. London, 1813. (3rd. ed.)

Rev. Eclectic Rev., 1st. ser. IX (1813). 221: On Sp stanza. Cf. Evans, B. Ifor. Keats. London, [1934]. 88-9: Mrs. Tighe's Spenserianism.

142. Times Literary Supplement. (London.) Leading article, Sept. 28, 1933. 637-8.

143. TUCKWELL, WILLIAM. Spenser.

Rev. Athenaeum. 1907. I. 14.

144. TURNER, CELESTE. Anthony Mundy, An Elizabethan Man, of Letters. Berkeley. Univ. of California Press, 1928.

See p. 26 and index. Cf. Forthcoming article by E. C. Wilson.

145. The Union: or, Select Scots and English Poems. Ed. T. Warton. Third ed., London, 1766.

94-5: A Pastoral in the Manner of Spenser. From Theocritus. Idyll XX. By "A Gentleman formerly of the University of Aberdeen." Cf. Chalmers' English Poets. XVIII. "Thomas Warton."

146. *Varietés Angloises. London, 1770.

163 ff.: Sp.

147. "Veritas." The Fairy Queene (in the theatre at Berlin).
Monthly Packet, n. s. XIX (1875). 647-8.
Takes only title from Sp.

148. The Vision. A Fable. Inscribed to Dr. Garth. By the
Author of [The Dissatisfy'd]. In the Examen Miscel-
laneum. Ed. Charles Gildon. London, for B. L. . . .
by John Chantry. 1702. [J. G. McManaway]
62-4: Sp named in a catalogue of poets.

149. VOLTAIRE, F. M. A. Oeuvres Complètes. Paris, 1878.
XIII: Essai sur les Moeurs et l'Esprit des Nations. (1st. ed. 1753).
p. 56: "Spencer avait ressuscité la poésie épique." XVIII, 579:
Épopée (Dict. Philosophique, 1st. ed. 1727). " Spencer, en Angleterre, voulut rimer en stances son poëme de la Fée reine; on l'estima,
et personne ne le put lire."

150. WALLER, EDMUND. The Second Part of Mr. Waller's
Poems . . . London, 1705. Preface to " The Maid's
Tragedy" &c. sig. u^v:
" In the meantime 'tis a surprising Reflection, that between what
Spencer wrote last, and Waller first, there should not be much above
twenty years distance: And yet the one's Language, like the Money
of that time, is as Currant now as ever; whilst the other's words are
like old Coyns, one must go to an Antiquary to understand their
true meaning and value. Such advances may a great Genius make,
when it undertakes anything in earnest! "

151. WARD, A. W. (ed.). Poems of John Byrom. Chetham
Soc., 1894.
I, pt. i, 49n: Quotes E. K. for correct use of " Thame "; ibid.,
55: FQ II, ix, 1, may have given Addison the idea for his Spectator
paper No. 275, Dissection of a Beau's Head.

152. WEST, GILBERT. Education, a Poem: in Two Cantos
Written in Imitation of the Style and Manner of Spenser's Fairy Queen. London, 1751.

153. WHITE, HENRY KIRKE. Remarks on the English Poets.
Warton. In The Poetical Works and Remains of Henry
Kirke White. Ed. Robert Southey. Philadelphia, 1855.
271: Warton's feeling for Sp. Cf. 272-3.

154. WHITEHEAD, CHARLES. The Solitary. London, 1831;
Victoria Victrix. London, 1838.
Use Spenserian stanza.

14

155. WHITEHEAD, WILLIAM. Plays and Poems . . . London, 1774. 2 vols.

II, 298-9: In "A Charge to the Poets." II, 95: Una's mirror in "On Ridicule." *Cf.* III, 11-2.

156. WILLIAMSON, GEORGE. Mutability, Decay, and Seventeenth-Century Melancholy. ELH II (1935). 121-150.

Influence of *Mutabilitie* on 17th. c. melancholy.

157. WILSON, J. Spenser and His Critics. In Critical Essays of the Early Nineteenth Century, ed. R. M. Alden. New York, 1921. [L. O. Hogan]

368-77: Sp.

158. WILSON, P. W. Review of Alan G. Smith's *William Cecil.* New York Times, Book Rev., Sept. 15, 1936, p. 9.

159. WOLFE, THOMAS. Of Time and the River. New York, 1935.

390, 588, 668, 868: Allusions to Sp and his high place among poets.

160. *WOLFF, MAX JOSEF. Die Renaissance in der englischen Literatur. Bielefeld, 1928.

Sp is the "high Renaissance."

161. WORDSWORTH, WILLIAM. Letter to Catherine Grace Godwin. Letters of the Wordsworth Family. Ed. W. Knight. Boston, 1907.

II, 403: Difficulty of using Sp stanza. Some 18th. century imitators. [E. Wayne Marjorum]

162. WRIGHT, LOUIS B. Middle-Class Culture in Elizabethan England. Univ. of North Carolina Press, 1935.

See index. *Rev.* Quart. Rev. CCLXVI (1936). 277-9, by Whitwell M. Dodd.

163. YART, ABBÉ ANTOINE. Idée de la Poésie Angloise. Paris, 1753. Copy in Yale University Library.

II, 107-8: From *Le Progrès de la Poësie.* Par Mme. de Worthley Montaigue. "Le grand Spencer parut avec une pompe brillante; il donna de la douceur à la Poësie, & de l'harmonie à la Prose; ses vers créateurs, représentent les vertus, les vices, les passions sous leurs formes précises: la nature sert l'enthousiasme du Poëte; il n'a point de parties dans son Poëme, qu'il ne remplisse de sa force, & qu'il n'anime de son feu." "Il n'est point suprenant qu'Adisson ait blâmé Spenser, & que Madame de W . . . l'ait loüé. Il est peu d'Auteurs qui ne méritent presque également la critique & l'estime, par des endroits différens. Adisson méprise les allégories de Spencer Madame de W . . . vante les descriptions de ce Poëte. " Voici un trait de sa vie, qui vas justifier l'Eloge de Madame de W . . . Spencer montra un jour au célebre Philippe Sydney, qui ne le connoissoit point, le neuvieme Chant du premier Livre de son Poëme. Sydney fut si ému de la description que le Poëte y fait du désespoir, qu'il ordonna à son Maître d'Hôtel de payer à l'Auteur cinq livres sterlings. Il continua de lire, & son émotion ne faisant qu'augmenter a mesure qu'il lisoit, il fit doubler la somme: mais ayant encore lû une Stance, & s'étant apperçu que celui à qui il avoit donné l'ordre de payer Spencer, ne l'avoit pas fait, il lui dit, que s'il ne payoit pas sur le champ deux cens livres sterlings au Poëte, il ne pourroit pas s'empêcher de lui donner tout son bien."

164. YATES, FRANCES A. John Florio. The Life of an Italian in Shakespeare's England. Cambridge University Press, 1934.

See index.

165. YEATS, W. B. Mr. Yeats at Seventy. New York Times, June 30, 1935. Sect. IV, p. E8.

IV.
VARIOUS TOPICS

IV. VARIOUS TOPICS

PORTRAITS

1. Archaeological Journal of the Royal Arch. Institute of Great Britain and Ireland XIX (1862). 296, 297.

   In the Institute's exhibit of enamel miniatures are two of Sp by H. P. Bone.

2. Bookman (Lond.) 72 (1927). 261-2. The Poet's Poet. Portrait.

3. British Museum Catalogue of Engraved Portraits. Ed. F. O'Donoghue. B. M. Publications, 1904-22. 5 vols.

   IV, 166-7: Lists 17 engraved portraits of Sp, e. g. Vertue, 1727; Bell's Poets, 1777, etc. V, 79: Head of Sp appears in engraved title-page of E. Phillips' *New World of Words,* 1678. V, 80: Plate II, *Worthies of Britain,* pub. by J. Bowles; plate I, *Poets and Philosophers of England* [F. I. C. and A. P.]

4. Catalogue of the Library of the Late Winston H. Hagen. The Anderson Galleries. 1918.

   No. 1437: Engraved portrait of Sp.

5. HENDERSON, PHILIP. London . . . The City Seen by the Poets. Bookman (Lond.) 83 (1932). 152. Portrait of Sp.

6. Monthly Mag. XIII (1802). 233: A portrait in possession of a lineal descendant of Sp's near Mallow, 1790; *ibid.,* XXVI (1808). 139: John Love of Castle Saffron had a Vertue print of Sp. *Cf.* Berkenhout, John. Biographia Literaria, 1777, p. 380.

7. New York Times, May 13, 1934. Portrait.

   Sect. 2, p. 2, col. 2: Mr. Gabriel Wells's presentation to Yale University of the Michael Rhysbrach bust of Sp. The bust was done prior to 1732. [L. O. Hogan]

8. Notes and Queries, ser. i. IV (1851). 74, by "Varro"; 101, by E. M. B. Spenser's Age at his Death.

   Refers to a portrait, dated 1593, showing Sp in middle age.

9. TWISS, HENRY. Mallow and Some Mallow Men. J. Cork Hist. and Arch. Soc. XXXI (1926). 69.

   Portrait owned by Mrs. Sherlock.

193

10. WELPLY, W. H. Edmund Spenser. NQ, ser. xiv. VI (1932). 241-2.
On the Castle Saffron portrait and the one owned by Edmund Spenser, 3rd.

11. WHITE, JAMES. Historical and Topographical Notes on Buttevant . . . 1911.
II, 264: Sp portrait at Castle Saffron said (1817) to have been removed.

AUTOGRAPHS

1. GREG, W. W. English Literary Autographs, 1550-1650, selected for reproduction and edited by W. W. Greg. In collaboration. . . . Oxford University Press, 1932.
Pt. II, Plates XXXIX, XL: Sp's autograph illustrated by official documents and discussed. *Rev.* The Library, ser. 4. X (1929-30). 107-8, by B. S. Mentions the careful identification of Sp's two "hands"; MLR XXVIII (1933). 384-6, by G. C. Moore Smith.

2. JENKINS, RAYMOND. See "Life, General References," No. 59.

3. JENKINSON, HILARY. On Autographs. History, n. s. VIII (1923-4). 98 ff.
99, 106, 108: Sp's two "hands" and the authenticity of some of the signatures attributed to him.

4. ROSENBACH, A. S. W. Books and Bidders. Boston, 1927.
148-51: Sp's autograph in FQ presented by him to Eliz. Boyle. *Cf.* Gollancz, I. in Carpenter, Ref. Guide, 55; Brooke, Tucker. Sat. Rev. of Lit. IX (June 3, 1933). 625-6.

SPENSER POET LAUREATE

1. BELLAMY, CHARLES H. The Poets-Laureate. Manchester Quart. XLVII (1928). 249 ff.
251: Sp should not be listed as laureate; he himself made no claim to the title.

2. BERKENHOUT, JOHN. Biographia Literaria. London, 1777. 379, 382.

3. Blackwood's Mag. LXIV (1848). 220 ff. Laurels and Laureates.
226: Sp's pension grant did not name him laureate.

4. Contemporary Rev. CIV (1913). 129-33. Poets Laureate.
130: Sp cited as appointed to laureateship in 1590.

5. SPENCER, NATHANIEL. The Complete English Traveller
. . . London, 1773.
   320: Sp made laureate.

6. WOOD, ANTHONY Â. Athenae Oxoniensis. Ed. P. Bliss.
London, 1813-20.
   II, 269: "Spencer, as I have been informed, was poet laureate to Queen Elizabeth." [F. I. C. and A. P.]

SPENSER AND PURITANISM: RELIGIOUS OPINIONS

See "Mutabilitie," Nos. 10, 13-6, 18, 30-3; "Spenser's Philosophy," Nos. 15, 16; "FQ, Sources," Nos. 110-3; "FQ, General," No. 67.

1. ALBRIGHT, EVELYN M. Spenser's Cosmic Philosophy and
His Religion. PMLA XLIV (1929). 715-59.
   Sp's cosmic philosophy is not entirely in accord with Lucretian teaching, but shows traces of the thought of Empedocles. *Cf. post*, No. 2.

2. BENNETT, J. W. Spenser's *Fowre Hymnes*: Addenda.
SP XXXII (1935). 131-57.
   Renaissance Christian Neo-Platonism in the *Hymnes*, which are a unified exposition of Neo-Platonic thought. *Cf.* "Four Hymns," No. 2.

3. BUCKLEY, GEORGE T. Atheism in the English Renaissance. University of Chicago Press, 1932.
   See index for Sp.

4. COLLINS, JOSEPH B. Christian Mysticism in the Elizabethan Age. Diss., The Johns Hopkins University,
1934.

5. DAVIS, B. E. C. Edmund Spenser: A Critical Study.
   110-6, 224-9, 236-43: Sp's philosophy and religion.

6. JUDSON, A. C. A Biographical Sketch of John Young,
Bishop of Rochester, with Emphasis on his Relations
with Edmund Spenser. Indiana University Studies
XXI (1934). No. 103. 1-41.
   36-9: Sp's ecclesiastical views probably did not differ sharply from those of Young. Sp's chief concern is with abuses which do not conform to the Christian spirit. He is not greatly concerned, apparently, with the controversy over forms. He probably did not sympathize with the "Puritans."

7. KNOWLTON, E. C. Spenser and Nature. JEGP XXXIV
(1935). 366-76.

8. LANDRUM, GRACE W. Spenser's Use of the Bible and his Alleged Puritanism. PMLA XLI (1926). 517-44.

Sp seems to have known best the Great Bible. Relation of this fact to his religious views. His Calvinism admitted, but not his Puritanism. Sp's possible sympathy with Precisionist or even with Low Anglican ideas. Appendix lists his Biblical allusions. *Cf.* Padelford, F. M. in Carpenter, Ref. Guide, 291; "Spenser's Reading," No. 10; "FQ, General," Nos. 19-21; "Mother Hubberd's Tale," No. 21. *Rev.* Shakes. Jahr. 64 (1928). 219; No. 11. Proceedings of Dr. Greenlaw's Seminary "C," 1926-7, by D. J. Savage. The Johns Hopkins University Library.

9. LEGOUIS, É. Edmund Spenser. New York and London, 1926.

Ch. II: Spenser's Religious Views.

10. OSMOND, PERCY H. The Mystical Poets of the English Church. London, 1919.

Ch. II: Edmund Spenser, Giles and Phineas Fletcher.

11. PADELFORD, F. M. Spenser and the Puritan Propaganda. MP XI (1913).

Rev. Shakes. Jahr. 50 (1914). 144-5.

12. PEARSON, A. F. SCOTT. Thomas Cartwright and Elizabethan Puritanism, 1553-1603. Cambridge University Press, 1925.

188-9: Sp's possible connection with Puritan movement is signified by his choice of Singleton as SC printer. Sp's Thomalin is the Puritan, Thomas Cartwright.

13. ROPE, H. E. G. Catholicism in Elizabethan Literature. The Month CLXII (1933). 250-4.

254: Nostalgia for Roman Catholic faith runs through all Elizabethan literary period from Spenser to Shirley.

14. SAVAGE, D. J. Spenser's Relation to Puritanism. No. 51. Proceedings of Dr. Greenlaw's Seminary "C," 1926-7. The Johns Hopkins Univ. Library.

15. SELWYN, E. G. Some Philosophies in English Poetry. Quart. Rev. CCLXIV (1935). 224-37.

225: Sp and the spirit of the Christian Renaissance.

SPENSER'S PHILOSOPHY

See "Mutabilitie," Nos. 3, 10, 14-6, 30-5; "Four Hymns," Nos. 2, 18; "Spenser and Platonism," Nos. 1-5, 7, 8; "Spenser and Puritanism," Nos. 6, 8-10, 12-4; "FQ, Sources," Nos. 3, 13, 21, 29, 116, 120; "Addenda," No. 16.

1. BENNETT, JOSEPHINE W. Spenser's Garden of Adonis. PMLA XLVII (1932). 46-80.

> Sp's cosmic philosophy is based on Neo-Platonic and Platonic thought. There is no trace in it of the Lucretian theory of origins.

2. ———— Spenser's Venus and the Goddess of Nature in the *Cantos of Mutabilitie*. SP XXX (1933). 160 ff.

> Sp's philosophy here is Neo-Platonic and Platonic and he is concerned with discussing a serious Platonic problem.

3. ———— Spenser's *Fowre Hymnes*: Addenda. SP XXXII (1935). 131-57.

> Renaissance Christian Neo-Platonism in the *Hymnes*, which are a unified exposition of Sp's Neo-Platonic thought.

4. DAVIS, B. E. C. Edmund Spenser: A Critical Study.

> Ch. IX : Philosophical Ideas. *Cf.* IV : Humanism. Sp a consciously philosophic poet; eclecticism of his humanistic philosophy illustrated by noting his use of familiar concepts from Plato, Aristotle, Ficino, Giraldi, Castiglione, Pythagoras (*via* Ovid), Lucretius, and old religious cults, etc. His natural philosophy is inconsistent and somewhat fatalistic. *Cf.* "Mutabilitie," No. 14.

5. DEVERE, AUBREY. Spenser as a Philosophic Poet. Littell's Living Age, 5th. ser. XLIX (1885). 579-97. Also Century XLVIII (1894). 765. "Recollections."

6. FOWLER, EARLE B. Spenser and the System of Courtly Love. Louisville, Ky., 1934.

> While accepting the outward and conventional practices of the courtly love system, Sp rejected its moral aspects. He adhered to a philosophy based on Platonic and Puritan concepts.

7. KNOWLTON, E. C. Spenser and Nature. JEGP XXXIV (1935). 366-76.

8. LEVINSON, RONALD B. Spenser and Bruno. PMLA XLIII (1928). 675-81.

> Suggests Bruno's influence on Sp. Denies influence of Lucretian scepticism which is at odds with the Christianized Neo-Platonism considered to have been Sp's "sole philosophy." *Cf.* "Mutabilitie," 14, 15, 30-3. *Rev.* Shakes. Jahr. 65 (1929). 225-6; Proc. Eng. Jour. Club, Dec. 12, 1928, by C. W. Lemmi. The Johns Hopkins University.

9. Literary Magazine and American Register V (May, 1806). 323-4. " The Influence of Climate on the Mind."

". . . but Spenser, that child of fancy, had on this subject [i. e. the title] a sounder philosophy than Milton. In his view of the State of Ireland, composed in the dialogue manner, one of the speakers conceives that the barbarity of that country proceeds from the very genius of the soil, or influence of the stars. But he is justly reprimanded by the other, in the following philosophical and pleasing expression: ' Surely, I suppose this but a vain conceit of simple men, which judge things by their effects, and not by their causes; for I would rather think the cause of this evil, which hangeth upon that country, to proceed rather of the unsoundness of the counsels, and plots which you say have been oftentimes laid for the reformation, or of faintness in following and affecting the same, than of any such fatal course appointed of God, as you misdeem; but it is the manner of men that when they are fallen in any absurdity, or their actions succeed not as they would, they are always ready to impute the blame thereof unto the heavens, so to excuse their own follies and imperfections.' The admirable Spenser is another instance to prove that an exquisite imagination may be combined with the soundest intellect, and it is now, perhaps, the first time that Spencer the poet has been quoted as Spenser the philosopher."

10. LOEWENBERG, J. Philosophy and Literature. Univ. of California Chron. XXXIII (1931). 267-92.

273: Sp's " disdain of the actual " as " prompted by the passion for a possible region of unexampled and ideal perfection."

11. RENWICK, W. L. Edmund Spenser. . . .

Ch. VI: Philosophy.

12. SAURAT, DENIS. Les Idées Philosophiques de Spenser. Arsbok, 1924. Yearbook of the New Society of Letters at Lund. I (1924). 251. Repr. as Ch. V in La Littérature et l'Occultisme. Rev. YWES V (1924). 155.

13. ———— La Littérature et l'Occultisme. Paris, 1929.

14. ———— Spenser and the Occult. New York, 1931.

Translation of La Littérature et l'Occultisme. Rev. New York Herald-Tribune Books, Feb. 22, 1931, p. 19.

15. ———— Literature and Occult Tradition: Studies in Philosophical Poetry. Translated by Dorothy Bolton. London, New York, 1930.

163-238: Sp's philosophical ideology is slight but his poetic philosophy is primarily concerned with his " feelings " for nature, and the vicissitudes of life. Sp is by nature a pagan, but he has outbursts of Christianity such as that at the close of Mutabilitie, VIII. Sp must certainly have known the Cabalists. Rev. Anglia Beibl. 42 (1931). 161-9, by Bernhard Fehr.

16. SAURAT, DENIS. La " Sapience " de Spenser et la " Schekhina" de la Cabale. Rev. de Litt. Comp. VI (1926). 5-15.
    Sp's debt to Cabalists in *Hymne of Heavenly Beauty*.

17. SMITH, CHARLES G. The Place of Love in Spenser's World-Order. No. 47. Proceedings of Dr. Greenlaw's Seminary " C," 1926-7. The Johns Hopkins University.
    Cf. Meylan, E. F. From Ficino to Heroet: the disintegration of Plato's theory of love. Paper read before the Mod. Lang. Ass., 1934. *Cf.* PMLA XLIX (*Proc.*, 1934). 1304. *Cf.* "FQ, Sources," Nos. 110-3.

18. SPENS, JANET. Spenser's *Faerie Queene*. London, 1934.
    Chs. II, VI: Spenser's Philosophy. Disregards a great deal of recent scholarship on the subject. *Rev.* YWES XV (1934). 214-5.

19. STIRLING, BRENTS. Two Notes on the Philosophy of *Mutabilitie*. *Cf.* " Mutabilitie," No. 33.

20. SYFORD, CONSTANCE. Lucretius in Sixteenth-Century England. PMLA XLVII (*Proc.,* 1932). 1334.

TREATMENT OF NATURE

Cf. also " Cantos of Mutabilitie" for Philosophy of Nature.

1. DARDEN, W. A. The Law of Nature in the *Faerie Queene*. No. 40. Proceedings of Dr. Greenlaw's Seminary " C," 1927. The Johns Hopkins Univ. Library.

2. DURKEE, CORA L. *Britannia's Pastorals* as a Spenserian Imitation. M. A. Thesis, Yale University, 1926.
    Ch. IV: " Spenser's Influence as a Poet of Nature."

3. FRAZER, W. The Shamrock: its History. Roy. Soc. Antiq. Ire., 5th. ser. IV (1894). 132.

4. JOHNSON, FRANCIS R. The Progress of the Copernican Astronomy among English Scientists to 1645 and Its Reflection in Literature from Spenser to Milton. Diss., The Johns Hopkins University, 1935.

5. KNOWLTON, E. C. Spenser and Nature. JEGP XXXIV (1935). 366-76.

6. ROBIN, PERCY A. Animal Lore in English Literature. London, 1932. See index.

7. Shakespeare Jahrbuch 36 (1900). 102. Sp's botanical knowledge.

8. Quarterly Review XXXVII (1828). 311.
   Sp "luxuriates" in forest description; CLXXVIII (1894). 341.
   Sp's first-hand description of animal life.

COLOR IN SPENSER

1. ALLEN, DON CAMERON. Symbolic Color in the Literature of the English Renaissance. PQ XV (1936). 81-92.
   References to Sp.

2. Blackwood's Magazine IV (1819). 705-6. Sp and Rubens; XXXIV (1833). 532.
   Sp offers subjects to the painters.

3. British Critic LV (1819). 362-3.

4. Edinburgh Review CXXI (1865). 302-3.

5. FLETCHER, J. V. Some Observations on the Changing Style of *The Faerie Queene*. SP XXXI (1934). 152-9.
   Sp's waning use of color.

6. HARD, FREDERICK. Spenser's Use of Chiaroscuro. No. 16. Proceedings of Dr. Greenlaw's Seminary "C," 1926-7. The Johns Hopkins University Library.

VIEWS ON ART AND POETRY

See "Areopagus," Nos. 3, 6, 8, 9.

1. BHATTACHERJE, MOHINIMOHAN. Studies in Spenser. Calcutta, 1929.
   Ch. III.

2. FRIEDLAND, LOUIS S. Spenser's Minor Poems. Diss., New York University, 1912.

3. HUGHES, MERRITT Y. Zeitgeist and Style. An Apology for Heinrich Wölfflin Against Martin Schutze. Sewanee Rev. XLII (1934). 482-91.
   Pt. IV, 491: Sp's admiration for baroque painting which he describes as "life-resembling."

4. LANGDON, IDA. Materials for a Study of Spenser's Theory of Fine Art.
Rev. Shakes. Jahr. 49 (1913). 220-1, by L. L. Schücking.

5. ——— Milton's Theory of Poetry and Fine Art. New Haven, 1924.
See index for Sp's theory.

6. LEGOUIS, ÉMILE. Edmund Spenser. New York and London, 1926.
Ch. III.

7. RENWICK, W. L. Edmund Spenser . . .
Chs. I, II.

8. WHITE, HAROLD O. Plagiarism and Imitation in English Literature, 1558-1625. Summaries of Theses, Harvard University, 1930. 218-21.
Sp incidentally discusses the subject of imitation as an element in the canon of critical theory. *Rev.* MLN L (1936). 198-9, by Douglas Bush.

SPENSER'S WOMEN

1. BRADFORD, GAMALIEL. Elizabethan Women. Ed. H. O. White. Boston, 1936.
Spenser's Women. *Rev.* New York Times, Book Rev., Mar. 15, 1936, p. 6, by Percy Hutchison.

2. British Quart. Rev. XLVIII (1868). 93-117.

3. DOWDEN, EDWARD. Heroines of Spenser. Cornhill XXXIX (1879). 663-80. Also Littell's Liv. Age, 5th. ser. XXVI (1879). 771-82.
Ideals of beauty; method of portraiture.

4. HEINEMANN, ELFRIEDE. Das Bild der Dame in der Erzählenden Dichtung Englands von Malory bis Spenser. Münster, 1929. [L. O. Hogan]

5. PURVIS, SUSIE E. A Comparative Study of the position of women in *The Faerie Queene* (the Radegund episode), *Love's Labour's Lost, The Princess, Man and Superman.* M. A. Thesis, Columbia University, 1916.

6. SCHELLING, FELIX E. " Sidney's Sister, Pembroke's Mother." A Consideration of the Elizabethan Woman

in her Sphere as a Patron of Learning. Tudor and Stuart Club Lecture, 1923. The Johns Hopkins Alumni Mag. XII (1924). 3-23.

7. Variorum I, App. vii; III, App. vii; IV, App. iv.

BIBLIOGRAPHY, GUIDES, INDICES, CONCORDANCES, ETC.

See "Addenda," Nos. 2, 29.

1. CARPENTER, F. I. A Reference Guide to Edmund Spenser. Chicago, 1923.

> Rev. TLS 22 (Aug. 23, 1923). 560; YWES IV (1923). 123, 256; MLR XIX (1924). 258-9, by G. C. M. S.[mith]; Nation CXVIII (1924). 237; JEGP XXIII (1924). 316-22, by L. S. Friedland; SP XXI (1924). 448-9, by T. S. Graves; Shakes. Jahr. 61 (1925). 146.

2. HEFFNER, RAY. The Spenser Allusion Book. Paper read before the Mod. Lang. Ass., 1932. *Cf.* PMLA XLVII (*Proc.*, 1932). 1335.

3. JOHNSON, FRANCIS R. A Critical Bibliography of the Works of Edmund Spenser. . . . The Johns Hopkins Press, 1933.

> For reviews, *cf.* "The Works, Introductory," No. 7.

4. MAAR, HARKO GERIT DE. Elizabethan Romance in the Eighteenth Century. Zalt-Bommel, 1924.

> App. II, III: A partial list of Sp imitations to 1785.

5. OSGOOD, C. G. A Concordance to the Poems of Edmund Spenser.

> Rev. The Nation (N. Y.) CII (1916). 314.

6. PARROTT, ALICE. A Critical Bibliography of Spenser from 1923-1928. SP XXV (1928). 468-90.

7. READ, CONYERS (ed.). Bibliography of British History. Tudor Period, 1485-1603. Oxford, 1933.

> Nos. 2579, 3950a, 3959, 3972: Sp.

8. Studies in Philology XXXII (1935). 525. Notice: Spenser Bibliography.

9. VAN PATTEN, NATHAN. An Index to Bibliographies and Bibliographical Contributions Relating to the Work of American and British Authors, 1923-32.

> 237: A very brief list of Sp scholarship.

10. WHITMAN, C. H. A Subject Index to the Poems of Edmund Spenser.
    Rev. JEGP XXI (1922). 702, by H. S. V. Jones.

11. WYLLIE, J. C. and R. W. CHURCH. A Spenser Bibliography for 1928-30. Mimeographed sheets. University of Virginia, 1931.

12. ———— *Ibid.*, Revised, 1932.

LANGUAGE, ARCHAISM

See " Style and Diction," Nos. 15-6; " Addenda," Nos. 50-1.

1. BACKE, W. Essay on Spenser . . . with regard to the Language.
    Rev. Archiv L (1872). 472-3.

2. BOEHM, K. Spensers Verbalflexion.
    Rev. Shakes. Jahr. 46 (1910). 191-2.

3. BRUNNER, K. Die Dialektwörter in Spensers *Shepherds Calendar.*
    Rev. Shakes. Jahr. 51 (1915). 222.

4. CHEVALLEY, ABEL. The Concise Oxford French Dictionary. Oxford, 1934.
    xi: Sp's "narre" not difficult to translate.

5. COLGAN, NATHANIEL. The Shamrock in Literature: A Critical Chronology. Roy. Soc. Antiq. Ire., 5th. ser. VIII (1896). 211 ff.
    218: Sp's use of shamrock (water-cresses?) in *Veue.*

6. CRAIGIE, SIR WILLIAM. The Northern Element in English Literature. University of Toronto Press, [1933].
    128: Dialect in SC.

7. DAVIS, B. E. C. Edmund Spenser: A Critical Study.
    Ch. VII: Imagery.

8. DRAPER, J. W. More Light on Spenser's Linguistics. MLN XLI (1926). 127-8.
    Some specific etymologies perhaps derived from Camden and Holinshed. *Cf.* MP XVII, 471 ff. *Rev.* YWES VII (1926). 161-2.

9. ———— Spenser's Use of the Perfective Prefix. MLN XLVIII (1933). 226-8.
    Sp's reading of Middle English must have been wide and detailed, with an interest in language *per se.* This conclusion is

15

based upon a study of the perfective prefix, of which 120 in Sp are
"justifiable." *Rev.* Shakes. Jahr. 70 (1934). 166; YWES XIV
(1933). 226.

10. DRAPER, J. W. An Aspect of Spenser's Middle English
Grammar. Paper read before the Mod. Lang. Ass., 1932.
Cf. PMLA XLVII (*Proc.*, 1932). 1335.

11. —— Classical Coinage in the *Fairie Queene*. PMLA
XLVII (1932). 97-108.

Gives the classical forms from which Sp derived many of his
proper names. Sp meant the names to be thoroughly understood
and such understanding was possible only among the educated aris-
tocracy. *Cf.* "Spenser's Reading," No. 26; "FQ, General," Nos.
59, 134. *Rev.* YWES XIII (1932). 193.

12. DRAYTON, MICHAEL. Legends. "To the Reader."
Poems, 1619.

312: Sp's use of *legends* and *cantos*.

13. DUSTOOR, P. E. Legends of Lucifer in Early English
and in Milton. Anglia LIV (1930). 213-68.

226-8: Sp's use of *archangel, Cherubim, Seraphim*.

14. Edinburgh Rev. XIV (1809). 135, 141.

Sp's use of *Losel* and *to sorn*.

15. FLEMING, CHARLES F. Spenser's *Faerie Queene*; Sans
Loy, Sans Foy and Sans Joy. NQ, ser. xii. IV (1918).
71.

16. Gentleman's Mag. XIX (1749). 66.

Sp's use of *leech* to mean *physician*.

17. GUILLIM, JOHN. A Display of Heraldrie. London, 1611.

See "Criticism before 1651," No. 26, for text.

18. GÜNTHER, F. Spensers syntaktische Eigenthümlichkei-
ten. Archiv LV (1876). 17-82.

19. HAGGETT, DOROTHY. Spenser's Original Contributions to
the English Language, Adapted from words of Ro-
manic and Classical Origins. M. A. Thesis, University
of Washington, 1928.

20. HERBERT, A. S. "Chevisaunce." TLS 30 (March 19,
1931). 234.

21. HOFFMANN, FRITZ. Das Partizipium bei Spenser.

Rev. Shakes. Jahr. 46 (1910). 191.

22. HOWARD, LEON. Elf, to wit, Quick. No. 10. Proceedings of Dr. Greenlaw's Seminary " C," 1928-9.

23. JONES, H. S. V. A Spenser Handbook.
    Ch. XXXII: Language and Versification.

24. JONES, RICHARD FOSTER. Richard Mulcaster's *View of the English Language.* Washington University Studies XIII (1926). 267-303.

25. KING, R. W. Spenser and Archaisms. Athenaeum. 1920. I. 252.
    Sp was not a "mere archaist."

26. MARSH, E. An Emendation in Spenser's *Prothalamium.* Lond. Merc. IX (1924). 300.

27. *MATTHES, PAULA. Das umschreibende "do" in Spenser's *Faerie Queene.* Tübingen, 1921 [1922]. [L. O. Hogan]

28. MAYHEW, A. L. Bewaile (FQ I, vi, 1). NQ, ser. vi. IV (1881). 89.
    Cf. ibid., 254, by Br. Nicholson.

29. PARKER, ROSCOE E. Spenser's Language and the Pastoral Tradition. Language I (1925). 80-7.
    Sp's pastoral language purposely more archaic than his non-pastoral. *Rev.* YWES VI (1925). 169.

30. Quarterly Rev. XXXIV (1826). 14-5.
    Saxon plurals in Sp.

31. ———— XXXV (1827). 191.
    Sp's systematic use of "does-s" and "do-s" and "did-s."

32. R., H. These Remarks on Spenser were transmitted to me by the Rev. Mr. J. Calton, of Marton, near Gainsborough, Lincolnshire. They were addressed to him by a Gentleman, his Friend. . . . Dated May 22, 1742. The History of the Works of the Learned. . . . 1742. London.
    II, 209-22: Chiefly on diction of Bk. I.

33. RAY, JOHN. A Collection of English Words not Generally Used. 1691. P. 85.

34. READE, GEORGE H. On a Prick-spur. Roy. Hist. and Arch. Soc., 4th. ser. III (1874-5). 325.
    Pricking, FQ I, i, 1, 1-2.

35. RYLANDS, GEORGE. English Poets and the Abstract Word. Essays and Studies by Members of the English Association. Collected by H. J. C. Grierson. XVI. Oxford, 1931.
    53-84: *Passim* for Sp's usage.

36. ROYSTER, JAMES F. E. K.'s "Elf ⟨Guelph, Goblin ⟨Ghibelline." MLN XLIII (1928). 249-52.

37. SCHULTZ, VICTOR. Das persönliche Geschlecht unpersönlicher Substantiva bei Spenser.
    Rev. Shakes. Jahr. 51 (1915). 259.

38. THOMSON, JAMES. The Castle of Indolence . . . London, 1748. "Advertisement" prefixed to "List of Obsolete Words."

39. *TRNKA, BOHUMIL. On the Syntax of the English Verb from Caxton to Dryden. Travaux du Cercle Linguistique de Prague, 3. Prague, 1930.
    Rev. Archiv CLXII (1932). 242-3. Sp's verb syntax and archaisms; Neophilologus XX (1935). 113-20, by A. Dekker.

40. WALLER, EDMUND. The Second Part of Mr. Waller's Poems. London, 1705. Preface to *The Maid's Tragedy.*
    Sig. u^v: Sp's antiquated words. See "Criticism after 1651," No. 150 for text.

41. WARD, A. W. Poems of John Byrom. Chetham Soc., 1894. I, pt. i, 49n.

42. WILLIS, JOHN. De Lingua Spenseriana ejusque fontibus.
    Rev. Archiv V (1849). 445-6.

43. WINKLER, GERDA. Das Relativum bei Caxton und seine Entwicklung von Chaucer bis Spenser. Diss., Berlin, 1933.

STYLE AND DICTION

See "Language, Archaism"; "Addenda," No. 30.

1. ALFORD, B. H. Spenser's *Fairy Queen.* NQ, ser. i. X (1854). 370. *Cf. ibid.,* 143, by F. J. C.

2. ATKINSON, DOROTHY F. A Study of the Punctuation of Spenser's *Faerie Queene.* Abstracts of Theses, University of Washington, 1931. 151.
    The punctuation of FQ, while in the main following the system of the age, reveals the conscious artist modifying conventional practice to suit his purposes.

3. BAROWAY, ISRAEL. The Imagery of Spenser and the *Song of Songs.* JEGP XXXIII (1934). 23-45.

4. BATESON, F. W. English Poetry and the English Language. Oxford, 1934.
   Ch. II, sect. 1: "Elizabethans . . . ." 30 ff.: Sp's style. *Rev.* TLS 34 (Mar. 21, 1935). 172; Criterion XIV (1935). 538-9, by F. C.

5. BULLOCK, W. L. A Comment on Criticism in the Cinquecento. PMLA XLII (1927). 1057-60.
   Calls attention to theories of literary language in Bembo and Speroni. *Cf. post,* No. 22.

6. ——— A Comment on Criticism in the Cinquecento. PMLA XLVI (1931). 287-8.
   Additions, etc., to earlier paper. *Cf. post,* No. 22.

7. DAVIS, B. E. C. Edmund Spenser: A Critical Study.
   Chs. VI, VII: Diction and Imagery.

8. FULLER, RONALD. Literary Craftsmanship . . . London, 1934. P. 273.

9. GREEN, ZAIDEE E. Observations on the epic similes in *The Faerie Queene.* PQ XIV (1935). 217-28.

10. KÖHLER, KARL. Das Epitheton ornans in der englischen Poesie von Chaucer bis Spenser. (Auszug). Freiburg, 1923. [L. O. Hogan]

11. LEA, KATHLEEN M. Conceits. MLR XX (1925). 389-406.
    393-7: Sp's use of the conceit.

12. LEGOUIS, ÉMILE. Edmund Spenser. New York and London, 1926.
    Ch. III.

13. LOTSPEICH, HENRY G. Classical Mythology in the Poetry of Edmund Spenser. Princeton University Press, 1932.
    13 ff.: Style in FQ.

14. MAXWELL, WILLIAM C. Word-Compounding in Spenser. Diss., University of Washington, 1925. *Cf. post,* No. 19.

15. MCELDERRY, BRUCE R., JR. Archaism and Innovation in Spenser's Poetic Diction. Diss., University of Iowa, 1925.

16. McElderry, Bruce R., Jr. Archaism and Innovation in Spenser's Poetic Diction. PMLA XLVII (1932). 144-70.

Sp's deliberate use of archaism has been exaggerated. His reliance upon dialect is slight, even in the SC, and almost negligible in later poetry. His innovations are "only very incidentally reckless or ignorant." Illustrative tables. *Rev.* YWES XIII (1932). 194. *Cf.* Renwick, W. L., *post*; Lounsbury, T. R. Studies in Chaucer. 1892. III, 59-65; Long, P. W., MLR XII (1917). 88; *post*, Nos. 21, 22.

17. Nicholson, Margaret E. Realistic Elements in Spenser's Style. SP XXI (1924). 382-98.

Analysis of passages marked by local color and realism. [F. I. C. and A. P.] *Rev.* YWES V (1924). 157-8.

18. Osgood, C. G. Verse in Spenser's Prose. Paper read befor the Mod. Lang. Ass., 1933. *Cf.* PMLA XLVIII (*Proc.*, 1933). 1430. Printed in ELH I (1934). 1-6.

Cites passages from *Veue* and *Axiochus* to show the strongly iambic character of Sp's prose. *Cf. post,* No. 23.

19. Padelford, F. M. and W. C. Maxwell. The Compound Words in Spenser's Poetry. JEGP XXV (1926). 498-516.

Sp's compounds are those of accepted diction or those coined or employed for conscious poetic purposes. Classification of the second type and frequency tables. The findings support possibility of dating *Mutabilitie* before Bk. IV. *Rev.* YWES VII (1926). 162; Shakes. Jahr. 63 (1927). 230-1. *Cf. post,* No. 23.

20. Pattison, Bruce. The Roundelay in the August Eclogue of *The Shepheardes Calender.* RES IX (1933). 54-5.

The roughness of this diction may be attributed to the influence of contemporary song tunes.

21. Pope, Emma F. Renaissance Criticism and the Diction of the *Faerie Queene.* PMLA XLI (1926). 575-619.

Introductory survey of the progress of critical opinion on Sp's diction from 1599 to the present. Evolution of Renaissance theory of poetic diction from inception through developments in Italy, France, and England. The theory comprises three elements: necessity for enriching vernacular, archaism as a literary device, preservation of all phases of decorum. Attempts to establish relationship between Sp's diction and this theory, concluding he is "in strict accord" with it. *Rev.* Shakes. Jahr. 64 (1928). 219. *Cf. ante,* Nos. 15, 16; "Areopagus," No. 1.

22. POPE, EMMA F. A Comment on Criticism in the Cinquecento: A Reply. PMLA XLVI (1931). 276-87. *Cf. ante*, No. 5.

23. PURCELL, J. M. The Date of Spenser's *Mutabilitie* Cantos. PMLA L (1935). 914-7.
    Applies stylistic tests to *Mut. Cf.* Albright, E. M., in SP XXVI (1929). 428 ff.; Bush, D., in PMLA XLV (1930). 954-7; Padelford, F. M., *ibid.*, 704 ff.

24. RENWICK, W. L. Edmund Spenser: An Essay. . . . Chs. III, VII.

25. SOHR, LUDWIG. Die visuellen Sinneseindrücke und akustischen Phänomene in E. Spensers poetischen werken. München, 1922. [L. O. Hogan]

26. STOLL, E. E. Poets and Playwrights.
    193-203: Classicism of Sp's style.

27. *THOMPSON, GILBERT. Select Translations from Homer and Horace. London, 1801.
    Preface, 6-7: Sp's similes. [Douglas Bush]

28. WELLS, HENRY W. Poetic Imagery Illustrated from Elizabethan Literature. Diss., Columbia University, 1924. Columbia University Press, 1924.
    Sp examples *passim*.

29. Word Study VII (Jan., 1932). 1. The Language of Edmund Spenser.

30. WYLD, HENRY C. Spenser's Diction and Style in Relation to Those of Later English Poetry. In *A Grammatical Miscellany offered to Otto Jespersen on his Seventieth Birthday*. Copenhagen, London, 1930.
    Compares diction and style of FQ with those of the school of Pope.

VERSIFICATION, STANZA, METRICS

See " Amoretti," No. 10; " Addenda," No. 31.

1. Blackwood's Magazine XII (1822). 66-7.
    Sp's " the noblest stanza in our language."

2. BELLOC, HILAIRE. Milton. Philadelphia, 1935.
    212, 216: Sp's sonnets.

3. BOUCHIER, JONATHAN. The Spenserian Stanza. NQ, ser. vii. III (1887). 409, 525; *cf. ibid.,* 525, by Herbert Hardy.

   Lists some poems using Sp stanza. *Cf. ibid.,* ser. vii. IV (1887). 137-8.

4. BRADFORD, GAMALIEL. Letters of . . . ed. Van Wyck Brooks. New York, 1934. P. 11.

5. BRADNER, LEICESTER. Forerunners of the Spenserian Stanza. RES IV (1928). 207-8.

   Two nine-line stanzas in *Tottel's Miscellany* use medial and final couplet in Sp's manner. *Rev.* YWES IX (1928). 173.

6. BRAY, SIR DENYS. The Art-Form of the Elizabethan Sonnet-Sequence and Shakespeare's Sonnets. Shakes. Jahr. 63 (1927). 159-82.

   172: Sp's sonnets. *Cf.* "Amoretti," Nos. 21, 22.

7. BREWER, ROBERT F. The Art of Versification and the Technicalities of Poetry. Edinburgh, 1918. See index.

8. British Critic XVII (1801). 223.

   Sp's facility in using his difficult stanza.

9. ———— XVIII (1801). 489n.

   Sp and Fairfax, the "great improvers of the heroic stanza," lack the polish found in pseudo-Rowley.

10. ———— XXXIV (1809). 368n.

    Sp's stanza and its relation to Chaucer.

11. ———— XLV (1814). 46, 278.

    Byron and the Sp stanza.

12. British Review XII (1818). 24.

    Nature of the Spenserian stanza. *Cf. ibid.,* V (1814). 398; IX (1817). 22-3; XI (1818). 327.

13. BUYSSENS, E. Spenser's *Prosopopoia,* lines 241-2. NQ, ser. xiv. VIII (1933). 190.

    On *aine* and *ame* rhymes in FQ and MHT. *Cf.* "Mother Hubberd's Tale," No. 11.

14. DAVIS, B. E. C. Edmund Spenser . . .

    Ch. VIII: Verbal Music, Verse.

15. Edinburgh Review CXVII (1863). 355.

    Sp's stanza unsuited to Homeric translation.

16. Espiner, Janet G. [Scott]. Les Sonnets élisabéthains.
Rev. de Litt. Comp., 15ᵉ· an. (1935). 107-9.
108: Sp's debt to the Italian not fully seen by Sir Sidney Lee.

17. Farnham, Willard. The Lost Innocence of Poetry.
Essays in Criticism by Members of the Department of
English, University of California. Berkeley, 1929.
42: Sp's fight against the English hexameter.

18. Fletcher, Priscilla. A Study of English Blank Verse,
1582-1632. Colorado College Publications, Language
series II (1907). 41-65.
42: Sp's imitation of Chaucer's versification.

19. Garrod, H. W. Aberration in Rhyme. TLS 26 (April
14, 1927). 265.
Cites instances from other Elizabethan poets to show that "substitution for a rhyming word" of an "unrhyming synonym" is not
peculiar to Sp. Rev. YWES VIII (1927). 185.

20. Gentleman's Mag. II (1732). 786.
FQ stanza tires the ear and limits Sp's reputation.

21. Gilchrist, Marie. Writing Poetry. Boston, 1932.
62-3: Sp stanza. Negligible.

22. Hamer, Enid. (Mrs. E. H. H. Porter). The Metres of
English Prosody. London, 1930.
158-65: FQ stanza. Cf. index also.

23. Hollowell, B. M. The Elizabethan Hexametrists. PQ
III (1924). 51-7.
Sp's interest in the movement, 1570-90, to introduce classical
prosody into English verse. Cf. "Style, Diction," No. 3.

24. Hulme, William H. The Most Popular English Verse
and Stanzaic Forms. West. Reserve Bull. XXIII
(1920). 53 ff.
64, 68: Sp's sonnet and FQ measures.

25. Jones, H. S. V. A Spenser Handbook.
Ch. XXXII: Language and Versification.

26. Koller, Kathrine. Studies in Colin Clouts Come
Home Again. Diss., The Johns Hopkins University,
1934.
Ch. II: Literary Problems: versification, etc.

27. LANZ, HENRY. The Physical Basis of Rime. Stanford University Press, 1931.
259: Diagrams for FQ stanza showing the "harmonic structure judged by the standards of modern pronunciation."

28. MAYNARD, THEODORE. The Connection between the ballade, Chaucer's modification of it, rime royal, and the Spenserian stanza. Diss., Catholic University, 1934.
Ch. VII: The Formation of the Spenserian Stanza. The Alexandrine a 16th. c. fad; Sp's stanza "had been in the air" for a considerable time before he crystallized it. Cf. ibid., 85, 100, 103, 107-27, 128-31 for relation of Sp's stanza to Chaucer's. Cf. post, No. 33.

29. Monitor (Dublin) II (1879). 299 ff., by N. W.
304: Sp's "artificial line."

30. NOTCUTT, H. CLEMENT. Spenser's Wonderful Line. Spectator 135 (1925). 305.

31. OSGOOD, C. G. The Voice of England. New York, 1935.
168, 391, 435, 442-3, 445: Sp's stanza.

32. PADELFORD, F. M. The Cantos of Mutabilitie: Further Considerations . . . PMLA XLV (1930). 704-11.
A study of prosodic and stylistic qualities (run-on lines, feminine endings, etc.).

33. POPE, EMMA F. The Critical Background of the Spenserian Stanza. MP XXIV (1926). 31-53.
Resumé of the controversy between exponents of the quantitative and the vernacular verse. Sp's need to devise a new meter for FQ; rejects relation of Sp's stanza to Chaucer's on the ground that "there is no relation of tone or quality" between them. Sp reviewed Italian metrical schemes, choosing Dante's terza rima. He transferred its tone and syllable quality into the nearest English equivalent. The stanza form is based on nine-line madrigal. Rev. YWES VII (1926). 160-1; Shakes. Jahr. 63 (1927). 231. Cf. ante, No. 28.

34. Quarterly Review XLIX (1833). 450.

35. RENWICK, W. L. Edmund Spenser: An Essay.
Ch. IV and Appendix.

36. RESCHKE, HEDWIG. Die Spenserstanze bei den Spensernachahmern des Neunzehnten Jahrhundert.
Rev. Engl. Stud. 53 (1919-20). 430, by Walther Fischer.

37. Retrospective Review IX (1824). 175.
Sp's use of the exemplars of heroic meters in Chaucer.

38. SCHIRMER, WALTER F. Das Sonett in der englischen Literatur. Anglia 49 (1925). 1-31.
    Passim for Sp's sonnet technique.

39. SÉLINCOURT, E. DE. Oxford Lectures on Poetry.
    117-21: Sp's musical ability gives unity to FQ by skillful use of a variety of techniques.

40. SHANNON, GEORGE P. The Heroic Couplet in the Sixteenth and Early Seventeenth Centuries, with Special Reference to the Influence of Ovid and the Latin Elegiac Distich. Stanford Univ. Abstracts of Dissertations II (1927). 127-34.
    128, 131: MHT couplets.

41. SHIPLEY, JOSEPH T. Spenserian Prosody; the Couplet Forms. SP XXI (1924). 594-615.
    Studies couplet forms of CCCHA, MHT, SC. Sp seems to have known the value of Chaucer's final *e* and is not mistakenly imitating Chaucer. *Rev.* YWES V (1924). 156-7.

42. STOCKDALE, PERCIVAL. Lectures on the Truly Eminent English Poets.
    Rev. Edinburgh Rev. XII (1808). 63-5. Weakness of Sp stanza.

43. STOVALL, FLOYD. Feminine Rimes in *The Faerie Queene.* JEGP XXVI (1927). 91-5.
    Frequency of feminine rimes in Sp's poetry. He seems to have used them deliberately as suited only to frivolous verse. *Rev.* YWES VIII (1927). 184-5.

44. WILLCOCK, G. D. Passing Pitefull Hexameters. MLR XXIX (1934). 1-19.
    7-10, 17-8: Experiments in metrical forms, SC.

45. WRINN, MARY J. J. The Hollow Reed. New York and London, 1935.
    58-9, 469-70: Sp stanza described and illustrated.

MISCELLANEOUS SUBJECTS, HOW TO READ SPENSER

1. CARLISLE, HELEN G. (Mrs. James M. Reid). We Begin. New York, 1932.
   330, 339: Sp.

V.
ADDENDA

V. ADDENDA

1. C., J. Biographical Sketches of Persons Remarkable in Local History. No. X. Edmund Spenser. J. Cork Hist. and Arch. Soc. III (1894). 89-100.

2. JOHNSON, FRANCIS R. A Critical Bibliography of the Works of Edmund Spenser Printed before 1700.
   Rev. German.-Roman. Monatss. XXII (1934). 406.

3. SPENSER, EDMUND. The Faerie Queene. Variorum edition.
   Vol. I: Rev. The Johns Hopkins Alumni Mag. XXI (1933). 421-4, by Frederick Hard.
   Vol. II: Rev. German.-Roman. Monatss. XXII (1934). 406.
   Vol. III: Rev. German.-Roman. Monatss. XXII (1934). 406; JEGP XXXIII (1934). 578, by H. S. V. Jones; YWES XV (1934). 210-1.

4. GOWEN, HERBERT H. Temperantia. London, 1891.
   Based on Bk. II.

5. Grub Street Journal, May 12, 1737. No. 385.
   Mentions Sp as one of poets included in The Muses Library.

6. SPENSER, EDMUND. Axiochus. Ed. F. M. Padelford.
   Rev. German.-Roman. Monatss. XXII (1934). 406; YWES XV (1934). 212.

7. MARSHALL, M. L. Representative Spenserian Sonnets. Dreamland Press, Landover, Md., 1927.

8. LIEVSAY, J. LEON. Spenser and Guazzo: A Comparative Study of Renaissance Attitudes. Diss., University of Washington, 1936. An important study.

9. BUSH, DOUGLAS. Mythology and the Renaissance Tradition.
   Rev. CR XLVII (1933). 147-8, by H. J. Rose.

10. CAMPBELL, LILY B. The Christian Muse. Huntington Library Bull., No. 8. 1935. 29-70.
    56-63: Discusses the Urania of TM and Hymnes in the light of DuBartas's L'Uranie.

11. Baconiana, n. s. I (1894). 191.

12. MOORE, G. S. The Influence of Dante on Spenser. The Moraga Quarterly III (1932). 60-8.

13. GILLETTE, ALLETTA M. Political Allegory in the Second Book of the *Faerie Queene*. M. A. Thesis, University of Washington, 1911.

14. STREATOR, G. I. The Influence of Mediaeval Allegory upon Spenser's *Faerie Queene*. M. A. Thesis, University of Washington, 1913.

15. WOOD, RUTH C. Ovid's *Metamorphoses* and Spenser's *Faerie Queen*. M. A. Thesis, University of Colorado, 1934.

16. SPURGEON, C. F. E. Mysticism in English Literature. Cambridge University Press, 1913.
    17, 24-5: Sp.

17. SEATON, ETHEL. Literary Relations of England and Scandinavia in the Seventeenth Century. Oxford, 1935.
    60-1: Daphnaida; 235-6: Veue of Ireland. See index also.

18. [DANIEL, GEORGE]. Democritus in London. London, 1852.
    286 n.: Pleasant Willie.

19. CRAIG, HARDIN. The Enchanted Glass. The Elizabethan Mind in Literature. New York, 1936.
    See index for Sp.

20. KNAUER, KARL. Lodovico Ariosto. German.-Roman. Monatss. XXIII (1935). 388.
    Sp and Ariosto.

21. ARMSTRONG, JOHN [LANCELOT TEMPLE]. Miscellanies. London, 1770. 2 vols.
    I, 164-6: Sp imitations. Material supposed to have been incorporated into *Castle of Indolence*, canto i. Copy in Folger Shakespeare Library. See " Criticism after 1651," No. 4. [J. G. McManaway]

22. Baconiana, n. s. IX (1901). 78.
    FQ and SC.

23. BARNARD, E. A Fragment in Spenser's Stile. [*ca.* 1742]. MS in library of J. G. McManaway.

24. BELL, EDNA F. Imitations of Spenser from 1706 to 1774. M. A. Thesis, University of Oklahoma, 1928.

25. Bradford, Gamaliel. The Journal of . . . , 1883-1932. Ed. Van Wyck Brooks. Boston, 1933.
4, 39, 73, 86, 241, 274.

26. Duff, W. Critical Observations on the Writings of the Most Celebrated Original Geniuses in Poetry. Being a Sequel to the Essay on Original Genius. London, 1770.
Summary of FQ stories with excerpts and comments. Copy in Folger Shakespeare Library. [J. G. McManaway]

27. Fragments from Old Letters E. D. to E. D. W. and second series. London, 1914.
I, 12, 123, 146, and II, 14, 43, 112, 137.

28. Revue de l'Enseign. des Lang. Viv. 47 (1930). 181.
Sp's influence on Keats.

29. Jones, M. LaV. Recent Interest in Edmund Spenser. Diss., University of Oklahoma, 1930.
A bibliography.

30. Dressler, Graham McF. A Study of Aphorisms in the Poetry of Edmund Spenser. Diss., University of Washington, 1936.

31. Winslow, Anne. Rhythmic Variations in Spenser's *Faerie Queene.* Vassar Journal of Undergraduate Studies V (1931). 179-93.

32. Fletcher, Jefferson B. Edmund Spenser. Encyclopedia Americana. New York, 1927.
XXV, 395-400: Revision of article in 1904-8 ed. *Cf.* Carpenter, Ref. Guide, 53.

33. Book-Auction Records XXXIII, pt. 3 (1936). 341.
Records the sale at Sotheby's, on May 4, 1936, of the Luthrell copy of *Axiochus.* The book is now in the library of Mr. Carl H. Pforzheimer of New York. See *ante,* pp. 50, 128, for another copy of *Axiochus.*

34. A Catalogue of the Manuscripts in the Library of Gonville and Caius College, Cambridge. Ed. J. J. Smith. Cambridge and New York, 1849.
96: No. 188. A Vewe of Ireland.

16

35. Catalogue of The Library of J. Walter K. Eyton, Esq. . . .
Comprising An Extraordinary Collection of Privately
Printed Books; . . . London, 1848.
180: Nos. 1418-9. FQ and Proth. editions.

36. Catalogue of the Valuable Library of An Eminent Collec-
tor [J. Wilkes] which will be sold by Auction, by Messrs.
S. Leigh Sotheby & Co., . . . March 12, 1847. [n. d.]
133: No. 2190. Todd's ed.

37. Sale Catalogue of Dr. Johnson's Library. With an Essay
by A. Edward Newton. [New York], 1925.
4, 14, 26: FQ editions.

38. *SNODGRASS, DOROTHY M. Shakespeare's Sonnets: Their
Relation to Other Sonnets of the Elizabethan Period.
M. A. Thesis, Stanford University, 1936.

39. PADELFORD, F. M. Robert Aylett. Huntington Library
Bull., 10 (1936). 1-48.
Robert Aylett (1583-1655), disciple of DuBartas and Sp; author
of didactic expositions of the virtues in Spenserian stanzas, and of
sacred epics; incorporated or adapted many stanzas from FQ; over
1800 Spenserian stanzas in extant poetry; pious regret that his
master, Spenser, did not devote talents exclusively to the Heavenly
Muse, Urania.

40. ———. E. W[ilkinson]., His Thameseidos. SAB, forthcoming.
A river-myth poem, published in 1600. Specific indebtedness to Sp
in phrasing. Cf. Brydges, Censura Literaria, II, 168; post, No. 48,
p. 496.

41. PEACHAM, HENRY. The Period of Mourning. Disposed
into sixe Visions. In Memorie of the late Prince. To-
gether with Nuptiall Hymnes, in Honour of this Happy
Marriage betweene the Great Princes, Frederick—Count
Palatine of the Rhene, and the Most Excellent, and
Aboundant President of all Virtue and Goodnes Elizabeth
onely Daughter to our Soueraigne, his Maiestie. 1613.
These Visions are reminiscent of VB and VP.
Vision II (E. 9); Vision I, ls. 19-20 (Cf. FQ I, i, 6, 5-6); Vision
III (Cf. FQ I, i, 1, 9 and 4, 1; II, xi, 22); Vision IV.
Minerva Britanna or A Garden of Heroicall Deuises, furnished and
adorned with Emblemes and Impresas of sundry natures, newly de-

vised, moralized, and published, by Henry Peacham, Mr. of Artes.
London, 1612. " Rura mihi et silentium." ls. 71-2; B4ʳ contains the
sonnet by E. S. reproduced in Carpenter, Ref. Guide, 133. [F. M.
Padelford]

42. Scot, Thomas. Philomythie or Philomythologie. 1622.
[First ed., 1616.]

> " A Supply of the Description of Monsier PANDORVS WAL-
> DOLYNNATVS, that merrie American Philosopher, or the Wise
> man of the New World, being antipode to Æsop, placed with him as
> parallel in the front. Done according to the simple truth of his owne
> naked deliuery." (Cf. Carpenter, Ref. Guide, 249 for reference to Sp
> in the address " To the Reader.")

>> " Vpon a stately wall Saint George doth ride
>> (Wanting a horse) in pompe and armed pride;
>> Beneath there is a Den, in that the Dragon.
>> This tells his name, whose worthy parts wee brag on.
>> It is his owne deuice, let all men know:
>> So is the rest which we in order show."

>> . . . .

>> . . . . . . " Wagers haue been laid
>> That let an enemie fart, he would out-run
>> An Irishman, for feare 't 'ad been a gun.
>> Where learned *Spencer* maketh harnas't *Feare*
>> Afraide the clashing of his armes to heare,
>> That apprehension he from hence did gaine,"
>> Our Monsieur did, what *Spencer* did but faine." [F. M. Padelford]

43. T. W. The Lamentation of Melpomene, for the death of
Belphæbe, our Late Queene. With a Ioy to England for
our blessed King. 1603.

> Aiii r and v : 12 lines, beginning " For loe; the Lampe that whilome
> burnt so cleare," echoes FQ I Proem 4; IV, i, 18; VB 10, 5-8; RT
> 574; FQ III, iv, 1, 1, 2.
> B2ᵛ, ls. 4-5: Cf. SC, June, 89 and Nov., 58-9.
> B2ᵛ, l. 18: Cf. Daph. 376.
> B4, ls. 2-3: Cf. FQ V, vi, 13, 8-9.
> A3, l. 12: Cf. Daph. 1, 232-3.
> Aiv, ls. 4-15: Cf. Daph. 456-90. [F. M. Padelford]

44. Houston, Percy Hazen. Doctor Johnson. A Study in
Eighteenth Century Humanism. Cambridge, Mass., 1923.

> 35, 115, 132, 133-6, 138, 146, 205, 210, 212, 238: Sp mentioned.

45. Jameson, R. D. A Comparison of Literature. London,
1935.

> Ch. VI : " The Distractions of the Classical Renaissance." 118:
> Sp.

46. KITTREDGE, GEORGE LYMAN. A Harvard Salutatory Oration of 1662. In Publications of the Colonial Society of Massachusetts. XXVIII (1935). 1-24.

Acct. of the commonplace book of Elnathan Chauncy (A. B. Harvard 1661, A. M. 1664) which contains many passages from Sp.

47. R. B. Adam Library Relating to Dr. Samuel Johnson and his Era, The. Printed for the Author. Buffalo and Oxford University Press, 1929.

III, 225: Johnson and Sp.

48. TAYLOR, HILDA. Topographical Poetry in England During the Renascence. Abstracts of Theses, Humanistic Series, University of Chicago V (1926-7). 493-7.

Passim for Sp.

49. WAGER, CHARLES H. A. To Whom It May Concern. Chicago, 1928.

49-50: The poets' love of Sleep; Sp.

50. FREDERICK, J. T. and L. L. WARD. Good Writing. A Book for College Students. New York, 1934.

32: Sp's words.

51. PALMER, ABRAM S. Leaves from a Word-Hunter's Note-Book. Being Some Contributions to English Etymology. London, 1876.

8-9, 10, 11, 25, 36, 44, 58, 70, 71n, 96 (and note), 103, 129-30, 143n, 147-8, 152, 162, 191, 197, 211-2, 215n, 247-8, 252, 264, 265n, 274-5, 286n: Sp's diction (etymology and archaisms).

INDEX